THE
WHITE
WORKING
CLASS
TODAY

Who They Are,
How They Think
and How Progressives
Can Regain Their Support

D1056867

THE WHITE WORKING CLASS TODAY

Who They Are,
How They Think
and How Progressives
Can Regain Their Support

ANDREW LEVISON

DEMOCRATIC
STRATEGIST
PRESS

Democratic Strategist Press
A Division of
The Democratic Strategist
www.thedemocraticstrategist.org
Email: editors@thedemocraticstrategist.org
Copyright ©2013 by Andrew Levison
Published 2013
Printed in the United States of America
ISBN 978-0-692-01979-5

Cover and book design by Margaret Johns, Sage Design
www.sagedesign.biz

Dedication

To Franklin Delano Roosevelt, Walter Reuther, Robert Kennedy and Martin Luther King, Jr.

They shared the dream of an America that provided social justice and a basic level of economic security for every one of its citizens—a dream that remains at the very heart of the progressive vision and agenda today.

Their lives and sacrifices moved America forward as a nation. From their example today's generation of progressives can draw not only insight but inspiration.

Table of Contents

PART TWO – HOW THEY THINK

PART THREE – HOW PROGRESSIVES CAN REGAIN THE TRUST AND SUPPORT OF WORKING CLASS AMERICANS

PART FOUR – APPENDICES – ACADEMIC RESEARCH AND PROGRESSIVE POLITICAL STRATEGY

Preface:
The White Working Class
and the Future of American Politics

As the smoke has cleared from the 2012 elections, it is now apparent that the coalition of progressives and moderates that re-elected Barack Obama has essentially reached a political and electoral stalemate in its struggle with conservatives and the GOP.

Although Democrats received more votes than Republicans—not only in the presidential race but also in the races for the Senate and House of Representatives—Republicans have proven themselves highly skilled at using the rules and procedures of Congress to paralyze the normal activity of government. Republican obstruction has insured that Obama and the Democrats cannot pass major legislation, make normal executive branch appointments, staff many existing agencies or enforce a range of laws already passed by Congress and now on the books.

Although the long-term demographic trends are favorable for progressives and the Democrats, there is little realistic hope that this basic stalemate can or will be broken in 2014, 2016 and even for some years beyond simply by maintaining or increasing the turnout of the core Obama coalition. Demographic change is inexorable, but it is also slow.

To create a stable Democratic majority anytime in the foreseeable future, the Democratic coalition that elected Barack Obama needs to win the support of a significant group of voters who now vote as part of the Republican coalition. As the 2012 elections demonstrated, the group that (outside the South) has the greatest potential in this regard is the white working class. These are the high school or community college educated men and women who work in blue collar or lower level white collar jobs and whose pay provides neither a genuine "middle class" income nor meaningful economic security.

In 2012, Obama and the Democrats were assisted by an extraordinarily favorable combination of circumstances in their outreach to this group—a uniquely aloof and unsympathetic Republican candidate, a series of profoundly provocative and insulting actions by GOP governors in critical Midwestern states and a weak but nonetheless discernible economic recovery in the months before Election Day. Democrats cannot count on these factors being repeated in the future; quite the contrary, the GOP, despite its intense ideological myopia, will not intentionally repeat exactly the same set of tactical and strategic mistakes it made in 2012.

As a result, both on the positive side and on the negative side, the white working class is now a unique—perhaps THE unique—swing voter group for the future. On the positive side, permanently increasing the level of Democratic support among white workers to the 40% Obama received in 2008 could actually insure a genuinely stable and reliable Democratic majority for many years to come. On the negative side, if in 2016 white working class support for the Dems falls to or below the 33% it hit in 2010, a GOP president becomes a very real possibility.

In order to successfully appeal to this critical group of voters, Democrats will need to do more than create a few clever TV ads or emphatically repeat Democratic campaign clichés left over from the 1950's. Four decades of isolation and mutual distrust have left many Democrats with little or no understanding of who white working class Americans are, why they think the way they do or how to win their support. To genuinely appeal to these Americans, Democrats will have to re-think their entire attitude and approach.

That, in a nutshell, is the purpose of this book.

Introduction: The 2012 Election

In November of 2011, a year before the recent elections, Ruy Teixeira and John Halpin of the Center for American Progress released an analysis of the demographic changes that had occurred since 2008 and what those changes implied for upcoming contests. Among other trends they pointed out that white working class voters, the majority of whom generally voted Republican, were continuing to decline as a percentage of the electorate—a fact which would inevitably improve Obama's chances.

The conservative press gleefully leaped on the opportunity to misinterpret this conclusion as nothing less than a nefarious *"Democratic plan to abandon working class whites"* and argued that it proved that Democrats were indeed the snotty, arrogant elitists that conservatives had always said they were.

The allegation was particularly absurd in the case of Teixeira, whose 1999 book, *The Forgotten Majority: Why the White Working Class Still Matters*, was the most forceful expression of the case for the continuing importance of the white working class in modern Democratic thinking. In his 2003 book, *The Emerging Democratic Majority*, which defined the demographic trends and objectives for the Democrats for the coming years, he and co-author John Judis calculated that the Dems would need to win around 40 percent of the white working class vote to win national elections in 2004 and 2008. This was a minimum level that would decline only gradually over the following election cycles.

In a *New Republic* article several weeks after the 2011 report was published, Teixeira emphatically clarified his real view about "abandoning" the white working class. As he said:

> My new report with John Halpin, "The Path to 270: Demographics Versus Economics in the 2012 Presidential Election," has generated a lot of comment, much of which focuses on the alleged need for the Obama campaign to "abandon" the white working class and embrace a coalition based on emerging demographics like minorities, Millennials, single women, and college graduates. Or to forget about trying to win in states like Ohio and put their chips on states like Virginia, Colorado, and North Carolina.
>
> But this more reflects what commentators wish to believe about the Obama campaign than what the report actually says. In reality, we do not argue that the Obama campaign needs to choose between, say, white working class and white college graduate voters, or between states like Ohio and Virginia. These are false choices.
>
> The data in the report show why this is so. Take white working class voters. We note in the report that this demographic is declining as a share of voters and that, given the typically poor performance of Democratic presidents among this group, this ongoing demographic decline should benefit Obama. It also means that Obama can win the presidency with a larger deficit among these voters than prior Democratic campaigns, including his own victory in 2008.
>
> *This is a simple recognition of electoral reality, not a call to "abandon" these voters. In fact, given the political proclivities of these voters and the current economic situation, Obama will have to fight hard to keep his deficit [i.e., the margin between him and his Republican opponent] with this group at manageable levels. This means Obama should pay a lot of attention to*

these voters and I predict that he will.[1]

Even as the debate over Teixeira and Halpin's analysis was going on, however, commentators were already beginning to focus on a much more practical issue—the surprising level of white working class support for an Ohio referendum defending unions. As Michael Tomasky noted in December 2011:

> Barack Obama is winning the Rust Belt back. The overwhelming repeal in Ohio of Governor John Kasich's anti-labor bill from last year shows that the GOP has gone way, way too far—too far for Democrats, obviously, but also for independents. It shows the potential for something else, too: the populist message can stick. "Class warfare" can work. It can take hold even with the people who allegedly despise our Kenyan leader the most: the white working class...
>
> Ohio's Question 2 lost 61 to 39 percent. The white working class, which Kasich won by 14 points in 2010, backed repeal by the very 61 percent that it took overall. This was a pasting, as Kasich acknowledged.[2]

The Ohio results raised the first major doubts about the viability of a "plutocratic" candidate like Mitt Romney as the choice to challenge Obama among white working class Americans. And then the early primaries in January, February and March strongly reinforced the doubts about Romney's ability to win white working class support. Although Romney vastly outspent his opponents and ran to the right of them on all major issues, he still did very poorly with white working class primary voters. He was hit by both Gingrich and Perry for the "vulture capitalism" of his Bain capital years and lost white working class voters to Gingrich and Santorum by significant margins, underlining the doubts about his upper class, elitist image and apparent indifference to ordinary Americans.

Headlines in the first three months of 2012 reflected his difficulties:

Jan 2 – Santorum's Opportunity—Working Class Republicans

Jan 13 – Can Mitt Romney's Opponents Capitalize on His Weakness with Blue Collar Voters

Jan 21 – Romney's Results Show Weakness with Working Class Voters

Feb 2 – Is Obama Winning Back Blue Collar Whites?

Feb 20 – Mitt Romney's Michigan Problem: Reagan Democrats

March 6th – Romney's Worsening Working Class Voter Problem

As most political observers were aware, however, there is always a great deal of volatility during primaries as voters use their responses to survey interviews to "vent" frustration with the political system as a whole and vote for minor candidates as a way of expressing discontent with the major choices. It was widely expected that once Romney emerged as the clear nominee his white working class support would rise.

And so indeed it did. By April an article in *Salon* magazine by Steven Kornakei was titled, "White Guys Versus Obama: He's Getting Blown Away Among Blue Collar Men."[3] And in early June, Nate Cohn reviewed the polling data and headlined his *New Republic* article, "Obama's Problem with White Non-college Educated Voters is Getting Worse".

Even as the Obama campaign confronted this challenge, they were simultaneously struggling with an opposing imperative—to overcome the "enthusiasm gap" that the polls suggested was afflicting many of his base supporters.

For many observers, Obama was faced with a clear trade-off. As

Ron Brownstein noted in June:

> By endorsing gay marriage, championing free contraception in health insurance plans (over resistance from the Catholic Church), and administratively legalizing young people brought to the U.S. illegally by their parents, Obama has repeatedly subordinated the concerns of older and blue-collar whites to the preferences of the Democrats' emerging coalition: minorities, young people, and culturally liberal college-educated whites, especially women. "He's taking positions that are strongly opposed by culturally conservative whites, basically conceding that he is going to do poorly among them, in a conscious effort to increase enthusiasm among the coalition that put him in office," says GOP pollster Whit Ayres.
>
> Each strand of that Democratic "coalition of the ascendant," as I've called it, is growing as a share of the electorate. But Obama's tightening embrace of its priorities nonetheless represents a historic gamble. Romney could still beat him by amassing large enough margins among the economically strained, culturally conservative older, and blue-collar whites whom Obama's recent decisions may further provoke.
>
> The president isn't conceding those voters, who once anchored his party's base: His attacks on Romney's Bain Capital experience largely target them. But far more than previous Democratic nominees, Obama seems willing to risk alienating them.[4]

The Obama campaign disagreed with the notion that Obama was not able to appeal to both groups at once and pointed to the fact that the polls continued to show him with a small but statistically significant lead. In an August *New Republic* article, Ruy Teixeira presented the case that this delicate balancing act could indeed lead to victory:

As has been widely noted, Obama's weakest voter group by far is the white working class. That is true today as it was true in the 2008 election, when Obama lost white working class voters by 18 points, but white college graduates by only 4 points... Huge deficits among these same voters routed the Democrats in 2010. And Obama appears to be weaker among this group today than he was back in 2008. Yet Obama is running ahead consistently in the national and swing state polls. Why is the Obama coalition not yet succumbing to its clear Achilles' heel?

There are two reasons. The first is that the rest of Obama's coalition has held up so well. The minority vote looks rock solid for Obama, coming very close to the 80 percent support level he received in 2008. Also, Obama may have actually gained ground among college-educated whites. In Pew polls, this group is averaging around a 2 point deficit for Obama, compared to 4 points in 2008.

This gives Obama a considerable buffer against expected weakness among white non-college voters. Indeed, if the minority and white college-educated vote hold up as well in November as they have in recent polling, Romney needs to generate a huge margin among white working class voters to have a decent chance of winning—closer to the 30 points Congressional Republicans won this group by in 2010 than the 18 point margin received by John McCain in 2008.

That brings us to the other reason Obama has been ahead so consistently in the polls. Romney has not been remotely close to that level of support among white working class voters. He's been averaging around the same margin McCain received in '08 with occasional readings as high as 23 points.

Even the latter margin is far off what he will need to win, given the size and leanings of the rest of the electorate.[5]

By the middle of the summer the major polling aggregates from Talking Points Memo, Pollster.com and Real ClearPolitics had settled into stable pattern with Obama holding an extremely small but steady lead. Among Democrats concern increasingly shifted to two key questions: Would the actual turnout of Obama's supporters on Election Day fall short of what the polls were suggesting? and Would some unexpected "October surprise" suddenly and dramatically alter the race?

In the following weeks daily campaign coverage followed a rapid roller-coaster ride from the Republican and Democratic conventions— with Bill Clinton's dramatic convention address and Clint Eastwood's dialog with an empty chair gaining major coverage—and then the up and down results of the three presidential debates.

Lurking beneath the headlines, however, was one underlying trend that was becoming clear regarding the white working class. As Tom Edsall noted in a *New York Times* article in late September:

> A key assumption underpinned Romney's [campaign in Pennsylvania]—that the working class whites who once dominated this great industrial center would back the Republican nominee...
>
> [But] even if there were a higher percentage of working class whites in the region, Romney would have faced an uphill struggle. A new survey ...reveals clearly that the white working class (broadly defined) cannot, at present, be described as a secure Republican constituency.
>
> ...The reason Romney has a strong, 13-point edge among all white working class voters, according to the [survey's] findings, is that in the South his margin is huge. In the rest of the country, the white working class is much more closely divided.

Among southern working class whites, Romney leads by 40 points, 62-22, an extraordinary gap.

The story in the rest of the country is different. In the West, where Colorado and Nevada are battleground states, Romney leads by a modest 5 points, 46-41. In the Northeast, which Obama is expected to sweep, except perhaps for New Hampshire, Romney holds a 4-point advantage among working class whites, 42-38. In the Midwest, where Ohio, Michigan and Wisconsin are in play, Obama actually leads among working class whites by 8 points (44-36).

There is a noticeable lack of zeal for either Romney or Obama among these voters. Only 66 percent of white working-class Americans said they are certain to vote, compared to 87 percent of college-educated whites and 74 percent of African Americans.[6]

Edsall identified one key difference between the North and the South:

Two Democratic operatives active in non-presidential campaigns in Pennsylvania argue that Romney just does not sell with non-southern working class whites. Doc Sweitzer, a political consultant whose clients include Kathleen Kane, the Democratic nominee for Attorney General, told me that cities and towns throughout the state "have all been hit by these corporate raider types" who buy and sell businesses in a manner similar to Romney's former firm, Bain Capital. "He just doesn't hunt here."

Steve Murphy, a media consultant working on congressional campaigns in Pennsylvania, characterized Romney's problem somewhat differently: "I don't think so much the argument is that he is anti-worker. It's just that they just don't like him. He seems like he is completely disconnected from people who have to work for a living."

...The hope harbored by Republican political professionals— that Obama was sufficiently unpopular among non-college whites to make up for Romney's shortcomings—has failed to take concrete form. The trouble Romney finds himself in today also suggests that the barrage of early advertising by the Obama campaign and allied groups attacking Bain Capital has proven to be a successful tactic, at least so far.

When Election Day arrived, the profound difference between the southern and non-southern white working class played a critical role in insuring Obama re-election. Ron Brownstein described the basic way in which this occurred:

President Obama won a second term by marrying the new Democratic coalition with just enough of the old to overcome enduring economic disenchantment and a cavernous racial divide.

In many places, particularly across the Sun Belt, Obama mobilized the Democrats' new "coalition of the ascendant," winning enough support among young people, minorities and college-educated whites, especially women, to overcome very weak numbers among blue-collar whites and college-educated men. But in the upper Midwest, where there are not enough of those voters to win, Obama attracted just enough working-class whites to hold the critical battlegrounds of Wisconsin, Iowa, and above all Ohio against Mitt Romney's forceful challenge.

...Exit polls show that the unstinting effort by his campaign and its allied super PACs to paint Romney as an insensitive plutocrat detonated with explosive force in those critical states, particularly Ohio, where nearly three in five voters said his agenda would favor the rich.[7]

In order to clearly understand the white working class vote in 2012, however, it is necessary to examine the results of the election in more detail.

Here is how voters with less than a 4 year college degree voted, compared with those who obtained a college degree*

WHITES		
	Less than 4 year college degree	College graduates
Vote for Obama	36%	42%

Thirty-six percent of voters with less than a four-year college degree voted for Barack Obama, four percent less than voted for him in 2008. With the strong turnout among other pro-Obama voting groups however, this reduced margin was still sufficient to insure his victory.

Looking more closely at the educational status of the voters in 2012, it quickly becomes clear that there was not a great difference in the level of support for Obama between the "narrowly" defined white working class—high school graduates—and the larger group of those with some college education. In fact, in this particular case, even college graduates voted for Obama in basically the same percentage as those with less education. It is only at the post graduate level that there is a sharp and major increase in Obama's support.

---

*Data on the voting patterns of demographic subgroups are usually derived from information in the major exit surveys. In 2012, however, the producers of these surveys did not release subgroup data for white Americans with less than a four year college degree. Fortunately the polling firm Democracy Corps conducted a very large (3,400 respondents) survey immediately after the election that provided similar types of data. The percentages given in the following charts are all drawn from that survey.

WHITES				
	High School Graduates	Some Post High School education	4 year college Degree	Post graduate education
Vote for Obama	36%	37%	37%	52%

Turning to gender, the difference between men with less than college educations and women with less than college educations is actually substantially more significant than the gap between the high school educated and those with some college.

WHITES WITH LESS THAN 4 YEARS OF COLLEGE		
	Men	Women
Vote for Obama	32%	40%

This gender gap is of critical significance for Democratic political strategy because if Obama had been forced to depend solely on the votes of white working class men, he could not have been elected. To the degree that there are different issues and messages that appeal to white working class men and women, this suggests that white working class women will be in general a more receptive audience.

Differences in age play slightly less of a role than differences in gender.

WHITES WITH LESS THAN A 4 YEAR COLLEGE DEGREE		
Age	Young (under 50)	Older (over 50)
Vote for Obama	38%	35%

As can be seen, white working class voters under 50 are somewhat more pro-Obama than their elders but the difference is not vast.

One quite dramatic distinction, on the other hand, is the difference between whites who are union members and those who are not.

Although in many areas of the country union members do not constitute a significant electoral force, in the critical states in the Midwest like Ohio they remain pivotal.

The following chart shows the level of support for Obama among white working class Americans in Ohio and Wisconsin who were members of unions compared with white working class Americans who were not members of unions.

NON-COLLEGE WHITE HOUSEHOLDS		
	Ohio	Wisconsin
2012 Union Household Vote for Obama	54%	60%
2012 Non-Union Household Vote for Obama	39%	42%

Source: http://www.washingtonpost.com/blogs/the-fix/wp/2012/11/20/can-unions-save-the-white-working-class-vote-for-democrats/

On the one hand, this clearly shows the very substantial pro-Democratic influence that union membership has on the political attitudes of white working class Americans—a 15 percent increase in support for Obama in Ohio and 18 percent in Wisconsin—but it also indicates an underlying geographical trend as well. Even among non-union white workers in those two states, the level of Obama support was substantially above the national white working class average of 36 percent.

The importance of geography is confirmed by a large public opinion study that used a distinct and more narrow definition of the term "working class" than simply levels of education. The study found a huge regional gap between the "white working class" vote for Obama in the South and in other regions of the country.

WHITE "WORKING CLASS" VOTERS				
	South	Midwest	West	Northeast
Vote for Obama	22%	44%	41%	38%

Source: http://publicreligion.org/site/wp-content/uploads/2012/09/WWC-Report-For-Web-Final.pdf

As we will see, this huge gap between support for Obama among white working class Americans in the South and those in the Midwest and other parts of the country reflects a series of underlying social and cultural differences between the two groups that make it necessary to visualize them as actually being two distinct white working class cultures—one rooted in the social conditions and "country" culture of the south and non-southern rural and small town areas and the other in the Rust Belt and other more urban and northern white working class areas. These distinct cultures produce two quite distinct political forces, one overwhelmingly and strongly Republican, the other, more evenly divided between Republicans and Democrats.

A final characteristic of the white working class vote in 2012 is one that does not show up in any of the charts above—the existence of the substantial number of white working class people who do not bother to vote on Election Day for either Democrats or Republicans.

William Galston of the Brookings Institution notes the importance of this group in 2012. First he presents the figures for all Americans:

> Overall, 128.7 million votes were cast, down from 131.5 million in 2008. And because the pool of eligible voters expanded by more than 10 million during that period, turnout fell sharply, from 62.3 percent of eligible citizens in 2008 to only 58.8 percent in 2012.

He then looks specifically at whites:

While we won't know for sure until the Census Bureau releases its results, a rough calculation suggests that five million fewer white Americans voted in 2012 than in 2008.

As Sean Trende has observed, demographic shifts can't explain this: "although whites are declining as a share of the voting-age population, their raw numbers are not." Most of the white voters who participated in 2008 are still alive, and those who aren't have been more than replaced by new white entrants into the electorate.

Incomplete evidence suggests that most of the white dropouts are working class voters who saw little to choose between an African American president they regarded as unacceptably liberal and a rich white venture capitalist who notoriously wrote many of them off as part of the "47 percent" content to receive government handouts.[8]

Obama's election, and particularly the role played by white working class voters in key states like Ohio, represented a substantial validation of Ruy Teixeira's continuing insistence on the decisive importance of those voters. Ironically, however, the massive turnout of the "Rising American Electorate"—the combination of minorities, youth, professionals and single women that Teixeira and Judis had called "the McGovern coalition" in The Emerging Democratic Majority—resulted in a substantial number of commentators asserting that by themselves this new coalition could be the foundation for a stable Democratic majority.

Teixeira emphatically disagrees:

According to the exit polls, [the white working class] is still an enormous group of voters—still larger than white college graduate voters—and there are good reasons to suspect that the exit polls may significantly underestimate the size of this group....

Progressives ignore that large a group at their peril. First and most obviously, increased support among this group could dramatically expand the progressive coalition. These voters, by virtue of their economic position, have clear potential to be a greater part of this coalition, if their suspicions about government ineffectiveness can be overcome. Secondly, progressives' already large deficit among the white working class—clearly their biggest political vulnerability—could easily become larger. If that happens, any fall-offs in support among their core and emerging constituencies could put the progressive majority at risk, despite continuing demographic trends in their favor. *Therefore, reducing the deficit among white, working-class voters should remain a key progressive objective.*[9]

It is also extremely important to note that when Teixeira cites statistics about the "decline" of the white working class, he is talking specifically and exclusively about the decline in their level of participation as voters, not their social and political significance as a demographic group. Because of their low levels of turnout and registration on Election Day as well as their gradual demographic decline, whites with less than a four-year college education have indeed contracted from 61 percent of the *electorate* in 1984 to 39 percent in 2008 *but this latter figure is emphatically not equivalent to their percentage of the population or the labor force.* In fact, as we will see in the next chapter, the kinds of occupations that most observers would comfortably describe as white "working class" still represent close to a majority of U.S. jobs.

This is profoundly important because the influence of the white working class in American politics and society is not limited to their votes on Election Day. In the day to day life of society—in on the job conversations, in their participation in community life and in their influence on their peers in political discussion and debate, white working class people who do not themselves vote nonetheless have a significant effect on American political life. To understand the full role and significance of the white working class in American politics, it is necessary to look beyond those who cast a vote on election day.

Part One

Who They Are

CHAPTER

1

The Surprising Size of "White Working Class" America – Half of all White Men and 40 Percent of White Women Still Work in Basically Blue-Collar Jobs

In the spring of 2012 an energetic argument about voting trends among white "working class" voters and the right way to properly define the group itself mushroomed across the pages of the *New York Times,* the *U.K. Guardian, The New Republic, The Washington Monthly* and a variety of other political journals.

As Tom Edsall noted in a round-up article in the *New York Times:*

> Political analysts, journalists and academics are fighting over white working-class voters—over how to define them and what their political significance is. Part of the reason for the furious tone of the argument is that this is an issue of central importance in American politics. And it's not just crucial for the presidential election: understanding what the white working class is and where it is going is fundamental if we want to understand where the country is going…

> …Part of the problem is that different people mean different things when they are talking about the working class. Is this cohort made up of those without college degrees; those in the bottom third of the income distribution; or those

in occupations described by the federal government as "blue-collar"?[1]

The most careful and systematic recent analysis of how to best define the white working class was presented by Ruy Teixeira and Alan Abramowitz in a 2008 Brookings Institution study. Teixeira and Abramowitz carefully compared the advantages and disadvantages of each of the approaches above and developed a sophisticated composite index that made use of all three forms of data Edsall noted as well as people's own self-description of their class position.[2]

In that same analysis, however, Teixeira and Abramowitz also noted that for several very practical reasons most polling companies, political strategists and media commentators today accept education rather than occupation or income as the best single way to define the term "working class."

On the one hand, although the traditional conception of the term "working class" and most people's mental image of working class individuals has historically been based on occupation, collecting useful data in this area presents serious practical problems. When polling companies call people on the telephone, getting them to provide clear, unambiguous definitions of their specific job and occupation is often extremely difficult and accurately categorizing those responses into broad categories like "blue collar" versus "white collar" frequently presents problems. In contrast, asking a person about the highest level of education he or she has obtained is generally straightforward.

The alternative approach of defining "working class" simply in terms of income level produces even greater complications. Low income individuals include all sorts of people—the retired, students, homemakers, the chronically ill or disabled and others who are not working at all and the group is simply not what political analysts and commentators really mean to refer to when they use the term "white working class." The inescapable fact is that "lower income" people and "working class" people are actually very distinct sociological categories.

While it avoids these problems, using education to define the term white working class does, however, also have its own downside. While, as we will see, education and occupation do indeed substantially overlap, they are not identical. When commentators use the term "the white working class" they are generally visualizing blue collar or other essentially physical or manual workers—a group that has very distinct social and cultural characteristics—rather than the more sociologically amorphous and hard to visualize social category of "less educated" individuals. In most people's experience, blue collar and other basically manual workers are significantly different from white collar office workers, sales workers or technical workers who happen to have less than a four-year college degree and it is the former group rather than the latter that people generally associate with the term "working class."*

The Disappearing White Working Class

In fact, there is a deep and unacknowledged political schizophrenia in American public attitudes toward the traditional, "blue collar" white working class. In the three or four months before elections journalists head to Ohio and Pennsylvania and send back reports from the blue collar diners, bowling alleys and pot-luck dinners in white working class neighborhoods in those states because it is universally agreed that they are key battlegrounds in the elections. Other reporters go on the road and file dispatches from NASCAR

---

*There is also a fourth, essentially economic or more precisely "political-economic" definition of the term working class—people who are employed by others and who essentially have to "take orders" rather than "give orders." This political-economic definition harks back to the 18th century concept of the "proletariat" and is chiefly concerned with the relations of power in society rather than with the social, cultural or political differences between groups of voters which constitute the primary concern of political strategists and electoral campaign managers. In his book, The Working Class Majority, Michael Zweig uses the economic definition to calculate that almost two-thirds of Americans can be defined as working class today and this broad vision of "the many versus the few" found practical application in the rhetoric and analyses of the Occupy movement.

races, tractor pulls, country music concerts and other parts of red state America to sample the mood of the other, "real" U.S.A. For a few weeks the papers and TV news programs are filled with images of the white working class—the America of weather-beaten, wood-siding houses with metal swing sets and cars with chipped and faded paint in the front yard, the America of deer hunters, roadside churches, Ford and Chevy trucks hauling john boats and off- road motorbikes to state parks on weekends and crowded bars that play commercial country music and show mixed martial arts on their TV's. This world suddenly becomes visible because it is recognized that this is where the election will be decided.

But then, two or three weeks after elections are over, the white working class suddenly disappears. Commentators quickly revert to describing America as a block of socially homogenous "middle class" voters while the profound social chasm that exists within the white electorate is completely ignored. Whites, other than pro-Democratic professionals, are routinely analyzed as rural or suburban rather than urban, red state rather than blue state and old rather than young. But they are rarely if ever distinguished as blue collar versus white collar.

Underlying this lack of attention to white working class Americans is the powerful image of the "modern digital economy"—the deeply rooted conviction that in the knowledge-based, post-industrial world traditional blue collar workers simply can't be very important— politically or sociologically. This is reflected in the major clichés and buzzwords of modern political commentary. In the 1990's images of a new white-collar electorate became popular—the famous "soccer moms", "office park dads" and "wired workers". More recently the *"new working class"*—"pink collar workers" or "waitress moms" among women and low paid, dead-end "lousy jobs" for young men—have also become journalistic clichés.

But traditional blue collar workers do not have a current cliché of their own. The 1950's era image of the "average Joe" or "ordinary guy" who was a basically decent fellow and reliable Democratic voter became transformed into the image of the conservative "Joe six-packs" and "hard hats" in the 1970's. In recent decades the images switched to geography and culture rather than occupation—the gun owning, pickup truck driving "rednecks" and "bubbas" who supported George W. Bush and the religious right. In the 2008 election the most significant—and misleading—images of blue collar workers were both starkly Republican—"Joe the plumber" and Todd Palin.

The White Working Class is More Than Just Industrial Workers

The basis for this relative disinterest in the traditional white working class is the notion that it represents a rapidly shrinking minority of the electorate and society as a whole. Because this decline seems almost self-evident, factual support for the view is usually limited to the presentation of just a few illustrative statistics—the most common being that manufacturing workers declined from 40 percent of the labor force in 1940 to 10 percent today.

There is, however, a profound fallacy in this approach. While the demographic assertion about the decline of industrial workers is technically accurate it is also deeply and fundamentally misleading. The number of manufacturing workers has indeed declined, but "industrial workers" represent only a small sub-set of the larger sociological categories "blue collar" or "working class."

In fact, when one takes the critical step of looking separately at the occupations of white men and white women rather than combining them together and focuses first on the occupations of white men, the striking fact that quickly becomes apparent is that there are still many white workers who are basically blue collar even though they do not work in large factories. They work in sectors other than manufacturing—as auto mechanics, construction workers, warehouse workers, truck drivers, police and firemen. Nor is this a recent phenomenon. Even in the 1950's industrial workers were not the only members of the American white working class. Longshoremen, teamsters, construction workers, security guards, night watchmen, janitors, cops, garbage collectors and many others were all part of the broad Democratic conception of "working class" men—the "ordinary guys" or "average Joes" whose support provided the foundation of the New Deal coalition.

But, oddly, in modern political commentary one literally never sees specific calculations of what fraction traditional blue collar workers constitute of the total white male labor force today. In most discussions the combination of the declining industrial work force and the growing white and pink collar "new white working class" composed of both men and women is treated as sufficient evidence to logically deduce that white male blue collar workers are no longer a critical political force.

This notion so deeply ingrained in modern political discussion that anyone who flatly asserted that the number of white men who still work in basically physical or routine manual jobs actually represent half of the white male labor force in America would be dismissed as simply unfamiliar with the data.

But, in fact, if one looks carefully at the detailed Bureau of Labor Statistics (BLS) tables that list the number of white men who work in some 300 major occupational categories (which includes those "not elsewhere classified", making it effectively include all white male workers) this is precisely what one finds. Almost exactly half of the white male labor force works in occupations that most political observers, commentators and ordinary voters would quickly and confidently define as basically "blue collar" or manual rather than white collar.

Blue Collar vs. White Collar*

Let us look first at white men and then at white women. Here is a chart that divides the number of white male workers in the major occupations that are tracked by the Bureau of Labor Statistics into the two basic categories "blue collar" and "white collar."

---

*The BLS sources for all of the statistics given in this chapter are described in detail in the section "Notes on the Data" at the end of this chapter.

OCCUPATIONS OF WHITE MALE WORKERS – 2007		
Total Employed (in thousands)	62,461	
White Collar Occupations	31,086	49.8%
Managers/ Executives/Professionals	21,907	
Sales/Clerical /Office Workers	9,178	
Lower Level Supervisors/ Foremen (Note: not included in either blue or white collar categories. See text)	2,826	
Blue Collar /Working Class Occupations	31,376	50.2%
Traditional Blue Collar Workers	22,722	
Blue Collar Service Workers	6,943	
Blue Collar Clerical Workers	1,711	

Note: in this chart the "traditional blue collar" category includes the two BLS top-level categories "production, transportation and material moving" and "Natural Resources, construction and maintenance" These contain essentially the same set of occupations as the three traditional post-war BLS categories "craftsmen", "operatives" and "laborers".

People who are familiar with the occupational categories used by the Bureau of Labor Statistics will note that—unlike the chart above—BLS statistics do not separate out the blue collar workers in the "service" and "sales, clerical and office" categories from the white collar or pink collar workers in those same two categories. The reason is that the BLS categorization schemes are not designed to quantify the political and sociological categories "blue collar" and "white collar" but rather for quite different demographic and commercial purposes.

Specific Occupations

As a result, it is necessary to look more closely at the list of detailed occupations that lie beneath the broad categories in order to properly estimate the overall numbers of essentially blue collar versus white collar white men. The complete BLS chart is available for examination.[1]

Traditional Blue Collar Workers – there are 196 different specific occupations listed in the two BLS categories "Production, Transportation and Materials Moving" and "Natural Resource, Construction and Maintenance." They range from carpenters, construction laborers and iron and steel workers to auto mechanics, heating and air conditioning repairmen, truck drivers, butchers, factory workers, machinists and tool and die makers.

Traditional blue collar workers include:

Manufacturing workers
- 400,000 welders: average weekly earnings $661
- 44,000 electrical and electromechanical assemblers: average weekly earnings $622
- 300,000 machinists: average weekly earnings $802
- 51,000 cutting, punching and press machine operators: average weekly earnings $637
- 1,100,000 Laborers and materials movers: average weekly earnings $508

Transportation workers
- 2,400,000 truck drivers: average weekly earnings $691
- 225,000 bus drivers: average weekly earnings $660
- 180,000 taxi drivers: average weekly earnings $570

Construction workers
- 1,100,000 carpenters: average weekly earnings $624

- 680,000 electricians: average weekly
  earnings $890
- 480,000 plumbers: average weekly
  earnings $793
- 190,000 roofers — average weekly
  earnings $521
- 115,000 sheet metal workers — average
  weekly earnings $733
- 1,200,000 construction laborers — average
  weekly earnings $596

Mechanics and linemen

- 680,000 auto mechanics: average weekly
  earnings $680
- 340,000 heating and air conditioning mechanics:
  average weekly earnings $862
- 140,000 phone and cable linemen and installers:
  average weekly earnings $873

Agricultural and logging workers

- 510,000 miscellaneous agricultural workers:
  average weekly earnings $415
- 47,000 logging workers: average weekly
  earnings $613

Blue Collar Service Workers. There are 46 different occupations listed in the service category. For men, it is over- whelmingly blue collar. The largest male occupations in this category include policemen, firemen, guards and prison workers, cooks, waiters, bartenders, and dishwashers, janitors, lawn care, pest control and grounds maintenance workers.

Blue collar service workers include:

- 515,000 police: average weekly earnings $992

- 245,000 firefighters: average weekly earnings..$1055
- 500,000 security guards: average weekly earnings..$519
- 1,100,000 janitors: average weekly earnings..$494
- 890,000 cooks: average weekly income..................$401
- 170,000 dishwashers: average weekly earnings..$327
- 990,000 grounds and landscape workers: average weekly earnings $433
- 34,000 baggage porters: average weekly earnings..$564

Blue Collar Clerical/Sales/Office Workers – Within the clerical, sales and office category there are actually a substantial number of blue collar occupations. The largest blue collar occupations in this category include meter readers, mail carriers, shipping clerks and stock clerks.

Blue collar clerical/sales/office workers include:
- 170,000 mailmen: average weekly earnings..$952
- 45,000 bill collectors: average weekly earnings..$597
- 670,000 stock clerks and order fillers: average weekly earnings.................................$471
- 260,000 shipping and receiving clerks: average weekly earnings.................................$553

Lower-level Foremen and Supervisors – culturally and politically speaking, lower level foremen and supervisors generally share the blue-collar culture of the men they work with and who are often their friends and neighbors. In traditional industrial sociology, however, they were frequently considered a distinct, socially ambiguous group because they represent management. As a result, in calculating ratios of blue-collar to white collar workers, they were frequently set aside in a special "neither fish nor fowl" category.

If low-level foremen and supervisors are left out of the calculation, the percentage of blue collar and white collar white men in 2007 was almost precisely equal—50.2 to 49.8 percent. Including lower-level foremen and supervisors as part of the white collar total only increases that total by about 2 percent.

It is important to note that the economic crisis of 2008 actually eliminated almost 2 million working class jobs between 2007 and 2009, lowering the blue collar proportion of the labor force from 50 to 48 percent. It is reasonable to assume, however, that a significant number of these working class jobs will eventually return unless America remains in a permanent economic recession.

The basic conclusion is clear. Taken as a whole, the rather startling fact is that somewhere close to 50 percent of white men today are still in basically blue collar jobs.

For many people, this is quite unexpected. With the disappearance of the vast auto and steel plants of the 50's and 60's it became easy to imagine that the large majority of white American men had become part of an amorphous white-collar majority. But it simply is not true.

The Earnings of White Working Class Men

It is also worth noting a few facts about these white workers' income. During the 1950's and 1960's the cliché of the "affluent worker" became popular as many commentators noted that some skilled blue-collar workers earned more than many white collar workers. Even today, it is often suggested that blue-collar workers earnings are not really substantially lower than most white collar workers.

The facts, however, show the opposite. While many skilled workers and union workers in fields where they have substantial bargaining power can earn "affluent" incomes, most blue-collar workers earn distinctly less than their white collar counterparts.

WHITE COLLAR VS BLUE COLLAR	
Occupation (men)	Median Weekly Earnings
White Collar	
Management, business and financial	$1,388
Professional	$1191
Sales and Office	$761
Blue Collar	
Natural Resources, Construction and Maintenance	$730
Production and Transportation	$661
Service	$559

Every major white collar category makes more than any blue collar category. There are many specific occupations where white and blue collar weekly earnings overlap, but, seen on a larger scale, the pattern is clear.

A second point to note is that weekly earnings for the specific Blue Collar Service and Blue Collar Clerical and Sales occupations presented in the preceding pages provide confirmation that the blue-collar workers in those categories are indeed essentially "working class" rather than "middle class." In most cases they earn less than skilled blue collar workers making them clearly part of the white working class in terms of income as well as occupation.

Finally, it is important to note that looking at median weekly earnings provides a much more "down to earth" picture of workers' financial situation than do annual figures. Looking at the weekly figures one can quickly convert them to the familiar hourly rates that Americans encounter in daily life—10 or 12 dollars an hour for laborers or other unskilled workers and 22 to 24 dollars an hour for construction and other skilled workers.

The Occupations of White Working Class Women

Now consider the parallel statistics for white women:

OCCUPATIONS OF WHITE FEMALE WORKERS – 2007		
Total Employment (In Thousands)	**53,740**	
White Collar Occupations	**41,218**	
Managers/ Executives/ Professionals	23,509	
Sales/Clerical/Office Workers	17,709	The Working Class total rises to 40% if the female Clerical and Sales category is assumed to actually be split 50/50 between basically blue collar and white collar jobs
Lower Level Supervisors/ Foremen (Note: not included in either blue collar or white collar categories. See text)	763	
Blue Collar /Working Class Occupations	**12,522**	23% in traditional Working Class Occupations for women
Traditional Blue Collar Workers	3445	
Blue Collar Service Workers	8,016	
Blue Collar Clerical Workers	1,061	

Note: in this chart the "traditional blue collar" category includes the two BLS top-level categories "Production, Transportation and Material Moving" and "Natural Resources, Construction and Maintenance".

As the chart above shows, 23 percent—about one fourth of white female workers are in traditional female blue collar/working class jobs. The number rises toward 40 percent when one includes the essentially working class jobs contained within the Clerical, Sales and Office category. Once again, however, it is necessary to look at the detailed occupations to see the real story.

Traditional Blue Collar Workers – There have always been many blue collar occupations for women—circuit board assemblers in electronics plants, laundry workers, sewing machine operators, bus drivers and packaging workers among others. While blue collar "women's work" often requires less gross muscularity than many male blue collar jobs, it frequently requires greater endurance, focus and tenacity making the jobs equally hard, mind-numbing, and exhausting.

Traditional blue-collar occupations for women include:
- 61,000 electronics assemblers: average weekly earnings $481
- 213,000 Miscellaneous assemblers: average weekly earnings $475
- 75,000 Laundry and dry cleaning workers: average weekly earnings $361
- 105,000 sewing machine operators: average weekly earnings $410
- 178,000 packers and packagers: average weekly earnings $398
- 155,000 inspectors, testers and sorters: average weekly earnings $549
- 238,000 bus drivers: average weekly earnings $502

Service Workers – the largest specific occupations in this category include many of the classic white working class jobs for women—maids, cleaning women, waitresses, cooks, dishwashers, hostesses, counter attendants, ticket-takers and child care workers. These are the kinds of low-level jobs that Barbara Ehrenreich very perceptively described in her book, *Nickel and Dimed*. They are generally low-paid, no-benefit jobs with constant pressure and close supervision. It is the jobs of this kind that led the London Economist to recently define the "modern" white working class as people who "work with their hands or stand on their feet all day." In fact, these jobs actually fit the traditional sociological criteria for blue collar work based on four major factors – (1) primarily physical rather than mental, (2) dull and repetitive, (3) closely supervised and (4) offering limited potential for advancement.

Blue collar service occupations for women include:
- 1,230,000 waitresses: average weekly earnings $381
- 624,000 cooks: average weekly earnings $381
- 200,000 hostesses restaurant and coffee shops: average weekly earnings $337
- 992,000 maids and housekeeping cleaners: average weekly earnings $376
- 539,000 building cleaners and janitors: average weekly earnings.. $400
- 590,000 hairdressers, and cosmetologists: average weekly earnings $462
- 970,000 child care workers: average weekly earnings.. $398

Clerical, Sales and Office Workers – the clerical, sales and office category for women is huge—larger than all the traditional white working class occupations combined. But, in fact, a substantial number of these jobs are more accurately described as "white (or pink) collar working class" rather than simply "white collar." Some of the major occupations in this category include cashiers, telephone operators, file clerks, tellers, receptionists, and the lowest-level retail sales workers.

In sociological terms, it is clear that there is a deep social schism within this broad occupational category. Female real estate brokers and executive secretaries obviously live and work in a profoundly different environment than cashiers or telephone operators. White collar or pink collar working class jobs for women are, in general, preferable to working on an electronic assembly line for a minimum wage or scrubbing floors and making beds in hotels but many of these jobs come close to fitting traditional sociological definitions of white working class status based on effort, monotony, lack of mobility and close supervision as well as in regard to broader issues like pay, benefits and social status.

Jobs for women in the clerical, sales and office categories that fit many of the traditional sociological criteria for "working class" occupations include:

- 1,700,000 cashiers: average weekly earnings $366
- 1,350,000 retail salespersons: average weekly earnings $421
- 307,000 tellers: average weekly earnings $490
- 46,000 telephone and switchboard operators: average weekly earnings $588
- 206,000 file clerks: average weekly earnings $583
- 400,000 office clerks: average weekly earnings $597
- 1,000,000 receptionists: average weekly earnings $529

As far as earnings are concerned, for women as for men, all of the white collar occupational categories earn more than any of the blue collar ones.

Occupation (women)	Median Weekly Earnings
White Collar	
Management, business and financial	$972
Professional	$912
Sales and Office	$600
Blue Collar	
Natural Resources, Construction and Maintenance	$537
Production and Transportation	$473
Service	$423

The bottom line result is simple: close to half of white men and 35-40 percent of white women in the labor force are still essentially "working class." Their occupations are basically blue collar rather than white collar and their earnings fall far below their white collar counterparts.

In one respect, this seems a new and startling conclusion. In another sense, however, it is something most people really suspected all along. The data that has been presented here dramatically illustrates that in the real world white blue-collar workers are a far more important social group than is generally recognized. They are not the desperate and jobless workers who "shaped up" in front of the factory gates every day to beg for work as factory workers did during the great depression. Many make decent money and vast numbers work as small independent contractors rather than hired employees. Nor do most white working class men still talk or act like the inarticulate, hulking laborers portrayed by Marlon Brando in the 1950's and Sylvester Stallone in the 1970's. But they are united by sociological traits and cultural values that define many aspects of their social identity. Unlike the affluent or highly educated they see themselves as *"real Americans"* who are *"just getting by"*, They are *"hard-working,"* *"practical"* and *"realistic."* They believe in *"old-fashioned traditional values"* and trust in *"character"* and real-world experience rather than advanced education. They rely on *"common sense"* not abstract theories. These characteristics have not basically changed since the 1950's when these workers considered themselves good Democrats and they remain important determinants of their political outlook today.

The fact that white workers are actually a far larger and more politically important group than the common wisdom of recent years has suggested explains why political reporters and campaign strategists suddenly find themselves focusing on the mood in blue collar diners, bowling alleys and pot-luck dinners in white working class neighborhoods in Ohio and Pennsylvania as election day approaches while other reporters go on the road and file dispatches from NASCAR races, tractor pulls and country music bars. If traditional blue collar white working class people were really as socially and politically marginal as the popular clichés suggest, this would simply not be necessary.

In fact, traditional white working class voters are still a central force in American politics—a far larger force than most political commentators recognize. This is a fact that would clearly emerge if public opinion polls could accurately categorize employed voters by their occupations. As the next section reveals, however, education is actually quite closely correlated with occupation, enough to allow public opinion researchers to use education as a valid proxy for the traditional occupationally based conception of white working class status.

Notes on the Data in Chapter 1

The data on detailed occupations comes from the following unpublished table provided by the BLS:

"employed persons by detailed occupation sex and race 2007-2009 - annual averages."

It can be downloaded at http://www.thedemocraticstrategist.org/_memos/Employed-persons-by-detailed-occupation-sex-and-race-2007-09_annual-averages.xlsx

In calculating the data that appears in the two tables comparing blue collar and white collar employment in this analysis, five changes were made to the original BLS presentation of the data. The changes are displayed in the revised excel file titled :

"Employed persons by detailed occupation sex and race 2007 and 2009 - revised."

It can be downloaded at http://www.thedemocraticstrategist.org/_memos/Employed-persons-by-detailed-occupation-sex-and-race-2007-09_annual-averages.xlsx

The four changes are as follows:

1. The top-level BLS occupational categories (e.g. "Management, Professional and related occupations") that were not included in the original BLS excel table were added to the revised excel file.

2. In the revised file the entire top-level category "service workers" was moved from above the "Sales and Office workers" category to below it instead.

3. The major blue collar occupations from the "Sales and Office workers" category were extracted and placed in a newly created category called "blue collar sales and office workers"

4. All "supervisors and managers" from the blue collar categories were extracted and placed in a newly created category called "first line supervisors and managers"

Apart from these broad changes no attempt was made to move individual occupations out of their positions in the original BLS tables.

The revised spreadsheet also has excel versions of the two tables included in the article (in the tab labeled sheet 1) and data extracted from the BLS table on occupation and employment (in the tab labeled sheet 3)

The data on earnings and occupation are derived from the following unpublished BLS table:

Table A-26. Usual weekly earnings of employed full-time wage and salary workers by detailed occupation and sex, Annual Average 2010

It can be downloaded at http://www.thedemocraticstrategist.org/_memos/ Earn26_2010.pdf

The same data was also provided as an excel file and edited for this analysis to present only the relevant information.

Earnings by Occupation – 2010 – revised.
It can be downloaded at http://www.thedemocraticstrategist.org/_memos/earnings-by-occupation_2010_revised.xlsx

CHAPTER

2

Education and Occupation Overlap – Three Quarters of High School Educated White Men are in Blue Collar Jobs.

One important benefit of the revised view of white working class occupations provided in the preceding sections is that it provides a missing sociological underpinning for the modern approach of most political analysts, pollsters and strategists who now define the term "working class" in terms of education. Since 2000, and stimulated by the demographic work of Ruy Teixeira in his 1999 book, *The Forgotten Majority – Why the White Working Class Still Matters* and his subsequent studies, public opinion analysts have increasingly come to visualize the "working class" as those survey respondents who have either just a high school diploma or less than a college education.

Teixeira's point of departure was the fact that in the modern economy people who had no more than high school diplomas were very severely limited in their occupational choices to either blue collar or the lowest level white collar jobs. Regardless of the precise nature of the work that was involved, individuals with only a high school education were confined to the kinds of jobs that offered relatively low wages, meager or non-existent fringe benefits, very limited job security and opportunities for advancement, low social status and a variety of other negative characteristics. This made these jobs substantially different from the jobs available to individuals with higher education.

The resulting insight that education could therefore be used either as a very close proxy for occupation in studying the white working class or be visualized as representing a new non-occupational way of defining the white working class was tremendously important for political analysis because education levels are, as we saw, relatively easy to collect on opinion surveys while obtaining useful data on occupations has always been fiendishly difficult. Today, in political and polling analysis, education has become the most widely accepted way to define white working class.

Few studies, however, have tried to directly relate the specific occupations that people hold with their level of education. But basic data is in fact available and provides a deeper sociological picture of people with high school or less than college educations.

Here is a chart that shows the situation for white men, once again from the BLS:

OCCUPATIONS OF WHITE MEN BY YEARS OF EDUCATION – 2008			
Occupation	High School or Less	Some College (including AA degrees)	BA or Above
Total	40%	26%	34%
White Collar	26%	50%	86%
Blue Collar	74%	50%	14%

Note: in this chart "blue collar" includes the three BLS top-level categories "Production, Transportation and Material Moving", "Natural Resource and Construction" and "Service" occupations. The "White collar" total includes the BLS categories "Sales and Office" and "Management and Professional". [It is worth noting that if the blue collar workers in the clerical and sales category were allocated to the blue collar category the total would be even higher].

What this chart shows is that for white male workers with no more than a high school diploma—74 percent—three-fourths of the total—worked in blue collar jobs while only 26 percent had white collar occupations. For those with "some college"—Associate of Arts degrees or some college credits but no diploma—exactly half were blue collar and half white collar.

The heavy concentration of the high school educated in blue collar jobs is hardly surprising. It is in high school where young men and women's social identities are formed and it is largely these social identities—the sense of "who I am"—that substantially determine the kinds of occupations and the level of education they seek when they graduate.

Across a wide variety of American high schools, the two basic social identities that always emerge are the opposed cultures of "Jocks vs. Burnouts", "Greasers vs. Preppies", "Punks vs. BOMC's (Big Men on Campus)", "Trash vs. Collegiates". The particular names that are used vary from region to region but they always reflect the basic divide between white working class and middle class students.

As anthropologist Penelope Eckert notes in her study, *Jocks and Burnouts—Social Categories and Identity in the High School*:

> The Jocks and Burnouts are adolescent embodiments of the middle and working class, respectively; their two separate cultures are in many ways class cultures; and opposition and conflict between them define and exercise class relations and differences...

> Although the majority of high school students do not define themselves as full-fledged members of one category or another, an important part of most adolescent's social identity is dominated by the opposition between the two categories.[1]

In terms of occupational choice, the Jock vs. Burnout distinction marks the division between those who are aiming for college and a middle class life versus those who are gradually accommodating themselves to a future in the white working class.

Many white working class students tend to orient themselves toward occupations they perceive as "manly". In Texas, for example, anthropologist Douglas Foley describes the white working class students' attitudes as follows:

> Going to college was "too hard" and "cost too much money." Most aspired to working class jobs like their fathers, such as driving a tractor, trucking melons, fixing cars, setting irrigation rigs, and working in packing sheds. Some wanted to be carpenters and bricklayers or work for the highway road crews…. [Working on road crews] was the rural equivalent of working in a factory or foundry. It was dangerous dirty heavy work that only "real" men did… They considered working with their hands honorable, a test of strength and manliness. In contrast school work was seen as boring "sissy stuff".

While college is considered unattainable, students like these still seek to graduate high school because even most white working class jobs now require at least a high school diploma. But they see the diploma as simply a piece of paper.

As sociologist Lois Weis notes in *Working Class without Work – High School Students in a De-industrializing Economy:*

> In spite of the deeply felt sense that schooling is the only way to "keep off burgers" (i.e. work at a Burger King) most concern themselves only with passing not with excelling, competing or even doing well. The language of "passing" dominates student discourse around schooling much as obtaining a union card dominated the discourse of previous generations of white working class males… most end up with C's and D's but they do pass…

The connection between a high school diploma and working class status is therefore extremely tight. Once in the labor market, men and women with only high school diplomas find themselves largely restricted to relatively dead end jobs and white working class lifestyles.

There is, however, also a second major group within the

white working class—the more "aspirational" individuals who go on to community college. Many skilled working class jobs like automobile mechanics and heating and air conditioning installation and repair that were previously learned in union apprenticeship programs or through on the job training now require an Associate of Arts degree. As a result the more ambitious and disciplined white working class students go to community college to get the necessary credential.

The very strong class distinction between students who attend community college and students in the 1,000 leading four year colleges is clearly indicated by their economic situation. As Tom Edsall notes:

> ...Student bodies in competitive colleges and in community colleges reflect two very different economic worlds. At the 1,044 competitive colleges, 76 percent of the freshman came from families in the upper half of the income distribution. In the nation's 1,000-plus community colleges, almost 80 percent of the students came from low-income families.[2]

OCCUPATIONS OF WHITE MALES / AA DEGREES		
	Technical	Academic
White Collar	43%	57%
Blue Collar	57%	43%

Within the community college world, the social distinction between the blue collar and white collar graduates is captured by their distribution between technical and academic degrees. Of the men with technical degrees, 57 percent were employed in blue collar jobs. Of those with academic degrees, 57 percent were in white collar jobs.

Looking at the educational data more broadly, in 2008, 40 percent of white men had no more than a high school education, 26 percent had some college and 34 percent had at least a bachelor's degree. Using a "narrow" definition of "white working class" as those with no more than a high school diploma, 75 percent were employed in blue collar jobs. Using a "broad" definition of white working class—people with less than a four year college degree, 66 percent were blue collar workers.

Thus, either three-fourths or two-thirds of those men who are "working class" as defined by education are also blue collar workers in occupational terms. The white working class as defined by education is not identical to the white working class as defined by occupation, but the two approaches very substantially overlap.

Among women the ratio of blue collar to broadly defined white collar workers at the various educational levels cannot be accurately calculated with the available data because of the huge clerical, sales and office category which contains a complex mixture of both groups. But, the general picture is as follows: around one-third of women workers have a high school education or less, one-third have "some college" but less than a college degree and one-third are college educated. At the same time, about 40 percent are blue collar in occupational terms. Again, the "working class" as defined by education and by occupation substantially overlaps.

The overlap between occupation and education is not only important because it allows public opinion data from high school and less than college respondents to be used as a valid guide to the opinions of the "working class." It is also critically important because it dispels the notion that the less-educated can be visualized as a unique and distinct social group, rather than simply as another way of describing working class Americans.

Notes on Chapter 2

The data on education and employment are derived from the following unpublished BLS table.

"Table 10. Employed persons by intermediate occupation, educational attainment, sex, race, and Hispanic or Latino ethnicity (25 years and over), Annual Average 2008 (Source: Current Population Survey)"
It can be downloaded at http://www.thedemocraticstrategist.org/_memos/Table10_Employed-persons-by-intermediate-occupation-educational-attainment-sex-race-and-Hispanic-or-Latino.pdf

CHAPTER

3

The Working Class Seems Invisible in Daily Life – Explaining the Social and Geographical Reasons Why They Seem to Have Disappeared.

For many people the data in the preceding sections will seem somehow implausible and dramatically in conflict with daily observation and common sense. In daily life it often seems as if working class America has largely disappeared. One simply does not "see" blue collar workers today in the way that one did in the 1950's.

And in fact, in a sociological sense, this is literally true—blue collar workers have not actually ceased to exist but sociologically they have become invisible. There are four main mechanisms by which this occurs.

First, the large majority of blue collar and other manual workers today now work in relatively small groups rather than large factory settings. This makes observers perceive them as individuals rather than as members of a large and coherent social group. On a typical day a person may come in close contact with 15 or 20 blue collar workers—workers like the power company lineman on the pole in front of their house as they leave for work or the phone men or cable installers working on the junction boxes on the side of their homes when they return. A person will speak with a brake repairman at Brake-O or Pep Boys and the delivery driver from UPS. He or she will pass baggage handlers in airports and security guards at malls. But because each of these encounters is with a single individual or small group rather than with large masses like the long files of workers who once walked into steel mills and auto factories at 7:45 every morning, the typical person only "sees" a succession of individuals and not representative members of a social group. We see individual workers continuously, but never consciously "notice" working class Americans.

Second, many blue collar workers today have much more frequent contact with white collar and professional workers and with customers or clients as well. As a result, they have become less distinct and recognizable in style, diction and behavior. Daily contact and interaction with customers has significantly reduced their physical isolation and cultural distinctiveness. By the 1980's a large proportion of the children of the workers of the 1950's no longer fit the traditional stereotype of the hulking, inarticulate, brutish blue-collar worker exemplified by Marlon Brando's character Stanley Kowalsky in the 1956 film version of *A Streetcar Named Desire* or Sylvester Stalone's *Rocky* in the 1970's. The typical 30 year old electrician or auto mechanic one talks to today is very unlikely to bring any of these stereotypes to mind.

Third, many workers are now also small businessmen. In large cities one can still walk by large construction sites where hundreds of unionized hard-hat workers are employed but in single family home and small commercial construction, you will see instead a collection of pickup trucks and vans with the signs of independent contractors stenciled on their sides. This vast web of small contractors includes not just electricians and plumbers but bricklayers, stucco contractors, insulation, sheetrock and heating and air conditioning contractors, grading and foundation contractors, paving installers, trim carpenters, welders, glaziers, roofers, stonemasons, cabinetmakers, landscapers and security and home entertainment system installers. Even after construction is complete there remains a still-vast network of lawn and garden contractors, equipment repair technicians, exterminators and other providers of ongoing services all of whom work as independent contractors rather than salaried employees. This same pattern is easily seen in gardening, automobile and appliance repair and janitorial and cleaning services among many others.

Many small stores and businesses also employ a wide range of manual workers—stocking clerks, dishwashers, drivers and delivery men. These men and women are perceived as "employees" rather than "blue collar workers". These small businesses range from bowling alleys and beauty shops to hardware stores and auto parts and body shops and employ huge numbers of working class people.

But finally, and perhaps most significantly, many workers are literally invisible during the day on the job. The large factories of the 50's were iconic images of America and pictures of large groups of workers entering and leaving the factory gates were common. Millions of workers today work in industrial parks and warehouse districts in every city in America but there is no iconic image of the place where they work. There are vast acres and miles of warehouses in all major cities, but workers are not visible in large crowds like those who once worked in automobile or steel factories. These workers work on loading docks and drive fork lift trucks down long aisles of reinforced metal shelves that rise two and three stories into the air. They roll metal carts and jack up wood pallets to store boxes of goods in bins, shelves and boxes but are rarely seen by anyone from outside.

Here is one description of this invisible part of America:

> Like nearly everyone else in Joliet without good job prospects, Uylonda Dickerson eventually found herself at the warehouses looking for work.
>
> "I just needed a job," the 38-year-old single mother says.
>
> Dickerson came to the right place. Over the past decade and a half, Joliet, IL and its Will County environs southwest of Chicago have grown into one of the world's largest inland

ports, a major hub for dry goods destined for retail stores throughout the Midwest and beyond. ...

Dickerson, grateful to have even a temp job, was taken on as a "lumper"—someone who schleps boxes to and from trailers all day long. As unglamorous as her duties were, Dickerson became an essential cog in one of the most sophisticated machines in modern commerce—the Walmart supply chain. Walmart, the world's largest private-sector employer, had contracted a company called Schneider Logistics to operate the warehouse. And Schneider, in turn, had its own contracts with staffing companies that supplied workers.

...Such subcontracting enables corporations to essentially take workers off their books, foisting the traditional responsibilities that go with being an employer—paying a reasonable wage, offering health benefits, providing a pension or retirement plan, chipping into workers' compensation coverage—conveniently onto someone else. Workers like Dickerson, of course, aren't accounted for when Walmart touts that more than half of its workforce receives health coverage.

Dickerson quickly discovered that the work wasn't easy, if there was any work at all. Each morning she showed up at her warehouse, she wasn't sure whether she'd be assigned a trailer and earn a day's pay. She says there were days that she and many temps were told simply to go home, without pay, since there wasn't as much product to unload as expected. Sometimes Dickerson was told they didn't have any trailers light enough for a woman, she says.

But on most days the warehouse teemed with lumpers, many of them wearing different colored t-shirts to signify the different agencies they worked for. Dickerson herself would work for two different labor providers within the same warehouse in a little more than a year.

The difficulty of a lumper's day often went according to chance. A lucky lumper might be assigned a container filled with boxes of Kleenex or stuffed animals, while an unlucky lumper might pull a container filled with kiddie swimming pools or 200-pound trampolines. For the heaviest lifts, Dickerson would be assigned a partner, and the two would split the pay for the trailer, moving the massive boxes onto pallets by hand.

The job was fast-paced and stressful. Dickerson says supervisors would walk along the warehouse's bay doors, marking the workers' progress over time. The supervisors, Dickerson and other workers say, often told them to speed it up if they wanted to be invited back.

"By the end of the day, your body hurts so bad," says Dickerson, who was among a small minority of females working as lumpers at the warehouse. "You tell them you can't do it the next day,... they'll tell you, 'We've got four more people waiting for your job.'"

For a while, Dickerson worked according to "piece rate"—she was paid not by the hour but by the trailer—a stressful pay scheme meant to encourage her and her colleagues to work faster and faster, and one that the labor movement worked hard to abolish in many industries in the 20th century. Each paycheck was different than the last, and most of them were disappointingly low, she says. In her year at the warehouse, Dickerson says she never had health benefits, sick days or vacation days. If she didn't unload containers, she didn't get paid. "It all depends on how fast you work," she says. "It's like a race. You're racing to get done with the trailer so you can get another one. Otherwise, you won't get enough money."

While the classic automobile assembly line was a familiar image of American life years ago, few Americans have any comparable vision of modern warehouse work. As Dickerson concludes:

"I don't think people know what the people in those warehouses have to go through to get them their stuff in those stores. If you don't work in a warehouse, you don't know."[1]

Warehouses are by no means the only such "unknown" working class environments. Most middle class people have never set foot inside an oil refinery, an electric power plant, an auto or motorcycle machine shop, a solid waste treatment facility or an overnight rest stop for long-haul truckers. Along with the other factors described above, this profound isolation of many working class jobs from outside eyes helps to explain why the white working class seems invisible in daily life.

Geography: The Rust Belt, Small Towns and the Urban Fringe

At the same time that their dispersion into small groups and "behind closed doors" working environments makes white working class Americans less visible in the workplace, they are also less visible where they live.

In the major industrial cities in the early Post-World War II period white ethnic working class neighborhoods were a well-known and easily recognized part of the urban environment. Many of these areas became iconic symbols of white working class America— Brooklyn in New York, Southie in Boston, Hamtramck in Detroit and the ethnic neighborhoods of the south side of Chicago.

As automobile ownership became widespread among white workers by the mid- 1950's and early 1960's, however, and more affordable homes in new suburbs became available, fewer and fewer white working class people remained in the tight-knit urban neighborhoods that were walking distance from the factories. These new suburban communities were not, properly speaking, "affluent" but rather modest and included a mixture of both blue-collar and white collar households. But they became the broad "middle" of American society in that era.

Since that time, however, with the rise of gated communities and exclusive suburban subdivisions and neighborhoods, the separation of whites with modest incomes from the affluent has become far more extreme. As one recent study noted:

> **Back in 1970**, the vast majority of Americans lived in neighborhoods that did mix people of substantial and modest means. No more. In fact, says a new study just released by the Russell Sage Foundation and Brown University, the share of Americans living amid intense income segregation has more than doubled.
>
> America's rich haven't just become richer, show the study data from Stanford University sociologists Sean Reardon and Kendra Bischoff. They've become far more likely to live among their own kind. The same for the poor...
>
> ...Nearly one out of three families in America's large metropolitan areas, the Stanford analysts found, spent 2007 in either a severely segregated rich or a severely segregated poor neighborhood. In 1970, by contrast, only one in seven American families lived in neighborhoods that rated as segregated rich or poor. In that same year, 65 percent of Americans lived in neighborhoods where over half the resident families rated as middle income. By 2007, that share of Americans living in middle-class neighborhoods had dropped to 44 percent.

...this segregation, *Newark Star-Ledger* commentator Tom Moran observed last week, is taking an ever heavier toll on our political psyche. Growing income segregation, explains Moran, "means people of different means don't rub elbows as much, their kids don't play together as much, the parents don't chat over the back yard fence." In this segregated environment, people know less and less about people not like themselves. They more easily embrace stereotypes.[2]

In fact, many white workers today do not simply live in different neighborhoods from the relatively affluent but in entirely different geographic areas. Many reside in three distinct locations: the rust belt, small towns and the urban fringe. We see these areas as we drive past them but, since they no longer sit next to giant automobile factories and steel mills, our eyes do not immediately process them as "working class" communities.

The geographic region that remains most associated with the traditional post-war white working class is the "Rust Belt" that stretches from Pennsylvania and upstate New York to Michigan, Ohio and Illinois. Although no longer the location of massive industry, to a significant degree this vast archipelago of working class communities retain their distinctive blue-collar character.

Here is a description of one such community:

Steubenville, Ohio – This place on the bank of the Ohio River is a vintage working-class community. Longtime residents have a memory of the steel mill's whistle, of crowds on downtown sidewalks and plenty of jobs that could let a person with only a high school diploma raise a family and own a home...

...Jefferson County used to be a Democratic bastion, thanks to the strong union presence, but the unions have been in decline along with the steel industry. The county is socially conservative and, like many blue-collar communities in this part of the world, has a lot of Reagan Democrats. The upshot is that Steubenville and the nearby towns are in a profound political and economic transition.

This was once a place that seemed geographically blessed, growing prosperous on a 1,000-foot-wide navigable river that led downstream to the Mississippi, the Gulf of Mexico and the world beyond. Steubenville had four railroad lines leading to all points of the compass. ...The banks of the Ohio became an industrial artery, with a series of mills, foundries, glassworks, ice factories and world-famous potteries.

It was a good place to grow up and get a job, as Dino Crocetti, born in 1917 on South Sixth Street in Steubenville, the son of a barber, discovered when he went off to work at the mill in nearby Weirton—though his honeyed voice led him to riches and fame under the name of Dean Martin.

Retired millworker John Meatris, 62, spent 41 years dealing with molten steel. He remembers how, when he was a child, downtown Steubenville was so crowded you could barely walk down the sidewalk on a Monday morning. He also remembers the soot falling out of the sky, coating everything to the point that you could write your name on a car windshield....

...In the corner of the steakhouse, sitting at the counter on a stool closest to the grill, John Abdalla monitors a slow night in the restaurant. He's the head of the Jefferson County Democratic Party and mayor of the village of Stratton, population 300.

His voice is hoarse, and he has tubes feeding oxygen into his nose from a small tank sitting on the adjacent stool. "I was a boilermaker for some 20 years," he says. "A lot of fly ash and asbestos. The lungs. Just shot on me."

The article then turns to another nearby community:

>...It's hard to imagine a place more stressed, and depressed, than Mingo Junction, home to another stunning monument to the Age of Steel, a mill with soaring blast furnaces and smokestacks but not a solitary worker. Thousands of people used to walk down the steep hill and across a narrow bridge above the railroad tracks to earn their living here.

>People have been hoping for years that the mill would reopen, and that the blast furnaces would again bring heat and light and jobs to the community. That is not going to happen, apparently; the mill has been purchased by a company that deals in scrap metal.

>Much of downtown Mingo Junction is boarded up and condemned. The senior center has run out of money and may soon close. The city hopes to save money by turning off hundreds of streetlights. So few people walk the streets that it could be a movie set for a film about a deadly germ from outer space.

>"We don't even have no gas station. No bank. Our grocery store's shut down," says Mike Benko, 51, a self-employed heating-and-air worker drinking a $1.75 light beer at the American Legion hall, one of half a dozen bars still serving Mingo's hardy holdouts and survivors.

>...In the corner, parked in her regular spot with a view out the window, is Cecelia Pesta, 88, whose parents started the market nearly seven decades ago.

>"It was a beautiful town," she says. "We had a lot of little stores. A lot of old-country people—Slovak people—lived here. But they're all gone."

A regular customer, Herb Barcus, 81, comes into the store. One of the employees quickly fetches him a stool so he can rest while his groceries are gathered for him. Barcus worked for 46 years as a boiler operator in the mill.

"That job was good to me," he says. "Bought a house. Put my kids through college. Had a decent pension."[3]

Towns like Steubenville were, of course, victims of the massive closure of American factories from the mid-1970's to the 1990's. Several well-conducted ethnographic studies have examined the effect of plant closings on working-class communities in Ohio, Wisconsin and New Jersey. They include Gregory Pappas' *The Magic City*, Kathryn Dudley's *The End of the Line* and Ruth Milkman's *Farewell to the Factory*. Pappas' study presents the most finely observed and detailed description of the day-to-day effects of unemployment and the struggle to adjust after a factory closing while Milkman's study provides the best description of the unique and powerful working-class culture that existed in the factory life of her subjects and the profound psychological effects of its disappearance on the unemployed workers.

Much of the production that had taken place in those communities was "offshored" to foreign countries but a significant fraction also moved a shorter distance to smaller, more isolated towns in more rural areas of the country where anti-union, pro-business local governments created a more "favorable business climate."

One perceptive analyst of this part of working-class America is Joe Bageant, author of the 2006 book, *Deer Hunting with Jesus*. Born and raised in the working-class town of Winchester, Virginia, Bageant left the town and region as a young man and then returned in 2000, seeking to study and then sympathetically interpret his former home and neighbors to liberals and Democrats for whom they are largely an enigma.

As Bageant says:

> Winchester is foremost a working-class town... you can make light bulbs at the GE plant, you can make styrene mop buckets at Rubbermaid or you can "bust cartons", "stack product" and cashier at Walmart or Home Depo. But whatever you do, you're likely to do it as a "team assembler" at a plant or as a cashier standing on a rubber mat with a scanner in your paw. And you're gonna do it for a working man's wage—for about $16,000 a year if you are a cashier, $26,000 if you are one of those assemblers.

> Yet this place from which and about which I am writing could be any of thousands of communities across the United States. It is an unacknowledged parallel world to that of educated urban liberals—the world that blindsided them in 2004 and the one they need to come to understand...[4]

Along with the relatively insulated small town communities like Winchester, another major area where working-class Americans live today is in the vast number of relatively nondescript "shallow rural" communities that encircle all major American cities and secondary urban areas.

The most perceptive observer of this distinctly working-class environment is Aaron Fox, an anthropologist and ethnomusicologist who, beginning in the early 1990's, became deeply involved over a period of 14 years, personally as well as academically, with the people and communities around Lockhart, Texas, located on the outskirts of Austin.

He describes Lockhart in his book, *Real Country – Music and Language in Working-Class Culture.*

> People choose to live here, *"out the country"* as they say, limping their trucks and used car lot specials thirty-five miles each way to Austin, Urbana, Savannah, Meridian and so

many other cities around America. If you stood beside the state highway, you'd see them slipping back out to its margins at sunset, back out for another night of beer drinking, cigarette smoking, music playing, slow dancing, talk-heavy sociability in those windowless beer joints that line the road, shielding their patrons from the gaze of cops and passerby's...

...to the stranger this is a place to pass through quickly and quietly, those fences and dogs and windowless beer joint walls telling the outsider to keep on moving, following the signs to the famous barbecue joint in town....

...unmistakably these are working-class people, too painfully thin or overweight or muscled or bent or broken to be any other kind, perfumed with cigarettes and beer, still sweaty from the day's labor or dressed-up in Chinese-made western-style clothes from the Wal-Mart.[5]

He then offers a more detailed description of the areas' very distinctly working-class character.

Most of Lockhart's working-class citizens are not farmers or employed directly in agriculture. A significant number travel to work in Austin, San Marcos, and San Antonio, where wages for both skilled and unskilled labor are higher and jobs more plentiful. For men this means jobs as truck drivers, electricians, factory and construction workers, and state and federal employees (e.g., road maintenance workers, postmen). For women this means jobs as nurse's aides, cleaners, waitresses, school bus drivers and clerical workers and assembly jobs in the high-tech factories of south Austin. The local economy includes a number of small manufacturers... More stable, if dirty and dangerous, job exist in the oil and agricultural services sectors (drilling equipment maintenance, feed lots and trucking). Many men operate informal small businesses in trucking, auto repair, or the building trades ...many women supplement family income with transient work as barmaids, supermarket checkers, waitresses, and cleaners. In a pinch, as in the case of an illness in the family, a divorce or a breakup, or the loss of a business, minimum wage jobs at convenience stores and fast food restaurants are a frequent resort.[6]

One important consequence of this geographic shift in where working people live is that the popular image of the white working class has increasingly merged with the popular image of rural or small town whites. In the early 1970's the most vivid images of the conservative working class was the image of Archie Bunker, Hard-Hat construction workers and anti-bussing protests in Boston's "Southie" and Cicero, Illinois—all distinctly Northern and urban locales. By the 1990's the new axis of political conflict had become the clash between Red States and Blue States, between the small towns of Sarah Palin's "real America" and the urban, coastal areas that voted consistently Democratic.

As Lisa Pruitt noted in an academic research paper titled, "The Geography of the Class Culture Wars":[7]

Just as liberal elites shun and ridicule the white working class, they similarly express disdain for rural and small town residents. Indeed, among denizens of the largest cities and "coastal elites," rural Americans have become a proxy for the working class—the uncouth, the uncultured, and—yes— the illiberal...

...social progressives reserve their greatest contempt—and increasingly also their ire—for whites in rural America, the vast majority of whom are working class... the culture wars

58

are now largely being fought—at least rhetorically—across the rural-urban divide.

As a result, the clichés of the "redneck", "bubba", "NASCAR Dad", "trailer park trash", "pick-up truck with a gun rack type-guy" are now stereotypes of both rural/small town and blue-collar/working class people at the same time.

Thus, the American working class has not really disappeared; it is an integral part of the "Real" America that is contrasted with the urban, coastal and educated sectors of the population.

CHAPTER

4

Understanding Workers as Individuals – Traditional Blue Collar Workers and Self-employed Worker/Contractors

The fact that white working class Americans are still a major part of American society and are socially and geographically separated from urban, educated America is not necessarily of any great political significance if they are not in any substantial way different from white collar Americans, businessmen and the affluent middle class.

This is, of course, what conservatives have argued ever since Richard Nixon began to appeal to the "Silent Majority" in the early 1970's. Since that time conservatives have popularized the view that, unlike the traditional notion of the "working class", it is actually "hard-working", "tax-paying" Americans with "traditional values" who are the real, coherent and homogeneous social group—a group whose interests are diametrically opposed to those of the poor and the "pointy-headed" educated elite. In the 2008 elections this notion was updated by Sarah Palin as a split between the "Real America" on the one hand and Obama's coalition of minorities, the young, educated, coastal and urban on the other. Mitt Romney, borrowing a concept from the ideology of Ayn Rand updated it again with the notion of workers, businessmen and executives all being "producers" while the Obama coalition were all in one way or another "parasites" or "moochers."

But do blue-collar, working class Americans actually still represent a distinct social group? Is there still a unique "working class" perspective and set of values that sets them apart from the white collar workers, businessmen and executives located above them in the social hierarchy?

The question is complex because many working class Americans will identify themselves as part of the "middle class" on opinion polls and in journalistic interviews. On this basis many social commentators have confidently dismissed the idea that there is any unique "working class" outlook or perspective as an obsolete relic of the past.

But this is far too superficial an approach. For one thing it is necessary to use ethnographic field studies to evaluate the question and not simply opinion polls. Moreover, there are very distinct differences between white working class Americans in the traditional industrial regions in the east and mid-west and white workers in the south and west. There are also key differences between those who are hired employees and those who are self-employed.

What Field Studies Reveal

The study that is generally considered one of—if not the—best ethnographic field study of working-class Americans since the 1970's is David Halle's study of workers in a New Jersey chemical plant—published under the title *America's Working Man*. The study appeared in 1984 when political observers were trying to understand the so-called "Reagan Democrats"—blue collar workers who no longer seemed to identify with the New Deal traditions of the Democratic Party but rather saw themselves as part of the Republican "forgotten majority."

Halle's study was extraordinarily detailed. He spent 7 years from 1974 to 1981 observing and socializing with his subjects on the job and in their homes as well as at taverns, racetracks, sporting events and fishing trips. His analysis of working conditions on the job included highly detailed sketches of work areas, control panels, plant equipment, work flow and work procedures while his analysis of the communities where the workers lived included extensive photos of individual houses and detailed maps of specific streets and neighborhoods. As Halle noted, it was only through such sustained and intense participant-observation that he was able to listen to workers talking casually and spontaneously about politics and social issues in a variety of different settings and over an extended period of time.

What Halle found was that the workers he studied actually had three distinct social identities that were operative at different times—one on the job, a second in the community and a third as citizens and Americans.

On the job, Halle found that the difference between the blue collar jobs in the plant and those of professional and managerial employees was fundamental. The working-class jobs were distinguished by four factors. They were primarily manual or at least physical in some degree. In addition, the jobs tended to be repetitive and dull, offer little chance of upward mobility and be closely supervised.

Halle found that the workers whose jobs exhibited these characteristics shared a distinct social identity within the plant. They defined themselves as "working men" (sometimes "working guys" or "working stiffs") and shared a clear sense of group solidarity. They were firmly pro-union and deeply distrustful of big business.

In the community, on the other hand, the workers Halle studied tended to call themselves "middle class" and saw themselves as suspended "in the middle" between the rich above them and poor minorities below.

This perception accurately reflected the reality of their everyday lives. With the rise of the automobile, the predominantly working-class urban neighborhoods that had surrounded the industrial areas of major northern cities had increasingly given way to more occupationally and socially heterogeneous suburban communities. As Halle noted, on one typical street where his subjects lived there were homeowners with the following occupations: a factory worker, a gas station owner, an electrician, a delivery driver, an independent truck driver, a storekeeper and a restaurant owner. Halle noted that "there is little reason for blue-collar workers to view these areas as working-class" and he used photographs to illustrate that there was "no such thing as a blue-collar house". Since the earnings of the blue-collar and the other families also overlapped it was entirely reasonable that the workers Halle studied tended to see themselves as "middle class" or "middle American" when thinking in terms of their homes and communities.

Halle also discerned a third social identity among his subjects— a national identity as Americans. This was a populist identity that counterposed "the people" to big business and the politicians who "ran the show."

Halle's meticulous research offered clear explanations for a variety of apparent anomalies that arose in standard opinion research (such as why working-class respondents sometimes defined themselves as "middle class" and at other times as "working-class" or "workingmen" on surveys).

More important, it provided an explanation for how the working-class voters of that era could support Republican politicians like Richard Nixon or Ronald Reagan in some elections while also continuing to support traditional New Deal Democrats for many other offices. Halle's answer was that in certain contexts and situations the workers' community identity as "middle class" or "middle Americans" was activated while in others their self-definition as "workingmen" was operative.

Another uniquely insightful study of northern blue collar workers—and particularly of the core set of distinctly working class values they held—was conducted by Princeton sociologist Michele Lamont in her 2000 study *The Dignity of Working Men*. Lamont recognized that asking workers to choose their most important values from a prepared list—as most previous studies had done—would essentially force their replies into a predetermined mold that might have little to do with their real-world thoughts and feelings, Lamont used instead entirely open-ended and non-directive questions. She interviewed 150 blue-collar workers, black and white, in the U.S. and in France, and compared them with middle class people in both countries. Her questions asked workers to describe people similar to them and people who were different, people that they liked and disliked and those to whom they felt superior or inferior. Follow-up questions probed why they felt as they did, spontaneously eliciting a complex pattern of moral judgments and values.

Both work and family did indeed emerge among the blue-collar workers' core values. But their real significance lay in how they were perceived.

For the middle class American men Lamont studied, work meant a profession or career, a frequently stimulating and often fulfilling sphere of activity that had to be balanced against the demands of family in daily life. For many of the working class men, in contrast, work was basically "just a job". For some, it might be interesting or challenging, (as it is for many construction workers, for example), but, even for them, it was their family life and not work that provided the basic meaning and satisfactions of life.

And central to workers vision of their family was the constant difficulty of supporting and preserving it in an often hostile environment. Lamont's workers repeatedly described having to "fight tooth and nail" to get where they are, of constantly having to "fight for what's ours". When asked to name their heroes, many of Lamont's workers chose their own fathers because "he held the family together" during hard times.

Seen from this perspective, work was viewed in two distinct ways. On one level, it was a sacrifice, a physically exhausting, hard and sometimes dangerous sacrifice that a worker made on behalf of his family. Yet, on another level, these same qualities made a worker's mastery of the difficulties and challenges of his job a tremendous source of pride and personal worth.

But, while they valued work itself, blue-collar workers had a much lower opinion of ambition and success. In Lamont's interviews, workers repeatedly said that, to them, money is not the most important thing in life, that the quest they see middle class people conduct for higher status seems to them unending and to offer little satisfaction.

In fact, while these workers generally did not feel resentment toward the middle class managers and professionals above them, saying, for example, that "I can't knock anybody for succeeding," their view of them was far from admiring. Middle class people were "cold and shallow", they did not really enjoy themselves, they were "worrying all the time", sacrificing their family, "missing all of life" and living "with blinders on".

Moreover, these workers sensed both a profound snobbishness and dishonesty among the middle class people they encountered. They perceived middle class people as "snotty", "snobbish" and constantly ready to "look down at people". They were "two-faced", "phonies", "show-offs" and willing to "screw people to get what they want".

Workers saw themselves, in contrast, as more authentic and sincere and aware of the important things in life. They placed friends and friendship above success and money, and, along with work, family and friends, saw honesty and good character as fundamental values. They admired people who were "honest", "straightforward", "no BS", "stand-up guys", who would "be there" for someone else in times of adversity and "carry their weight" in the struggles of daily life. As a value, they saw strength of character as far more important than success.

This very deep sense that blue-collar workers had of a fundamental difference between their personal values and perspective and that of middle class white collar workers appears in other sociological field research as well. As sociologist Jeffery Torlina reported in his book, *Working Class: Challenging the Myths about Blue-Collar Labor:*

Several men reported feelings that white-collar people are not as good "on the inside." An eighteen-year-old construction worker: "I think that people who work [i.e., working-class] are going to be better people inside; they are going to have better personalities, they are going to be more down to earth and in touch with other people." ...A twenty-seven-year-old excavator described white-collar people simply as "Snobby, stuck-up." This was reiterated by a forty-five-year-old painter: "They're arrogant, very arrogant people."

The painter continued:

...we're family men. That's the difference. We're blue-collar, nine to five or eight to five, whatever you want to call it, seven to three o'clock, family men, where our families are important to us. We are not traveling around the world; we are not salesmen that are away from our families for a week or two weeks. We're not at the country club socializing, playing golf, trying to get ahead and making that our priority. "Who do I have to hang around or who do I have to buy a drink and what-not, and who do I have to socialize with in order to get ahead?[1]

This is a startlingly different vision of the core "values" of working Americans then the usual media portrayals which invariably focus on a handful of conservative "hot button" issues like abortion and gun control. Yet, it is the perspective that spontaneously emerges as workers simply describe the kinds of people and the outlooks on life of which they approve or disapprove.

In fact, this distinct combination of viewing work, family, friends and good character as central values in life while according a much lower value to wealth, achievement and ambition is instantly familiar to trade unionists and others who work directly with American workers as an accurate picture of the pattern of distinctly "working class values" that American workers actually hold. It appears unfamiliar only because, for so long, the term "values" has been applied instead to a fixed set of conservative positions on a certain group of moral and social issues.

This general outlook is shared by working class Americans across the country but there is a profound difference between the outlook of workers in the traditional industrial areas of the country and the small town and rural areas of the South and West.

In the traditional industrial areas of the Rust Belt and North there are two near-universal historical memories that shape the outlook of most working people:

First, there is the memory of a lost past of good jobs, economic security, close knit urban communities and a decent "middle class" life. The industrial jobs of the 1950's and 1960's were not just relatively well paid—allowing a man to support his family on his wages alone—but provided substantial fringe benefits like pensions and health care. Unions were seen as crucial providers of these benefits and, together with the local Democratic clubs and ethnic churches, created a powerful sense of community.

Second, there is the memory of the gradual and literally agonizing "hollowing out" of industry, the closing of factory after factory and the gradual descent into an economy of low-wage jobs, temporary jobs, working more than one job and living without any hope of pensions or health insurance. Along with this objective economic deterioration there was a simultaneous loss of the community institutions and sense of community solidarity.

The description of Steubenville in the last section provides a vivid picture of how this shared historical memory and historical experience profoundly shapes the attitudes of workers in these communities. It was Romney's utter, condescending indifference to this entire historical experience and what it meant to the people of these communities that played a key role in convincing them that he could never genuinely represent them.

In the more rural, small town regions of the South and West, on the other hand, the historical memory of blue-collar workers is very different. With the exception of certain limited industrial areas like the textile mills in the Carolina's and the steel mills of Birmingham, large factories were relatively rare. Workers worked in small workgroups, often together with the owner or manager and unions were nonexistent.

The result was a cultural memory and social identity that was profoundly different from that in the Rust Belt and the North.

Aaron Fox, the anthropologist noted in the preceding section, perceptively describes the way the people he was observing defined themselves and their social identity.

> "Most considered themselves to be "middle class" or "working people" in the pervasive language of America's post-war class compromise... For most of these people, however, "country" was the clearest and most resonant term with which they summarized their political and cultural identity as hard-working and underpaid manual laborers, as prototypical independent and free Americans and as members of a functional local community. The phrase "we're just country people" recurs frequently on my tapes and in my notebooks..."Country" simultaneously named the real and imagined place where they lived...
>
> ...tomorrows exhausting shift at the plant—or the nursing home or driving the school bus—is the looming horizon of "the real" toward which working-class Texans constantly look... but one can detect the faint outlines of an imagined paradise... a "rural" past both distant and close, both mythical and clearly remembered...[2]

As Fox perceptively explains in his study, country music was and is actually a unifying thread and a major repository of modern working-class culture, even in northern states and urban areas. It expresses a distinctly working-class philosophy and outlook on life and happiness—a set of attitudes about work and family, about the meaning of being a "man" or a "woman" and the distinct fabric of dreams and disappointments, triumphs and regrets that arise from a culture deeply rooted in hard work and economic limitation. This is why since the 1960's country music has completely transcended its original rural and Southern roots to become a basic part of the overall national white working class culture.

Along with the differences between geographic regions, however, there is also another important social cleavage within the white working class—between men who work for a "boss" in large groups versus the self-employed worker contractors and the two or three men who work with them.

Self-Employed Worker/Contractors

The following profile is of a reasonably typical "worker-contractor" in the single-family home construction industry. The specific individual profiled below is a real person but the characteristics noted about him tend to be quite representative of his broader occupational and demographic group.

1. He is 28 years old, married with one two-year-old child. He is a skilled carpenter who acts as the general contractor on some jobs and as a sub-contractor on others. In all cases he works as the head carpenter on the job and never as a hands-off supervisor.

2. He has one permanent partner—who is also a close friend—and he hires another skilled carpenter he knows well when large jobs come along. He also hires one or two unskilled laborers for each project, rarely keeping them on for more than one or two jobs. When working as the general contractor on a job, everyone else he brings in to work is treated as an

69

independent sub-contractor, bidding the job and supervising their own crew. Many are also personal friends.

3. He owns $30,000 worth of tools and equipment as well as his truck. He earns $35,000-$40,000 in a normal year, $55,000 in a good year when he finds basically continuous year-round work. He keeps a separate bank account for his business, his wife does all the business bookkeeping and they file an IRS Schedule C, small business tax return.

4. He calls himself both "workingman" and a "small businessman" depending on the context and does not see any contradiction between these two roles. His perspective is a mixture of both identities, and varies depending on the particular issue. He does not have health insurance or a retirement plan and wishes he did. But he also wishes that hard-ass building inspectors, most zoning rules, IRS payroll tax reporting and workman's compensation paperwork would all just go away.

5. He lives 20 miles outside the city limits of a large urban area on a two acre lot with a small, one story house. He calls himself "basically a country boy" (or sometimes a "redneck" when he is among friends) although he has never actually lived in a genuinely rural area.

6. He used to do serious dirt bike racing when he was in his early 20's, but a second metal pin in his leg after another racing accident and a new-born child made him give it up. He still works with the pit crew on many weekends and goes deer hunting during the season with his father.

7. He did not attend church regularly when he was in his early 20's, except for special occasions, but he and his wife have now started to attend because, with their child leaving infancy, they feel that " kids have to be part of a church so they can learn good values while they're young."

8. He listens to rock music on the radio when he is working alone and he and his partner go to local concerts. But he also

listens to country music and puts the radio on a country station whenever there are other workers around. He never gets into serious discussions about politics sitting around at lunch or at other times on the job. He just accepts "born again" Christians, Rush Limbaugh talk radio fans, troubled military veterans and a vast variety of others as all part of the normal social world of the job. He does not personally know a single liberal or firmly partisan Democrat, however. "There just aren't any of them around here", he says.

9. He has no problem with any of the African-American and Latino subcontractors he works with regularly. He has several black friends going back to his high school days and occasionally goes to after-work bars and rock concerts with them when the occasion arises. In general he prefers to hire Latino as temporary laborers rather than African Americans, however, because he considers them better workers.

10. He is basically bored by politics and pays very little attention to any political news and debates. He has voted Republican ever since he registered to vote, largely because everyone else in his circle did and because he felt that the Democrats *"just always seemed crazy, like they were living in a different world."* He voted for Obama in 2008 because Obama seemed *"smart"*, *"cool"* and *"really ready to deal with all the problems"* while McCain seemed *"out of it"* and *"too old"* (He thought Sarah Palin was also *"cool"*—and at the same time *"pretty hot"*— but he also thought she was *"just not ready to run the county".*)

To fully understand construction workers like this individual, however, it is ultimately necessary to also understand the business and the culture in which he works—the culture of construction work and workers.

Construction work is of unique importance in contemporary working-class culture. With the decline of factory labor in industries like steel and auto, construction work has become not only the most important locus of classic working-class jobs but also the most important single center of the distinct occupational traditions and value systems of working-class America. Although as many or more blue-collar American men may work in warehouses, long-haul trucking and loading docks as on construction sites, the quintessential "working-class" American today is the construction worker.

Construction work is profoundly different from classic assembly line work. As sociologist Jeff Torlina concluded about his extended interviews with some 31 blue collar workers, many of whom worked in construction:

> Rather than depictions of subservience, alienation and meaninglessness that describe blue-collar life in social science textbooks, it became clear that these workers were proud of their trades and their products. They felt important in their skills and their efforts, and many of them regarded manual labor as the essential ingredient in an honorable and meaningful life.[3]

Torlina actually worked for many years as a full-time brick and cement mason in a family-owned masonry company, a work history that gave him a unique insight and bond with the men he interviewed. One of the key facts that emerged in the interviews he conducted is the extensive degree of complexity and knowledge involved in the jobs of most construction workers. On the surface, for example, the carpentry involved in framing a house appears to be simply a matter of "hammering nails" in accordance with a blueprint or supervisors orders. But, in fact, the task is highly complex. It is, for example, an entirely open secret in residential construction that most of the time architects' blueprints are simply wrong:

As Torlina notes:

...the men reported the commonplace necessity for them to override at least some aspect of a plan when the design was incorrect. Both factory and construction workers said that they could not always follow the blueprints. A thirty-seven year-old welder in a locomotive factory reported, "A lot of the engineering decision making and a lot of the blueprints they come up with, and what the real-life issue is, is totally different. They can have stuff on blueprints that really don't make sense."

Another said:

...I just take [the blueprints] inside the office and tell them that their prints are no effin' good. I just go ahead and fix the problem myself, which takes no longer than any problem anybody else runs into." The sixty-year-old machine operator from a turbine manufacturing plant went further. He said the production process depends upon shop workers taking it upon themselves to fix problems with the designs: "You know how many guys on the floor bailed out guys in management because they did it their way and not the freakin' process way or the way the boss told them to do it? Workers," he said, "had to understand more than the engineer who drew the blueprint."[4]

In residential construction the fact that blueprints virtually always contain errors or designs that do not work in practice is accepted as an entirely normal part of the construction process. As the worker/ contractor described above explained it with a laugh, "We look at the blueprints kinda like what captain Barbossa said about the 'pirate code' in the movie, *The Pirates of the Caribbean*. They ain't be rules, matey, they be more like guidelines."

In fact, even construction work that appears simply "mindless" to outside observers actually has more in common with the constant repetitive practice of a professional musician or dancer who is seeking to acquire true mastery. As Torlina notes:

> Skill is a product of repetition. The only way a mason can learn to put a perfect finish on a concrete floor or to build a block wall that is perfectly plumb, straight and level is to have performed those tasks thousands of times. ...It may take years to develop the unconscious feel for laying a brick so that it is always level from end to end and side to side. Repetition is what teaches a mason to take the perfect amount of mortar from the pan in just the right place on the edge of the trowel. ...there is much more complexity to the work than meets the inexperienced observer's eye.[5]

Another sociologist who spent years actually working in construction, is Kris Paap, the author of the study "*Working Construction—Why Working-class Men Put Themselves—and the Labor Movement—in Harm's Way*". Papp spent two and a half years, not simply observing construction workers as a sociologist, but actually working as a full-time union carpenter on three different kinds of construction sites. As a woman in a male-dominated industry, this provided her with an absolutely unique perspective.

One key insight that actually working in construction rather than simply observing it from outside provided Paap was something that anyone who has actually worked on construction sites understands— that the powerful sense of group solidarity and identity as "workers" that construction workers feel—the deep sense of "us vs. them" membership—is rooted in the raw, literally physical sense of strength and mastery that comes from years of hard physical labor—a kind of strength and endurance that is utterly different than the kind of muscularity developed in a health club or using an exercise machine. As Paap says:

I was aware of a "vitality", a very physical joie de vivre that emerged from the collective interactions and implicit cultural celebrations of what it meant to be a working man among working men. Put most simply, I had "sensations" of being masculine, manly and a man among men and that these sensations were positive."[6]

As Paap notes, men do not consciously perceive this sensation as being specifically "masculine." Rather, it is felt as being simply "strong and manly", in contrast to weak and "wimpy" desk-bound workers. It is an insight that explains a great deal of the powerful sense of distance and alienation that many workers feel toward middle class liberals and political candidates who try to communicate with them. Deep down, many feel—in an intensely literal and physical sense—that *guys like that will never understand how me and my buddies really feel."*

Paap worked in a variety of settings—large scale building projects where large numbers of carpenters worked together to build massive plywood forms into which wet concrete was poured, commercial buildings (retail malls, restaurants) where the carpenters' main task was to nail up the vertical wall studs and 4' x 8' panels of sheetrock that comprised the walls and smaller, single family home residential jobs that required fine "trim" carpentry.

One of Paap's central concerns was to understand why construction workers seem surprisingly supportive of their employers and identify with their interests instead of seeing them as "bosses" whose demands should be resisted. She quickly identifies one critical factor:

Union employers have the ability to send workers back to the union hall (that is, to lay them off) without providing any warning or justification beyond the statement that "work is slow"... [This] creates a tremendous vulnerability— essentially a total lack of protection from arbitrary firing—for the workers who are thus dependent to a greater and lesser degree upon the goodwill of their supervisors. The pressure is on to prove oneself as a good, worthy and cost-efficient worker.[7]

She later adds:

> ...because of the transitional nature of worksites, the need for [management] goodwill is significant ...construction workers no sooner start working on one job than they worry where the next will come from. Thus the goodwill of one's employer and the ability to "get on steady" with an employer (be retained across building projects) are no small matters.[8]

Paap's subsequent analysis then attempts to trace how this structural insecurity underlies and generates many of the racial and sexual attitudes construction workers display.

A second factor (one that Paap also notes), however, is that in construction, unlike in large factories, there is a network of close and personal social relationships between workers and supervisors on various levels. As Herbert Appelbaum wrote in his 1982 study, *"Royal Blue—the Culture of Construction Workers"*.

> Many [construction workers] are friends or drinking buddies with their foremen. Construction workers do not view foremen as instruments of all-powerful corporations as might be the case in the auto or chemical industries. [Moreover]Each foreman or superintendent tends to set up a circle of friends or relatives who become a labor pool from which he hires... a journeyman who expects to work steadily must make himself known to as wide a circle of foremen and superintendents as he can.[9]

This is powerfully reinforced by the relationships that develop between the myriad of contractors and subcontractors who have to work closely together on a construction job.

As Applebaum says:

Subcontracting also leads to family-like relationships between the general contractor and his family of subcontractors. Many general contractors use the same group of subcontractor firms over the years. General contractors like to repeat with good subs. If the relationship is continuous over a protracted period, the general contractor and his subs will often develop a close personal relationship. They will socialize and engage in recreational activities together. Similarly the workers will come to know each other and will work well in the field. Many of them will become close friends.[10]

When one adds to this the powerful sense of teamwork and collaboration that is a fundamental part of construction work, it becomes clear why even unionized construction workers do not respond to their bosses with the "us vs. them" perspective of union factory workers in the 1950's.

The same considerations are even more powerfully relevant in the vast non-union sector of construction that is responsible for most individual single family homes and small commercial buildings in the South, West, Southwest and other areas of the country. This sector is entirely comprised of small contractors and subcontractors connected by personal relationships and word-of-mouth reputation. Many of these small contractors and subcontractors work alone. Others hire a small number of steady helpers—often family members and relatives—and on other occasions employ short-term laborers for particular jobs.

Republicans would like to imagine that these "worker-contractors" are a new class of typical Rotary Club/Chamber of Commerce small businessmen like the traditional Republican real estate developers and used car dealers. But, in fact, these "worker-contractors" are quite different. As Joe Bageant says in his keenly-observed book, *Deer Hunting with Jesus*:

A self-employed electrical contractor is not a small business person or an entrepreneur. He is a skilled worker who construction companies refuse to hire because they do not want to pay social security or workers comp or health insurance for employees. Instead they contract with him and he assumes the cost of those programs and takes orders from a manager and shuffles through the farce that he is one of America's ever-growing crop of dynamic, self employed entrepreneurs.[11]

Torlina makes a similar point. As one of his interview subjects notes:

An amazing amount of them [tradesmen who worked together in housing developments] were people that had the same scenario happen to them that happened to me. They start out working for a larger company. [The siding installer] worked for GE, again; he worked there for eleven years and a lot of the guys he worked with were laid off—without a job. So he looked around and saw [the power company] is doing the same thing. The telephone company, steel companies are closing up, the [nearby] Ford plant, which used to be a great job if you could get in, well they're all gone. Everything is closing up. These big companies are all downsizing and there really isn't any security anymore. So a lot of us got the point where we realized the only security you had was in your own drive and your own ability and, not so much by choice, almost by necessity, got into the trades.[12]

These worker-contractors do not act or think like typical small businessmen, but neither do they think like the unionized automobile or steelworkers of the 1950's. Their perspective is a mixture of working-class and small business views that are not completely integrated but rather compete and interact in complex ways.

The Distinct Social Outlook of Worker-Contractors

Democrats have generally taken little cognizance of the distinct social outlook of these worker-contractors and have continued to appeal to them using the language and rhetoric of the 1950's. Throughout the 1970's and 1980's the dominant Democratic approach was to repeat traditional, trade-union/populist slogans and promises even though it was becoming increasingly apparent that these messages were growing more and more remote and unresponsive to the day-to-day problems and needs of these new "worker/contractors" as they themselves perceived them.

Conservatives like Rush Limbaugh, on the other hand, had a much clearer understanding of this sector of working-class America. In a *New York Times* profile, Limbaugh explicitly credited his success to his ability to act as a "small business advisor" to these blue-collar small businessmen, offering them a mixture of cultural conservatism and basic small business philosophy in a language they easily recognized and understood.

In fact, while Democratic advocates often seemed like very alien, white-collar and college-educated outsiders—(the kind of people workers immediately recognize as those who *"never did a hard day's work in their life"*)—not only Rush Limbaugh but Bill O'Reilly, Sean Hannity and many of the other talk radio hosts actually seemed like very familiar figures to their working-class audience. It is only necessary to visualize Limbaugh, O'Reilly and Hannity dressed in short-sleeved white shirts, wearing very clean, un-dented hard hats on their heads and holding clipboards in their hands in order to imagine them giving orders on a construction site. They all have the very distinct, "pushy", "no nonsense", "take-charge" style and approach of typical supervisors and general construction managers.

This influence of the conservative talk-show hosts is then reinforced and amplified by the small group dynamics of the construction industry. More than in many other fields, construction requires teamwork and collaboration among the various craftsmen involved—a teamwork that must be constantly renegotiated as new sub-contractors cycle through a construction project.

As a result there is a widespread attitude of *"go along to get along"* in the construction industry. Political or social arguments are generally avoided and the group simply readjusts to accommodate the range of opinions that exists at any given time. When a strict "born-again" Christian joins the group, for example, other workers temporarily cease swearing or making jokes about the topless bars. When minority workers are present, racially prejudiced workers temporarily refrain from making derogatory comments.

In this kind of opinion environment, conservative talk-show ideas that are expressed by highly opinionated workers simply become integrated into the overall group perspective. Workers who disagree are much more likely to simply mumble *"whatever"* and wander off rather than to initiate a political debate.

In previous eras, these conservative ideas would not have remained unchallenged. In the 1930's a group of workers eating lunch would have often included an intense and passionate union organizer energetically preaching the gospel of solidarity and union brotherhood. In the 1950's such a group would often have a good "union man," ready to argue in favor of his local and defend the Democratic Party as the party of "the working man".

Today, in contrast, there are no such ideological counterweights, and the result has been evident in the one-sided dominance of conservative ideas in working-class America since the 1980's. Progressives and Democrats frequently puzzle over why conservative ideas have such sway over groups like construction workers but, in a nutshell, this is the basic answer, one that has always been just as clearly evident to observers "in the field" as it has been invisible to those outside.

Part Two

How They Think

CHAPTER

5

How Working People Think about Politics – "Cubbyholes," "Frames" and the Sociological Perspective

Any serious Progressive political strategy for regaining the support of working class voters must be based on one central building block: an underlying model of how ordinary workers think—of how they process, store and organize political ideas and opinions.

In the current political discussion among Democrats and progressives, there are essentially two major "folk-models" of how ordinary voters process political information—the "cubbyhole" model and the "media framing" model. Each has profound implications for political strategy.

The "Cubbyhole" Model

The "cubbyhole" or "bin" model of the mind pictures each individual opinion as stored in a separate mental compartment from which it is accessed and recalled whenever needed—a model that is actually not unreasonable as a model of the mind of a professional politician like a congressman or political commentator. Most national politicians have dozens or even hundreds of perfectly memorized statements expressing opinions on specific issues that they can recall from memory and recite even in their sleep. Political commentators and other people deeply involved in politics have similarly organized mental filing systems. In the case of ordinary working people on the other hand, it is obvious that the model does not really reflect the way that they normally process political information.

Nonetheless, there are two practical implications for political strategy that are commonly drawn from this view.

First, the cubbyhole model tends to suggest that the individual opinions stored in the mental bins are clear, stable and meaningful. If a person says he favors a particular program or policy on an opinion survey, the implicit assumption that is suggested by the bin model is that that opinion will very strongly influence and even possibly determine the person's vote and other political activity in regard to the issue.

This assumption has at times led progressives to overestimate how much real and reliable support—support that does not evaporate the moment it is seriously challenged—is really available for various initiatives. In the case of health care reform, for example, the initial polling on the major planks of the proposed reform showed they were all solidly popular and fostered the expectation that—even after the inevitable Republican criticism and attack—the bill as a whole would remain substantially more popular with most Americans than turned out to be the case. The early polls were not wrong, they just could not predict where those specific opinions fit within voters' larger conceptual frameworks or how they would be processed and combined with other considerations as time went on.

The second implication of the bin model for political strategy is that, if an average voter encounters a conflict between two of his or her opinions, he or she will resolve the conflict by simply making a direct comparison between the two opinions and choosing the one he or she judges more important. In the case of an election, a voter is visualized as ranking all of his opinions from most important to least and voting for the candidate who advocates the views he or she considers most important.

This second concept underlies one of the most enduring progressive notions about the working class—that economic issues represent (or at any rate ought to represent) the "real" issues for working Americans and that, as a result, workers should be willing to vote for progressives based on the economic policies they advocate while dismissing as secondary other social or values issues on which working people and progressives tend to disagree.

This conception has its original historical roots in the 18th century Marxian notion of "false consciousness" but the modern version of the argument can be traced to Scammon and Wattenberg's, *1970 The Real Majority*, a book which challenged the idea that economic issues were inevitably more important than other issues and argued that Democrats had to moderate their positions on the new "social issues" in order to accommodate working class opinion rather than dismiss such concerns as secondary. From there the debates evolved into one aspect of the arguments between traditional liberals and New Democrats that occurred in the early 90's. During the mid-2000's, a particularly lyrical updating of this *"economic issues are the real issues and cultural issues are a distraction"* perspective was provided by Thomas Frank in his book, *What's the Matter with Kansas?*

In the last half-century no major progressive populist candidate within the Democratic Party has ever built a major national base of support among working class voters by taking this traditional *"just run on the real issues"* approach. But the perspective remains powerful within the progressive community because it justifies and validates the use of a consistent and uncompromised progressive political platform. The degree to which the "just run on the real issues" approach is based on a rather limited conceptual model of how working Americans actually think about political issues is not, however, adequately recognized as a significant limitation.

The Media Framing Model

The second major "folk-model" of how working people think is the "media framing" model. In this conception, media organizations and other interest groups like advertising agencies or political organizations create organized narratives that provide a unified framework for visualizing and understanding an issue.

There are a wide variety of both academic and popular interpretations of how media framing works but in the daily political discourse among Democrats in the major American newspapers, weekly opinion magazines and websites there are basically three major assumptions about the framing process that are widespread:

1. Media frames are internalized as complete units, not as a collection of bits and pieces.
2. It is either the first frame to be invoked, the most frequently repeated frame or the most dramatic and memorable frame that finally becomes the conceptual filter and mental framework within which an issue is subsequently contemplated and analyzed.
3. When forced to choose between two alternative frames, people choose either one frame or another, they do not "mix and match" elements from both.

When applied to politics, this popular folk-model has three important implications. First, that public opinion is basically shaped by the major messages delivered by the media. Second, that persuasion is achieved by repeatedly hammering home a basic core message and, third, that during political campaigns, when voters are inevitably exposed to competing frames, conservative frames must be challenged with equal and opposite progressive frames rather than with isolated facts or opinions. Frames can only be replaced by alternative frames, not by piecemeal information.

It is also notable that in both the cubbyhole and media framing models the average person is pictured in isolation from his or her social and cultural environment. A voter's thought process is basically visualized at the moment that he or she is answering opinion poll questions on the phone or is sitting in a living room watching political ads on TV.

The Social Dimension

Yet, in reality, no one really doubts that the social and cultural environment in which working Americans live is central to the way they develop and organize their political attitudes.

At the most basic level, working Americans political opinions are deeply shaped by the four basic value systems into which they are socialized beginning in childhood. These value systems are rooted in the major social institutions of working class life—the church, the military, small business and the school system. These institutions systematically inculcate the values they represent— patriotism, religious piety, free enterprise and the "American system of government"—the last being essentially the Constitution, the Bill of Rights and democratic elections.

Each of these major social institutions provides both extensive written expositions of its institutional value system and also vast numbers of individuals—local small businessmen, Chamber of Commerce members, clergymen and women, members of the military—in every small town and city neighborhood who serve as teachers, role models and local cultural transmission mechanisms.

The value systems of these major social institutions are imparted to almost every individual American citizen through a lifelong process of socialization conducted both within specific institutions (at church on Sunday morning, in the workplace from 9 to 5, in the armed forces from the moment basic training begins to the day of mustering out) and more generally through school, the legal system, the media and other channels of social influence.

These four value systems are highly integrated. Although frictions between the value systems of dominant social institutions have at times appeared in American history (such as the conflict between the "social gospel" of progressive Christianity and the business community's "social Darwinism" at the turn of the century) for the last half century or so the four major American institutional value systems have been overwhelmingly harmonious.

One important consequence of this tight integration is that, to most ordinary Americans, the four dominant and interlocking value systems do not seem like a conscious political ideology at all but rather like an entirely natural and obvious expression of "the way things are" or "just plain common sense." Many people who have only been exposed to the dominant value system literally cannot conceive of how anyone could possibly think differently. People who believe in alternative value systems (e.g., Islam, communism) can only be conceptualized as being literally "crazy" or "irrational".

As a result, by the time typical working Americans reach the age where they begin to pay attention to political issues, they already have internalized a firm set of interlocking value systems that define what is right and wrong, true and false and good and bad.

Individual life experiences, however, profoundly modulate and shape the way these value systems are internalized and understood. In some cases life experiences reinforce and intensify identification with the basic value systems—serving in the armed forces, working a father's small business, being home schooled by conservative parents or engaging in evangelical proselytizing all increase a person's sense of belief and commitment. On the other hand, seeing one's family crushed by medical bills, searching fruitlessly for a job, being dishonorably discharged from the military or dealing with a friend or sister's unplanned pregnancy leads other individuals to modify or reject various components of those value systems.

As the sociologist Jennifer Sherman noted about one of her subjects in her study of poor whites in rural California:

For Greg Smith, morality did not follow a single, clear-cut set of rules established by a church or other institutional source of moral authority, although undoubtedly some of his moral understandings were influenced by his church life and religious beliefs. Overall, his concept of morality was based in his own experiences and seemed flexible enough to suit his preferences and personal contradictions.

Moral discourses in Golden Valley, as in the United States as a whole, do not form a single coherent ideology but rather a conglomeration of ideas drawn from social, cultural, religious and psychological sources...morality in Golden Valley has numerous forms that are at times obviously incongruent with one another, many of which are not based in any formalized doctrine of religious or similar origin.[1]

While some of the life experiences that modify the acceptance of the basic value systems are entirely unique, others affect vast groups of people. In the 1930's, unemployment and conditions in the factories and mills of industrial America led millions of working people to join trade unions, a choice which provided not only material benefits but a new value system that modified the traditional faith in "the free market" and created the hybrid political ideology of the "mixed economy" or "welfare state" in the period after World War II. In the 1950's unionized workers saw the traditional American value systems and their new trade union inspired values of solidarity, economic security and full employment as entirely compatible.

The generation of white working class Americans that came of age after 1970, on the other hand, had a very different kind of widely shared life experience. There was widespread anger and bitterness among the largely working class veterans of the Vietnam War over the way they had been treated—by both the government and society as a whole. There was pervasive resentment of liberal social policies like school bussing and quotas. There was profound frustration—

particularly among construction workers and others who ran small businesses—with new health, safety, and environmental regulations and there was a barely contained fury at the failure of the government to control runaway inflation.

The result was the growth of a widely shared and deeply felt anti-government perspective—a general sense of alienation from government and hostility to taxes, deficits, government programs, regulations, bureaucrats and almost anything connected to government activity.

Using Common Sense

It is the combination of an individual's unique life experiences and the historical experiences he or she shares with others of the same generation that forms a distinct mental filter or perspective through which the basic social value systems learned in childhood are understood.

As a result, when ordinary working Americans are confronted with a completely new political issue they generally consider it in terms of both their basic value systems and also their life experiences. In the case of the "morning after" birth control pill, for example, they will consider their basic religious beliefs, their personal experience with birth control and pregnancy and also a variety of other individual considerations before forming their opinion.

Working people generally refer to this process of thought as using *"common sense"* or applying *"my personal philosophy"* to a question and it is familiar, indeed almost universal, in both the sociological and anthropological ethnographic field literature and also in popular and journalistic accounts of how working class people think about political issues.

(People with more advanced education also use a similar "common sense" process of thought in some situations, but for political opinions they rely far more heavily on various kinds of formal recognized authorities—scientific research and information, the views of specialists and experts, the opinions of elite publications and so on).

Two Kinds of Working Class Conservatives – True Believers and the "Open-Minded"

As a result of this way of thinking about political issues—comparing basic value systems with personal experience—there are two characteristic kinds of groups that regularly form in working-class political life.

The first is composed of people whose personal experience is completely compatible with the basic value systems they internalized while growing up. This congruity powerfully intensifies their confidence in those values and makes those value systems seem absolutely "right" and completely unchallengeable. If they further perceive that these values are under attack they become passionate defenders. It is from this group that the "conservative base" emerges and—when politically mobilized—becomes the "religious right", the "tea party patriots", "minutemen" and "militiamen".

The second group is those whose personal experience has led them to have some doubt or to reach alternative conclusions to those that follow from the basic value systems. In most cases they do not completely reject the basic social values but rather balance them with other considerations to reach a personal conclusion.

The typical pattern of thought for someone in this circumstance is an "on the one hand, on the other hand" kind of ambivalence or "open-minded" approach. The usual way it is expressed in popular speech is in formulations like, *"Now don't get me wrong. I believe a man has the right to make as much money as he can. But I don't know, there's just something wrong when a guy can get a 100 million dollar bonus for screwing up."* Or *"You know, I believe government should leave people alone and stay the hell out of their business but I don't think a little kid should be denied health care when he really needs it."*

90

Conventional opinion polls generally do not try to distinguish between "true believer" and "open-minded" forms of political thinking, but they can actually be clearly observed when a sufficient range of data is available. For example, the Center for American Progress's, *2009 State of American Political Ideology Survey*[2] collected opinions on an unusually wide range of issues, making it possible to see patterns that are usually obscured. The survey was completed in early 2009, before the Republican attacks on Obama took hold, so it provides a useful "baseline" picture of public opinion before it became polarized into pro-Obama and anti-Obama camps.

Not surprisingly there was very strong support among white working class Americans for many of the core propositions of the major social value systems:

	Agree	Disagree	Neutral
The Military			
Military force is the most effective way to combat terrorism and make America safer.	68%	19%	17%
Small Business			
Free market solutions are better than government at creating jobs and economic growth	57%	9%	34%
Limited government is always better than big government	60%	13%	26%
Religion			
Do you have a favorable opinion of Christians (Pew research/all voters)	87%	19%	10%
Our country has [not] gone too far in mixing politics and religion and forcing religious values on people	40%	42%	18%

Data for white respondents with a high school degree or less

But calling these views "conservative" actually reflects a widespread confusion between two related but very distinct sociological concepts: cultural traditionalism and conservatism.

Within the framework of the essentially universal respect for the major "traditional" social institutions and culture there is a profound division between essentially conservative and more progressive or open-minded outlooks in working class life. This profound division is generally not understood or even perceived by many liberals and progressives because both points of view are expressed entirely within the language and cognitive framework of working class cultural traditionalism.

To take a simple example, a person expressing sincere concern for the hardships illegal Mexican immigrants face and a desire that some kind of long-term solution to their legal status be found is expressing a clearly "liberal" or "progressive" view. But if he or she is doing do so at a Wednesday night prayer meeting in a weather-beaten roadside evangelical church in rural Georgia and justifies the view by quoting Jesus' words about concern for "the least of these" and the parable of the good Samaritan, many progressives would hesitate to define this person as being the same kind of "real" or "authentic" progressive as themselves.

In the State of American Political Ideology survey this distinction between conservatism and cultural traditionalism can be seen in the fact that this same sample of working class individuals who endorsed a set of traditional values also supported a wide range of clearly "progressive" programs and views. 72 percent or the respondents endorsed a "transition to renewable energy" and 64 percent supported "guaranteed affordable health care for every American." 52 percent agreed that "Iraq proved that America cannot impose democracy on other nations".

This combination of a broad "ideological conservatism" (which is actually divided between cultural traditionalism and genuine ideological conservatism) and more specific "operational liberalism" is a well-known and constant feature of American public opinion.

Estimating the Balance Between "True Believers and the "Open-Minded"

More interesting data which emerged from the Center for American Progress' survey relates to the way working Americans balance their support for the basic value systems in American society with other considerations. For example, a key question for Democratic political strategy is how much of working class support for the basic social value systems is intense and passionate—resembling the attitudes of the tea party supporters—and what proportion reflects a more moderate and restrained, "open-minded" commitment to those values.

The CAP survey asked its respondents to indicate on a scale of 1-10 the intensity of their agreement with the basic values noted above, making it possible to get a sense of the balance between the more extreme or passionate and more moderate currents of opinion within white working class America.

	Strongly Agree	Mildly Agree	Neutral	Mildly Disagree	Strongly Disagree
The Military					
Military force is the most effective way to combat terrorism and make America safer.	50%	18%	17%	5%	10%
Small Business					
Free market solutions are better than government at creating jobs and economic growth	40%	15%	33%	5%	4%
Limited government is always better than big government	46%	13%	26%	6%	7%
Religion					
Our country has [not] gone too far in mixing politics and religion and forcing religious values on people	34%	7%	18%	10%	30%

Data for white respondents with a high school degree or less.

93

What this chart shows is that the strong majority support (averaging around 55-60 percent) for the propositions reflecting the basic value systems is actually divided into two parts—a substantial but less than 50 percent majority group who support those propositions emphatically and passionately and a smaller group of about 15 percent who show some degree of reserve or ambivalence.

As we will see in the next chapter, this has clear implications for Democratic strategy. The first passionate group is almost certainly closed to Democratic candidates and messages while the more ambivalent group is likely to be more open to persuasion. Democrats need to clearly distinguish between the two sectors of working class America and target their messages and efforts accordingly.

A Closer Look at the "Open-Minded"

The CAP survey also rather dramatically reveals the ambivalent *"on the one hand, on the other hand"* kind of thinking that characterizes the second, more moderate group. The chart below shows the number of respondents who asserted their agreement with both progressive and conservative views that—on the surface—were logically incompatible.

Ideologically Incompatible Statements	Percent agreeing with both statements
Military	
Military force is the most effective way to combat terrorism and make America safer **And** America's security is best promoted by working through diplomacy, alliances and international institutions.	41%

94

Small Business	
Government regulation of business does more harm than good **And** Government regulations are necessary to keep business in check and protect workers and consumers	31%
Government spending is almost always wasteful and inefficient **And** Government investments in education, infrastructure and science are necessary to insure America's long-term economic growth	52%
Religion	
Homosexuality is unnatural and should not be accepted by society **And** Religious faith should focus more on promoting tolerance, social justice and peace in society and less on opposing abortion or gay rights	20%
Human life begins at conception and must be protected from that moment onward. **And** Religious faith should focus more on promoting tolerance, social justice and peace in society and less on opposing abortion or gay rights	38%

Data for white respondents with a high school degree or less.

What this shows is that a very significant percentage of the working class people in this survey hold and balance both progressive and conservative views in their minds. Focusing on just the economic issues above, the quite remarkable fact is that between one-third and one-half of American workers do not hold consistently conservative ideological views but rather entertain a mixture of both progressive and conservative ideas that they balance with an "one the one hand, on the other hand" approach based on "common sense" or "personal philosophy." On the pressing issue of health care reform, this same pattern was evident. A July 2009 Pew survey found that 66 percent of high school educated respondents agreed that "Government needs to do more to make health care affordable and accessible". Yet, on the very same survey, 60 percent also asserted that "I am concerned that the government is becoming too involved in health care."

How the Different Mental Models Explain "Open-Minded" Thinking

To consider what this implies for Democratic political strategy, it is necessary to begin by considering how the different "folk" mental models interpret this ambivalent kind of thinking.

In the cubbyhole or bin model, individuals who take political issues at all seriously should resolve directly contradictory views like these in favor of one view or the other. If they do not do so, it is generally taken to mean that the person simply does not think seriously or systematically about political issues—in political science jargon, they hold "non-attitudes"; in common language, they are described as too "scatterbrained" or "spaced out" to have a serious opinion.

In the media framing view, inconsistent positions like those above indicate the existence of basically incompatible conservative and progressive frames, one or the other of which must dominate depending on which one is first or most effectively invoked.

In the sociological view, seemingly incompatible propositions like these usually represent conflicts between attitudes drawn from basic value systems on the one hand and personal experience on the other, the decision regarding which one to favor in a particular case being decided by a person's "common sense" or "personal philosophy."

There are a number of implications of this third approach that will be explored in the following chapters. The first and most fundamental is simply that the usual broad generalizations about workers being generally "conservative" is fundamentally wrong.

CHAPTER

6

White Working Class Moderates— the Key Group Progressives Can Persuade.

The conventional way of analyzing the opinions of white working class voters is to note their views on a variety of subjects and then compare those opinions with the opinions of white voters who have graduated college or gone on to post-graduate educations.

The results are predictable. Aside from certain "pockets" of populist views on subjects like corporations, Wall Street and profits, across a wide range of issues white working class voters' opinions consistently appear to be more conservative than the more educated. On this basis, analysts and commentators invariably proceed to create a composite stereotype—a "typical" white worker who is significantly more conservative than his more educated counterparts across a wide range of issues. Based on this political composite columnists and pundits then quickly conclude that winning the support of this typical white working class voter requires "moving to the right" and appealing to his or her basically conservative views.

This cliché of "the typical white worker as a conservative" has a long history in political thinking. In its modern form it first appeared in 1970 in Scammon and Wattenberg's book, *The Real Majority* in which a fictional 40 year old machinist from Ohio took his place alongside similar clichés about "conservative Hard Hats" and the TV character of Archie Bunker. Since that time it has survived largely unchanged as "the Joe Six-Pack vote," "The Bubba vote", "the NASCAR vote" and "gun-rack on the pick-up truck vote."

But on the most basic level, this is simply the wrong way to think about white working class people.

For one thing, very often the differences between more and less educated white voters on specific issues are not large—often as little as 10 or 15 percent. This kind of difference is simply not enough to justify maintaining a stereotype of one group as being fundamentally more conservative than another. When comparing the views of two different groups of 30 individuals on a particular topic, for example, a 10 percent difference between the two groups will only represent a difference in the views of three of the 30 individuals. This is hardly enough to reasonably characterize one group as basically "conservative" and the other as "liberal" or "progressive".

Three Kinds of Workers

Far more important, however, is the fact that the stereotype of the "average conservative white worker" fails to capture the most important fact about these voters—that most are not "average." On the contrary White working class Americans are profoundly split into three distinct groups.

- The first is the substantially diminished but still significant group of "liberal" or "progressive" white workers. At the heart of this group are members of trade unions or retired unionists in the northern and rust belt cities who are still committed to the New Deal ideology of the early post World War II trade union movement—a combination of an economic liberalism that pictures the Democrats as the party of the "common man" or "ordinary guys" and Republicans as country club plutocrats along with a cautious social liberalism supporting "color-blind" racial justice and equality. Once, when 40 percent of industrial workers were in unions, this progressive ideology among the white industrial working class was a major force in the North and Midwest. It is now a fraction of its former size but is still significant enough to produce majority support for many Democratic candidates among white union workers. Obama's victory as well as the remarkable grass-roots pushback against anti-union measures in Wisconsin and the successful referendum campaign against SR-5 in Ohio demonstrated the continuing residual power of this ideology.

- The second major group is the conservative "true believers"— the white working class men and women who are deeply immersed in the Rush Limbaugh/Fox News world view. For all practical political purposes, these voters can be viewed as completely immune to persuasion. Other than long-term one-on-one efforts at complete ideological conversion, they will not be swayed by ads, leaflets, canvassing, news events or other political communication.

- The final group is the white working class moderates who are not fully convinced by either the conservative or progressive narratives. They are ambivalent or "open-minded" and describe themselves as having *"not completely made up their minds,"* or *"seeing some truth on both sides."*

Conventional opinion polling obscures the existence of these three very distinct groups within the white working class but they are familiar figures to local trade union officials, political canvassers and grass-roots organizers who have day-to-day contact with working class Americans.

The Grass Roots Perspective

The most extensive progressive grass-roots operation aimed at reaching and communicating with white working class voters today is run by Working America, the community affiliate of the AFL-CIO. Working America's members are working class moderates—88 percent of them white and many church-going gun owners who rarely if ever talk to progressives.

Working America has 3 million members and its field canvassers generally conduct anywhere from 10,000 to 20,000 or 25,000 one-on-one doorstep conversations a month in nine major states (Ohio, Wisconsin, Michigan and Pennsylvania Colorado, Minnesota, Oregon, Virginia and Missouri) as well as conducting smaller outreach efforts in others. During the 2008 campaign Working America spoke to a remarkable 1.8 million people.

In short, while its work is little known, Working America has more face-to-face, in-depth contact with and a deeper understanding of moderate and conservative working class voters than does any other progressive group in the U.S. Here is the basic approach they take to these workers:

> "Working America engages not the fixed 30-35 percent or so at each end of the political spectrum (including the firm conservatives who are not and never will be with us on the issues) but rather than 30-40 percent in the middle—working class moderates whose personal ambivalences make them swing voices in the public policy debates."

In another internal memo Working America describes its view as follows:

> One third of the people we talk to are with us. One third will never be with us. The challenge is to reach the middle third.

Thus, from the perspective of the most important progressive grass-roots organizing effort among white working class voters, the core approach to political organizing is not based on a superficial stereotype of a single "typical" or "average" white worker who is generally conservative but rather on targeting the key group of "ambivalent" or "open-minded" white workers.

Looking at the Data

The reason this "open-minded" or ambivalent form of thinking is largely ignored in American political commentary is that it is far more difficult to capture on standard opinion polls than are straightforward divisions of opinion between "yes" and "no" and "agree" or "disagree." In fact, most opinion polls are very carefully constructed to minimize or eliminate ambiguous responses and to direct respondents into providing clear yes or no answers. A "good" question is one that produces a clear and unambiguous response; a "bad" question is one that produces a response that cannot be so easily categorized.

A recent survey by Pew Research in the spring of 2011 provided a wide and unique set of questions that allowed a more precise measurement of the proportion of white working class voters who fit in the "open minded, ambivalent" category. In the 2011 Pew Political Typology survey a number of the questions were presented as matched pairs of opposing conservative and progressive propositions. Respondents could "strongly agree" or "weakly agree" with the first proposition, be "neutral" about both propositions or "strongly" or "weakly" agree with the second, opposing proposition. As a result, this unique question design made it practical to calculate the proportions of the respondents who were "true believers" in a wide range of conservative or progressive views (i.e., those who "strongly agreed" with one view or another) versus those who were relatively ambivalent or open-minded.[1]

At first glance, some of the results on the survey seem to confirm the stereotype of the "conservative" white working class. 68 percent of the sample, for example "strongly" agreed that "Religion is an important part of my life," 54 percent *"strongly"* agreed that "it is necessary to believe in God to be moral and have good values" and 53 percent *"strongly"* believed that "most people who want to get ahead can succeed if they are willing to work."

But, as the last chapter indicated, within the framework of this essentially universal respect for "traditional" social institutions and culture, however, there is a profound division between essentially conservative and more progressive or open-minded outlooks. This profound division is generally not understood or even perceived by many liberals and non progressives because both points of view are expressed entirely within the language and cognitive framework of white working class cultural traditionalism.

The distinction quickly becomes apparent when one looks at the data in the Pew survey. Consider the charts that appear after the following notes on the data:

Some Important Notes on the Data

There are several important facts that must be kept in mind when examining the charts on the following pages:

First, the Pew survey[2] was conducted in the spring of 2011. This was at the height of the debt ceiling debate and before the occupy Wall Street protests or Obama's shift to a more consistent progressive stance on economic issues. As a result, on some questions opinions may have shifted since the survey was done.

Second, in political opinion research, the term "working class" is now generally applied to either individuals with a high school education (or less) or else to individuals with less than a four-year college degree. Ruy Teixeira, who pioneered this approach, defines the first as the "narrow" definition of "working class" and the second as the "broad" definition.

Based on the "conservative white worker" stereotype, an analyst would tend to expect that the opinions of the larger, "less than four year college degree" group would be substantially more liberal or progressive than the opinions of only those who have just a high school education since the former group also includes individuals with some college experience.

Surprisingly, however, in this particular survey the difference between the responses of whites in the "narrow", high school educated group and the "broader" less than four year college degree group was consistently quite small, amounting to only a few percentage points and in no case changed the conclusion that would have been drawn by examining the results for the white high school educated respondents alone.

As a result, with this particular data it is possible to work exclusively with either the broad or the narrow definition of working class without having to constantly refer back and forth and discuss the differences between the results for two definitions. The key reason for choosing one rather than the other therefore becomes either (1) the difference in sample size between the two or (2) their degree of sociological precision.

In this sample, the white, less than four year college degree subsample included 1303 individuals, producing a simple margin of error of 3.6 percent. The white high school or less group included 678 individuals, producing a simple margin of error of 4.9 percent.*

These are both very exceptionally large subsamples of white working class individuals. Most typical survey subsamples of these groups contain less than one-third this number of respondents with correspondingly larger margins of error.

All else being equal, one would ordinarily tend to choose the subsample with the largest number of respondents and smallest margin of error. But the smaller high school or less group is sociologically much more homogeneous in occupational terms and closer to what most people think of as the traditional "white working class." Approximately 75 percent—three quarters—of white men with at most a high school diploma work in traditional blue collar or manual service occupations.[3] In contrast, among white men with less than a four-year college degree, only about two thirds are in traditional working class jobs.

Since the conclusions that are drawn from the data are not affected by the 1.3 percent difference between the margin of error between the larger and smaller group, for this study of the white working class it makes sense to use the "narrow" definition of working class and focus our attention on the opinions of just those with a high school diploma or less. This is the group that most closely resembles the traditional image of "white working class" individuals.

A few other points also need to be mentioned in passing:

The percents in the charts do not add to exactly 100 because of "don't know" and other unclassifiable responses.

In the published reports of the Pew Political Typology Survey the data are combined into a series of composite categories derived by factor analysis (i.e., categories like "the disaffected") and not by standard categories like age, education and so on. However Pew also releases the underlying data to researchers without these factor-derived categories and indexed by standard demographic and political variables (i.e., education, income, etc.).

It is important to keep in mind that these data include both men and women—"waitress moms" as well as "hard-hat dads." Although the sample size makes disaggregated analysis of the sexes significantly imprecise, on a number of issues men do indeed tend to be more "conservative" than women.

Only a subset of the full set of questions on the Pew political ideology survey are framed as direct choices between contrasting progressive and conservative views—the distinctive format that makes them uniquely suitable for this analysis. For brevity, however, this subset of contrasting questions will simply be referred to as "the Pew survey" rather than more precisely as "the contrasting questions subset of the Pew survey" whenever the Pew data is mentioned.

The full set of charts and dataset—for both the narrow (high school or less) and broad (less than BA) groups can be found at: http://www.thedemocraticstrategist.org/_memos/Charts-and-Data-for-Almost-everything-you-read-about-the-white-working-class.doc

Note: The MOE given above is the simple MOE assuming that the sample was completely random. In reality the Pew methodology is more complex and tedious to calculate for each individual question but the resulting MOE based on the Pew method is actually smaller than the MOE's presented here rather than larger so the simple MOE is entirely adequate for this discussion.

Moral Issues

When questions about moral issues are not framed as abstract statements of approval or disapproval for traditional "morality" in general but rather as questions about the more practical question of whether government should be made responsible for enforcing conservative morality, only 29 percent of white working class voters turn out to be conservative *"true believers"* who strongly agree with the idea. In fact, a significantly larger group of 43 percent strongly disagrees and holds that the government is actually "getting too involved" in the issue.

But even more significant, nearly a quarter of the respondents are somewhat ambivalent or open-minded on this issue. As the chart below makes dramatically clear, they represent the key swing group whose support can convert either side into a majority.

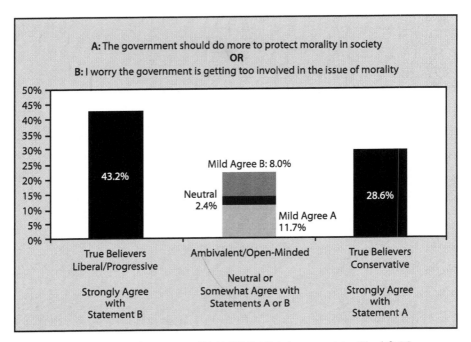

Source: http://www.people-press.org/2011/05/04/typology-group-profiles/ Q-37gg

The same pattern is also apparent even with the much more specific and controversial issue of homosexuality. Quite surprisingly, about equal numbers of white working class respondents are "strongly" in favor of accepting it as are in favor of discouraging it. At the same time, the key swing group of almost 15 percent is ambivalent or open-minded.

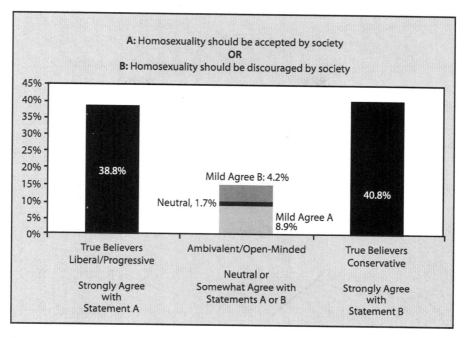

A: Homosexuality should be accepted by society
OR
B: Homosexuality should be discouraged by society

Mild Agree B: 4.2%

Neutral, 1.7%

38.8%

40.8%

Mild Agree A
8.9%

True Believers
Liberal/Progressive

Ambivalent/Open-Minded

True Believers
Conservative

Neutral or
Somewhat Agree with
Statements A or B

Strongly Agree
with
Statement A

Strongly Agree
with
Statement B

Source: http://www.people-press.org/2011/05/04/typology-group-profiles/ Q-37u

These results illustrate a pattern that runs through all of the Pew data. When conservative "true believers" (i.e. those who "strongly" agree with a conservative position) are separated from the ambivalent or open-minded, they turn out to be a minority rather than a majority of white working class Americans. The majority is composed of people who are either opposed to or somewhat ambivalent about hard-line conservative views.

Immigration

Hostility to immigrants is one of the two areas in the Pew survey (as well as in other surveys) where white working class Americans display the greatest degree of "conservatism." For example, 56 percent of the white working class respondents in the Pew survey either strongly or somewhat agreed that recent immigrants "threaten traditional American customs and values," which is one of the highest percentages favoring a "conservative" view in the entire set of Pew questions.

Yet even in this area, the number of respondents who "strongly" agree with this proposition is less than a majority and is almost exactly equaled by the total of those who either disagree or are ambivalent.

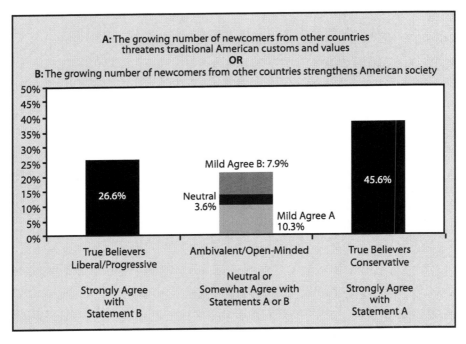

Source: http://www.people-press.org/2011/05/04/typology-group-profiles/ Q-37dd

It is only when immigration is framed in starkly economic terms as a competition between immigrants and American workers over jobs and resources rather than directly as a cultural/ethnic issue that a majority of American workers "strongly" express a conservative view. This is displayed in the chart below where an unambiguous majority of 53 percent "strongly" agree that immigrants are a burden because they "take our jobs, housing and health care."

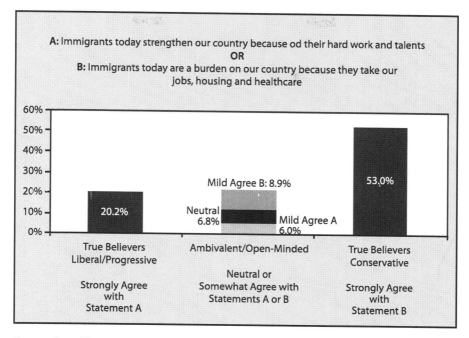

A: Immigrants today strengthen our country because od their hard work and talents
OR
B: Immigrants today are a burden on our country because they take our jobs, housing and healthcare

Mild Agree B: 8.9%

Neutral 6.8%

Mild Agree A 6.0%

20.2%

53,0%

True Believers Liberal/Progressive

Ambivalent/Open-Minded

True Believers Conservative

Strongly Agree with Statement A

Neutral or Somewhat Agree with Statements A or B

Strongly Agree with Statement B

Source: http://www.people-press.org/2011/05/04/typology-group-profiles/ Q-17g

These results confirm the undeniable strength and intensity of white working class antagonism to recent immigrants, but the fact that when the question is framed in explicitly cultural/ethnic terms there is almost an even split between those who are "strongly" hostile and those who are not still suggests the degree to which it is still inaccurate to stereotype most white working class people as conservative "true believers" in regard to immigration.

Military and International Affairs

When the questions in the Pew survey shift to military and international affairs, the distinction between liberal/progressive views and conservative views no longer involves an underlying split between relatively tolerant and intolerant attitudes toward minority social groups like Atheists, Gays and Latinos. Rather, the division becomes one between those who support a single-minded reliance on military force as the solution to all problems versus those who favor a more cautious approach that emphasizes using military force in a limited and careful way.

Consider the following chart:

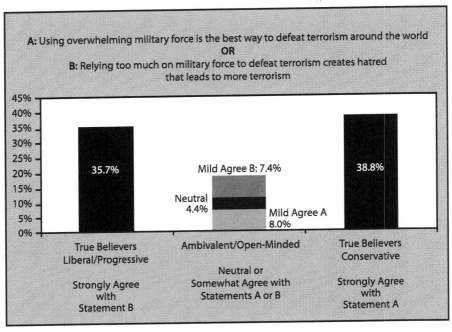

Source: http://www.people-press.org/2011/05/04/typology-group-profiles/ Q-37bb

Despite the fact that on basically all major opinion polls there is always near-universal support for *"our men and women in uniform"* among white working class Americans, only slightly more than one third of the white working class respondents endorse "overwhelming military force" as the best way to fight terrorism. An almost equal number sees the single-minded reliance on military force as counterproductive. Most important, it is, once again, the ambivalent or open-minded 20 percent of the respondents that represents the critical "swing" group on the issue.

The same pattern is repeated with questions that enquire about balancing the interests of U.S. allies versus "going it alone." The "true believers" on both sides are minorities while 25 percent fall in the category of the ambivalent or open-minded.

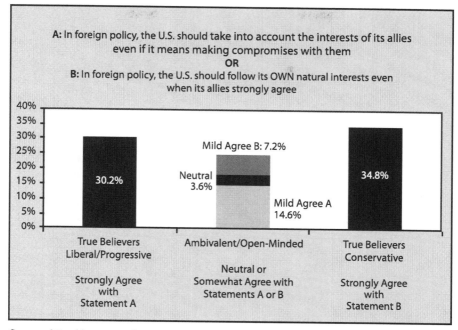

A: In foreign policy, the U.S. should take into account the interests of its allies even if it means making compromises with them
OR
B: In foreign policy, the U.S. should follow its OWN natural interests even when its allies strongly agree

Mild Agree B: 7.2%

Neutral 3.6%

Mild Agree A 14.6%

30.2%

34.8%

True Believers
Liberal/Progressive

Ambivalent/Open-Minded

True Believers
Conservative

Strongly Agree
with
Statement A

Neutral or
Somewhat Agree with
Statements A or B

Strongly Agree
with
Statement B

Source: http://www.people-press.org/2011/05/04/typology-group-profiles/ Q-37cc

Economic Issues: Wall Street and Big Business

Regarding white working class attitudes toward big business, even the most conservative analysts of public opinion do not hesitate to acknowledge that there is a strong and deeply enduring strand of suspicion and hostility. This cluster of views, which is usually labeled "populist" in journalistic accounts, has remained quite stable since the 1960's, even though attitudes on a vast number of other subjects have changed dramatically since that time.

As the two charts below reveal, these "populist" sentiments remain quite strong in white working class America today. 54 percent of the white working class respondents in the Pew survey strongly felt that business corporations *"make too much profit"* and 70 percent strongly felt that they have *"too much power"*. On this topic, even when the ambivalent or open-minded respondents are added to the defenders of corporate profits and power, the combined group still remains a minority.

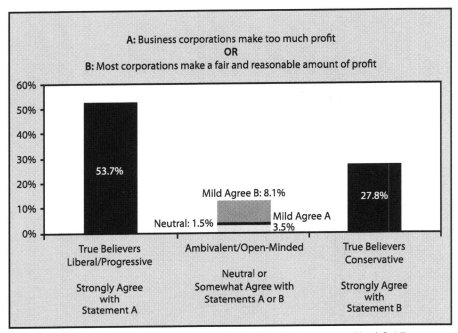

Source: http://www.people-press.org/2011/05/04/typology-group-profiles/ Q-37gg

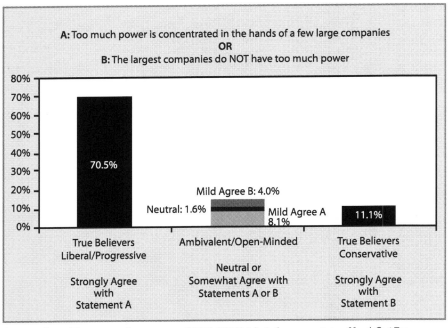

Source: http://www.people-press.org/2011/05/04/typology-group-profiles/ Q-17m

One reason why attitudes of this general kind have remained relatively stable for many years is that they are broad and abstract enough that they have not become the subject of intense, continuous and specific conservative attack. Until this year they have not been "hot button" issues in most election campaigns nor are they the kind of opinions that are energetically refuted on a literally a daily basis by talk radio hosts and commentators on Fox News.

However, one specific topic that has indeed been widely and fiercely debated in the last several years is the role of Wall Street in the economy. In the immediate aftermath of the 2008 Wall Street and bank "bailouts," the financial community was genuinely shocked by the intensity of the popular backlash against the financial sector in general. In response, business, the financial industry, conservatives and the Republican Party all joined in an energetic effort to "push back" against this backlash and mounted an energetic defense of Wall Street, banks and the financial sector.

These widely circulated defenses (which formed the basis of Mitt Romney's presidential campaign rhetoric) argued that the executives and traders on Wall Street and in the financial industry are the only real "job-creators" in the American economy, people without whom not a single job could ever be created at all. The extravagant bonuses and lavish lifestyles common in the financial industry were and are similarly justified on the grounds that they are the indispensable reward for the vast risk-taking and effort that is required to channel capital to job-creating ventures. The passionately pro-free market writings of Ayn Rand, previously popular among only a tiny audience of libertarians and free-market ideologues, suddenly became national best sellers and a serious ideological view in the national debate.

Given the substantial extent of this business "pushback" against all criticism of Wall Street and the financial industry in the last three years, it is reasonable to wonder if the attitudes of white working class people might actually have become less hostile on this particular subject than they are on the more abstract issues of corporate profit and power.

In fact, however, white working class antagonism to Wall Street still remains high. Over 45 percent of white working class respondents on the Pew survey "strongly" agreed that Wall Street "hurts the American economy more than it helps." When those who "mildly" agree are added, the percentage rises to 55 percent. In contrast, only 19 percent of the sample strongly supports the view that Wall Street "helps" the American economy more than it hurts it. Even when all the ambivalent or open-minded are added in, the total barely rises above 40 percent.

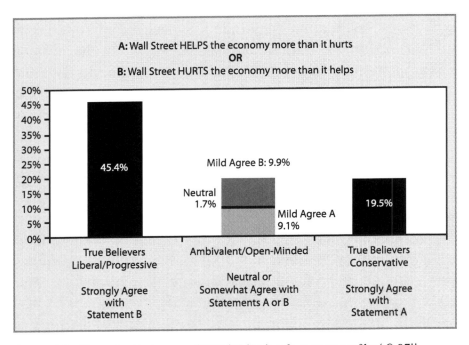

Source: http://www.people-press.org/2011/05/04/typology-group-profiles/ Q-37ii

The Pew survey provides therefore quite strong evidence for the persistence and strength of a powerful "populist" element in white working class thought, one that has not been reversed even by the extensive efforts at persuasion mounted by Wall Street and the business community.

Ever since the early 1970's, however, the most important response of business, conservatives and Republicans to white working class populism has not been the direct ideological defense of business and Wall Street but rather a broad attempt to displace the anger that is expressed in working class populism away from the business and financial communities and onto a variety of other targets.

Three groups and institutions are very specifically targeted in this ideological campaign:

First, white working class people are encouraged to blame liberal policies aimed at helping the poor for many of the problems faced by working Americans. Since the 1970's the poor have been described by conservatives as a separate class of the lazy and immoral who, unlike honest working class people, live on government benefits paid for by the taxes of white working class Americans. In the 1970's and 1980's it was the cliché of "welfare queens;" in the aftermath of the housing collapse, it was widely argued that it was "irresponsible" borrowers (and particularly minorities unfairly favored by government) rather than predatory lenders and financial institutions who were ultimately to blame for the housing crisis.

Second, working people are encouraged to blame educated middle class liberals for promoting policies that deprive working class people of jobs and prosperity in order to advance elitist social agendas. Most centrally, environmental rules and policies are described as destructive and unnecessary interventions in the free market that eliminate working class jobs and suffocate economic growth.

Third—and most important—the approach encourages working people to blame government itself for the economic problems of working Americans. Government, it is argued, imposes unnecessary taxes on working class people and distributes the proceeds to other, undeserving groups and programs while it also issues useless and overbearing regulations.

The Pew survey provides data that indicates to what degree working Americans have come to agree with these three perspectives.

Economic Issues: Poverty

The two charts below and on the next page display the findings of the Pew survey on this issue:

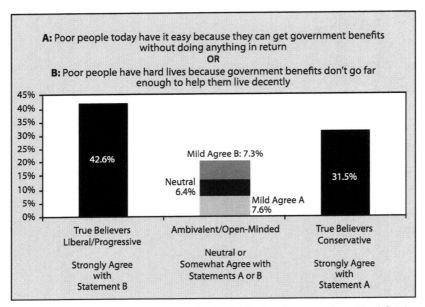

Source: http://www.people-press.org/2011/05/04/typology-group-profiles/ Q-17c

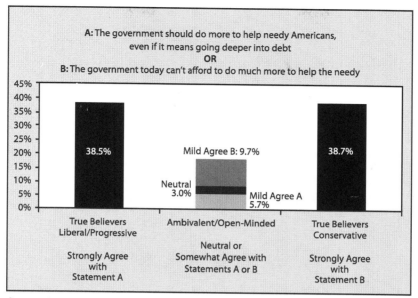

A: The government should do more to help needy Americans, even if it means going deeper into debt
OR
B: The government today can't afford to do much more to help the needy

Source: http://www.people-press.org/2011/05/04/typology-group-profiles/ Q-17d

As can be seen, only 31 percent of white working class people strongly agreed that the poor "have it easy" because they can get government benefits without working. In contrast, 43 percent strongly believe that government benefits don't go far enough to help them live decently.

It is reasonable to suspect that these responses would be different if the question made a clear distinction between unemployment compensation, upon which many working people depend and "welfare" or unspecified "government handouts" which have historically been associated with minorities. But nonetheless, this is a significant result, and it is supported by the fact that just as many white working class Americans strongly support doing more to help the "needy"—even if it means going deeper into debt—as reject the idea.

Thus, on this issue the general pattern seen in the Pew survey appears once again. Only a minority of white working class Americans "strongly" agree with the conservative position. A larger group disagrees and the balance of opinion lies among the ambivalent or open-minded.

Economic Issues: The Environment

The chart below shows that 38 percent of white working class Americans feel strongly that environmental laws and regulations are "worth the cost" while an almost exactly equal number feel strongly that they "cost too many jobs and hurt the economy." The pivotal swing group of the ambivalent or open minded, in contrast, constitutes about 18 percent of the total.

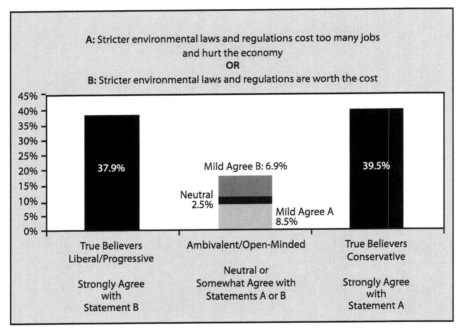

Source: http://www.people-press.org/2011/05/04/typology-group-profiles/ Q-37r

Equally significant, when the question is posed in a more general way, essentially asking if the respondents generally support government action to "protect the environment," the results are quite dramatically lopsided in support of environmental protection. 58 percent of white working class Americans strongly support the proposition that the nation must "protect the environment."

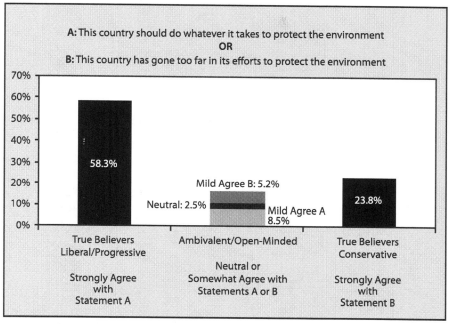

Source: http://www.people-press.org/2011/05/04/typology-group-profiles/ Q-37q

Economic Issues: The Role of Government

Given the fact that hostility and opposition to "big government" has been the central plank of the Republican platform since the Reagan era and the most consistently, intensely and ferociously asserted view across the entire conservative media it would be remarkable if it did not find a substantial degree of support within white working class America.

As the chart below shows, when opposition to government is stated as an abstract proposition, there is indeed widespread agreement with anti-government views in white working class America. When the defense of government is expressed with the rather weak proposition that it "does a better job than people give it credit for", only 22 percent of white workers strongly agree while 57 percent of white workers strongly assert the opposite view—that government is "almost always wasteful and inefficient." This is the highest level of support for a "strong" conservative view in any of the questions reviewed thus far.

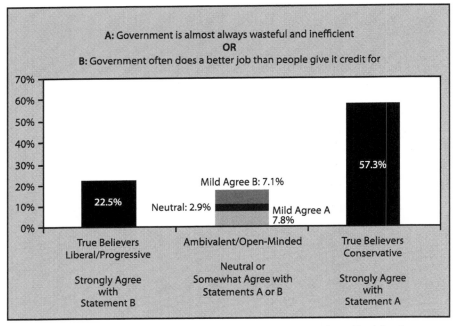

Source: http://www.people-press.org/2011/05/04/typology-group-profiles/ Q-17a

The level of opposition to government does decline significantly, however, when the question is posed at a more specific level—as support for the proposition that "government regulation of business is necessary to protect the public interest." In this case, while 47 percent of the respondents on the Pew survey strongly agreed that regulation of business "usually does more harm than good," the percent that disagreed or are ambivalent about this proposition was exactly the same.

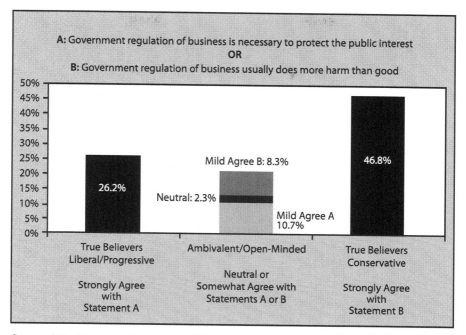

Source: http://www.people-press.org/2011/05/04/typology-group-profiles/ Q-17b

The Pew survey discussed here did not ask questions about support for particular government programs, but it is a well-known generalization that on a very wide range of such specific topics, white working class voters generally express favorable views. Ever since the 1960's a cliché of political science has been that the American people and the white working class in particular are "ideological conservatives" regarding big government in the abstract but are also "operational liberals" who support a wide range of specific government programs.

The Overall Picture

In order to summarize the wide range of data that has been presented thus far, consider the following chart:

Average – All Pew Questions Above	Liberal/ Progressive True Believers	Ambivalent/ Open-Minded	Conservative True Believers
	38.5%	18.3%	37.9%

This chart simply averages the percentages presented in all the charts shown in the preceding pages.*

What this chart shows is that an average of 38 percent of the respondents to the various Pew questions can be classed as conservative "true believers" who express strong support for conservative views while an almost exactly identical number can be classed as "true believers" in a liberal/progressive perspective. In contrast, about 18 percent of the white working class respondents in the Pew survey turn out to be ambivalent or open-minded.

The conclusion is unavoidable. The majority of white working class Americans are simply not firm, deeply committed conservatives. Those who express "strong" support for conservative propositions represent slightly less than 40 percent of the total. The critical swing group within white working class America is composed of the ambivalent or open-minded.

This is an extremely surprising result since virtually all political commentary about the white working class today is based on the assumption that these voters are generally quite deeply conservative and that conservatives very substantially outnumber liberal/ progressives in white working class America.

One reason for the strength of this preconception among political analysts lies in the fact that most discussions of white working class opinion actually only focus on a subset of "values" or "social" issues and set aside all the "populist" issues regarding big business.

---

*Note: These calculations also include the results from several additional, largely similar questions on the Pew survey that have not been presented in the preceding pages. The full set of questions on which these aggregate percentages are based can be found at http://www.thedemocraticstrategist.org/_memos/Charts-and-Data-for-Almost-everything-you-read-about-the-white-working-class.doc

In fact, when the overall data from the Pew survey are broken out into several major subcategories or "clusters" of political issues, two distinct patterns appear. As the chart below shows, attitudes about "populist" issues regarding big business and profits weigh the overall average in one direction while views about other domestic issues including morality, immigration and attitudes toward the poor, educated elites and government weigh the overall average in the opposite direction.

Averages for Key Issue Clusters	Liberal/ Progressive True Believers	Ambivalent/ Open-Minded	Conservative True Believers
Domestic Issues	34.6%	18.3%	42.8%
"Populist" Issues	53.7%	17.0%	19.5%
Military Issues	35.4%	21.8%	35.5%
Grand Total	38.5%	18.3%	37.9%

As can be seen, on the distinct subset of "populist" issues about corporate profits, power and the role of Wall Street a majority of white American workers—54 percent—strongly agree with a liberal/ progressive view. In contrast, only 20 percent strongly agree with the conservative, pro- business perspective. At the same time, however, on the range of other domestic issues about 43 percent of the Pew sample appear as conservative "true believers" who strongly agree with the conservative position in contrast to only 35 percent who strongly agree with the progressive view.

This rough split—conservatives constituting a percentage in the low 40's and liberal/progressives a percentage in the mid-30's—will feel oddly familiar to most political observers. But this is a coincidence that arises simply because it corresponds to the percentages commonly seen within the general population (rather than among white working class individuals in particular) on polling questions about domestic "social" or "values" issues other than those regarding big business. The lower percentage of liberals compared to conservatives also corresponds with the widely repeated generalizations about the ideological self-identification of the American people as a whole—that on Pew and Gallup polls[4] 36 to 40 percent describe themselves as conservative and 18 to 21 percent as liberal.

However, these familiar statistics are actually not at all relevant to the present discussion because they describe the U.S. population as a whole and not specifically white working class voters. But, if anything, the common stereotypes of the white working class would strongly suggest that conservatives should constitute an even larger proportion of the white working class total than they do of the general population and that liberal/progressive individuals should be an even smaller percentage of white working class people than of the general population.

But the quite unique data from the Pew Political Typology Report simply do not support this deduction. The questions on the Pew survey are specifically designed to map a uniquely wide range of ideological views in a way that most opinion surveys are not and the sample size is vastly larger than the white high school subsample that is available on virtually all other opinion studies. As a result the data provides strong evidence that the common clichés are wrong—that the majority of white workers are not strong conservatives and there is a distinct group of ambivalent or open minded white working class Americans who represent the critical swing group in working class politics.

This alone is a quite substantial challenge to the conventional view. Yet a deeper analysis of the Pew numbers provides results that are even more surprising. When a more sophisticated method of calculation is used, the number of genuinely consistent conservative ideologues—"Fox News/Talk Radio" true believers—in white working class America actually turns out to be significantly lower than the 38 percent suggested by the simple and straightforward average of all the percents on the various Pew questions.

Looking at the percentages in the initial chart in this section, it is easy to unconsciously make the assumption that the 38 percent of conservative true believers (or the equal number of their liberal/progressive counterparts) represent two stable groups of ideologically consistent conservatives or liberal/progressives—the kinds of consistent and committed ideological partisans one would expect to find attending the annual meetings of the Campaign for America's Future on the left or the Conservative Political Action Council on the right and loudly cheering the remarks of every single one of the speakers.

But this is not necessarily the case. If a particular Pew chart shows that 38 percent of the sample strongly agrees with the conservative view on one particular survey question (regarding immigrants, for example) and an identical 38 percent agrees with the conservative view on a second survey question (about military force, for example), even though the two percentages are the same, the two groups may be composed of quite different individuals.

The obvious real world example of this kind of situation is the existence of many "single issue" conservative (or liberal/progressive) groups and individuals. The person who is a passionate anti-abortion activist may not also be firmly opposed to higher taxes on millionaires or to exclusive reliance on overwhelming military force. On a multi-issue opinion poll, a person of this sort will be counted among the 38 percent of conservative "true believers" on some questions but not on others.

To estimate the size of the ideologically consistent true believers—the "Fox News/Talk Radio" ideologues who accept a wide range of conservative views (or the "Rachael Maddow/MSNBC" ideologues who embrace a similar range of liberal/progressive views)—requires a distinct method of summarizing the Pew data. In essence, the question that needs to be answered is "what percent of the white working class respondents on the Pew survey are people who strongly support a *very wide range* of either conservative or liberal/progressive positions."

One way to calculate this is to score each individual respondents' position on each one of the questions in the charts on the preceding pages on a scale of 1 to 5 (with 1 being equal to *"strongly agree with the liberal/progressive view"*, 2 being equal to *"somewhat agree with the liberal/progressive view"* and so on). Once this is done, averaging an individual's scores on all of the questions above makes it possible to derive a single summary "ideological" average for each individual survey respondent.

Individuals whose overall average is in the range between 1 and 2 are those who strongly agreed with a very wide range of liberal/progressive propositions. Those whose overall average ranges from 4 to 5 are those who strongly agree with a wide range of conservative propositions.*

The following chart shows the results:

	Liberal/ Progressive True believers (Score on a 1 to 5 liberal-conservative scale = 1 to 2.5	Ambivalent/ Open-Minded (Score on a 1 to 5 liberal-conservative scale = 2.5 to 3.5)	Conservative True believers (Score on a 1 to 5 liberal-conservative scale = 3.5 to 5)
Percent of Respondents: All Issues	25.9	46.6	27.5

These totals for conservative and liberal/progressive true believers are about 10 percent lower than they appear in the simpler calculation. The conservative true believers are 28 percent instead of 38 percent, the liberal/progressive true believers are 26 percent of the total rather than 38 percent. Rather than being about 18 percent of the total, the ambivalent/open-minded represent 47 percent—almost half—of the total.

There are two qualifications that can be noted. As with the simple calculation, the percentage of conservative true believers does indeed expand when one only looks at domestic social and values issues and sets aside the "populist" aspects of white working class opinion. On non-populist domestic issues the conservative true believers constitute 38 percent of the sample rather than 28 percent and liberal/ progressives only constitute 22 percent rather than 25 percent.

And it is also important to keep in mind that these results are for both men and women. On a substantial number of issues the opinions of white working class men alone would indeed be more conservative. For many kinds of sociological analyses this is an extremely important qualification. For analyzing likely voting behavior, where the votes of both sexes count exactly equally, it is less so.

But regardless of these two qualifications, three overall conclusions are essentially inescapable.

1. The majority of white working people are not strong conservatives. Those who express "strong agreement" with conservative propositions are distinctly less than 50 percent.

2. The ambivalent or open-minded are the key swing group in working class America. They represent a minimum of 20 percent of white working class respondents across wide range of survey questions using the most restrictive possible definition and substantially more using less restrictive definitions.

3. The genuinely consistent white working class conservatives— the "Fox News/Talk Radio" hard-line ideologues—represent only about one fourth of the white working class total.

This is a very surprising and disruptive set of conclusions for those who passively accept the popular clichés. But they do, in fact, correspond quite well with the "real world" conclusions of people who actually have face-to-face daily contact with this segment of the electorate.

For example, as noted at the beginning of this analysis, Working America, the community affiliate of the AFL-CIO, describes the persuadable voters within working class America that its door to door canvassing has revealed as "the 35-40 percent in the middle—

working class moderates whose personal ambivalences make them swing voices in the public policy debates."

Equally, Democracy Corps, the progressive polling and focus group organization that has done the most in-depth opinion studies of white working class voters, summarized a series of focus groups[5] studying the difference between working class "true believers" and the more open-minded in the following way:

> The self-identifying conservative Republicans who make up the base of the Republican Party stand a world apart from the rest of America... these voters identify themselves as part of a 'mocked' minority with a set of shared beliefs and knowledge, and commitment to oppose Obama that sets them apart from the majority in the country. They believe Obama is ruthlessly advancing a 'secret agenda' to bankrupt the United States and dramatically expand government control to an extent nothing short of socialism... they overwhelmingly view a successful Obama presidency as the destruction of this country's founding principles....

> ...The Republican base voters are not part of a continuum leading to the center of the electorate: they truly stand apart. For additional perspective, Democracy Corps conducted a parallel set of groups in suburban Cleveland. These groups, comprised of older, white, non-college independents and weak partisans, represent some of the most conservative swing voters in the electorate.... Though we kept discussion points constant between the two sets of groups, on virtually every point of discussion around President Obama and the major issues facing our country, these two audiences simply saw the world in fundamentally different ways.... Conservative Republicans fully embrace the 'socialism' attacks on Obama and believe it is the best, most accurate way to describe him and his agenda. Independents largely

dismiss these attacks as partisan rhetoric detracting from a legitimate debate about what many of them do see as excessive government control and spending.

Finally, it is notable that the results of this analysis—while they are completely opposed to the common wisdom—are actually strikingly in accord with the basic realities that journalists as well as many liberals and progressives encounter in their own personal experiences.

- In group interviews on construction sites and in diners or coffee shops, journalists and reporters generally report that not all the workers in the group are hard-core conservatives but that the group is split between conservatives and more ambivalent or open minded individuals.
- That hostility to illegal immigration and government in general are the most intensely felt "conservative" opinions among working class Americans. On other subjects, in contrast, opinions vary much more widely.
- That there are very distinct and dramatic "pockets" of populist views where white workers (particularly in the North and rust belt Mid-West) express deeply anti- corporate and anti- big business views.

In short, the conclusion is simple. The majority of America's white working class voters are not small-scale replicas of Sean Hannity, Rush Limbaugh or Glen Beck. The majority of white working class Americans are cultural traditionalists but not firm conservatives. They are deeply suspicious of progressives and the Democratic Party, but they are not irrevocably committed to the political right and the GOP.

The Political Implications

There are four major implications of this analysis:

First, Democratic political strategists should forget— no, indeed, actively reject—the notion that "the typical

129

conservative white worker" is in any possible way a useful political concept. It is empirically false, politically destructive, psychologically misleading and morally corrosive. It needs to be put on the same dusty shelf for outmoded political concepts as "welfare queens" and "Midwestern Republican moderate politicians" The "typical conservative white worker" notion simply does not provide an adequate mental framework for trying to understand white working class America.

Second, using the term "moderate" to describe the substantial group of workers who are not conservative true believers does not in any way imply that they actually conceptualize their philosophy as seeking some sort of abstract "middle of the road," centrism along the lines promoted by beltway commentators who endlessly dream of finding some magical policy agenda that is exquisitely balanced precisely midway between left and right. Quite the contrary, working class people often have very firm and uncompromising, gut-level commitments to their views which is the exact opposite of a philosophical commitment to "find the middle on everything" centrism. On the contrary, what distinguishes the ambivalent or open-minded white workers from the true believers is their distinct "on the one hand but on the other hand" method of analysis and their reliance on "common sense" rather than ideology for political decision-making.

The political implication of this is simple: these voters will listen to progressive arguments that respect their open-minded, "there may be some truth on both sides" mode of thought. They will simply ignore or flatly reject stale 1950's rhetoric and traditional Democratic stump-speech clichés.

Third, an obvious approach that at first glance seems suggested by this data is for Democratic messaging to relentlessly appeal to the cluster of populist views of white workers in the hope that constant repetition will eventually "overwrite" or replace the conservative framing with which white working people are more familiar. Traditional advertising strategy has long relied on the consistent, heavy handed repetition of a single, simple ad message as an effective way of convincing consumers to buy product X instead of product Y.

But the problem with this approach is that the "populist" views that white workers do indeed quite undeniably hold are not stored in a neat and separate cognitive compartment where they can be invoked and appealed to in isolation. White workers views about corporations, banks and profits are embedded in a series of larger cognitive frameworks that also contain their views about work, fairness, taxes, debt, corruption, distrust of government and alienation from the political system.

The most insightful and systematic study that has been done of these larger cognitive frameworks has been by Stan Greenberg's Democracy Corps in its "economy project."[5] What their research has revealed is that there are at least five interconnected clusters of ideas about the economy that all play a part in the political decision-making of white workers. In consequence no simplistic *"Just keep hammering em' over the head with the populist stuff until it sinks in"* approach will be successful.

Finally, the Democracy Corps research also confirms the grass-roots insight of Working America that, above all else, what ambivalent or open-minded white working

131

class Americans want is *representation*. White working class Americans feel, entirely correctly, that "no-one is looking out for them" and that they can no longer trust the traditional political system.

Here's how a Working America memo expresses it:

> While the working class swing voters that make up our constituency are confused and angry, they are not ideological. They aren't thinking about the Constitution and the Founding Fathers, or eliminating all government agencies. They want economic solutions and a sense that their civic participation can make a difference up against powerful special interests.

To put it simply, until the Democratic Party seriously comes to terms with its failure to genuinely represent white working class Americans, it will not be able to win their firm political support.

Taken together, what these four conclusions suggest is a dramatically—indeed fundamentally—different approach to winning the support of white working class voters. The first step, however, is quite simple: Democrats must put aside the useless fiction of "the typical conservative white worker" and to begin to deal with the complexity of white working class political opinion as it actually exists in America today.

CHAPTER

7

Values: the Split Between Tolerance and Intolerance In White Working Class America

The basic distinction outlined in the previous chapters—between "true believers" and the "open-minded"—overlaps a closely related psychological dichotomy between "tolerant" and "intolerant" attitudes and individuals. When white working class people are described as being basically "conservative"—as they often are—it is usually the individuals who are both intolerant and "true believers" who are being visualized—the kind of individuals who sound like Rush Limbaugh or other talk radio hosts.

But in fact, across a wide range of issues there is a profound split between tolerant and intolerant individuals in white working class America—a split that is nearly invisible to educated liberals because it exists entirely inside the overall framework of the traditionalist world-view and culture of working class life.

In this chapter we will look at how this division between tolerant and intolerant and conservative and progressive views expresses itself in the three major areas where struggles over "values" are fought—religion, racial attitudes about immigrants and opinions about the military.

Attitudes About Religion

Most political analyses approach the subject of religion with a basic vision of religious Americans as essentially arrayed on a single "liberal to conservative" continuum—one that combines both their political views and their degree of religious piety. In this way of thinking about religious voters, the highly religious and the highly observant, the politically conservative, the evangelicals and fundamentalists all tend to be visualized as clustered at one pole of this dichotomy while the less intensely religious, less devout and more socially and politically moderate members of the mainline denominations are visualized as clustering toward the other.

In this perspective, working class Americans are typically visualized as generally on the conservative end of the spectrum in all respects—in their views about religion itself, about "values" issues related to religion and also in their choice of evangelical rather than mainline denominations.

The 2008 Pew Religious Landscape Survey[1], a massive study that interviewed 35,000 Americans, confirmed that working class Americans—those with a high school or less than a college education—are indeed somewhat more heavily concentrated in the evangelical denominations than in mainline ones. 80 percent of evangelicals have less than a college degree, in contrast to 67 percent of the followers of mainline denominations. Over a third of the members of mainline denominations have college degree while only a fifth of evangelicals do.

	High school	Some college	College grad	Post grad	Number of Survey Respondents
Total	50%	23%	16%	11%	35,300
Evangelical	56%	24%	13%	7%	9,400
Mainline	43%	24%	20%	14%	7, 400

This does not mean that mainline denominations can be visualized as composed of the college educated and middle class. As the chart shows, two thirds of the mainline denominations members also have less than a college degree. But what it does indicate is that evangelical denominations are indeed quite overwhelmingly working class in composition.

Cutting sharply across both evangelical and mainstream denominations, however, is a fundamental split between two very different religious philosophies within American Christianity, a split between those whose religious outlook and philosophy is fundamentally tolerant and those whose outlook is fundamentally intolerant.

Among Democrats there is often a tendency to automatically assume that this split follows the same pattern as religious liberalism and conservatism or theological piety as a whole—that tolerant views are concentrated among relatively liberal Christian denominations or secular voters and that intolerance increases in direct proportion to increasing religious faith. On this basis, many Democratic discussions of religion tend to assume that large categories of religious voters—such as frequent church-goers or self-described "evangelicals" or "born-again" Christians—can be assumed to be generally intolerant and attracted to the religious right.

But, in fact, the fundamental cleavage within the Christian sector of the electorate between tolerant and intolerant interpretations of Christianity follows an entirely different pattern. Because the division is rooted in two distinct interpretations of the message of Jesus Christ and the meaning of the Christian faith itself, it can be found across the ideological spectrum and at every level of religious dedication and denominational choice. It appears within the ranks of both occasional churchgoers and deeply engaged weekly participants, it appears in the congregations of Baptists and Pentecostals as well as Lutherans and Presbyterians, among evangelicals and fundamentalists as well as among mainstream denominations, it appears among the most theologically conservative, devout and pious as well as among the more relaxed and flexible.

The first modern in-depth exploration of this fundamental cleavage among American Christians was presented by the sociologist

Alan Wolfe in his 1998 book, *One Nation After All*. His book is based on extensive interviews he conducted with over 200 individuals in eight carefully chosen communities during the late 1990's. Wolfe uncovered one particularly striking indication of the central importance of tolerance when he asked his sample if they agreed with the statement that, "There are many different religious truths and we ought to be tolerant of all of them". Of his 200 interview subjects, 167 agreed (75 of them "strongly") and only 19 disagreed.

Wolfe emphasized that there is a fundamental division among even deeply religious Americans between those whose faith is combined with tolerance for other religious opinions versus those who see their own views as right and all other views as wrong.

As Wolfe notes:

> It is more in accord with the way middle-class Americans understand their religious commitments to posit the existence of two different kinds of deep faith: one which is genuinely absolutist in its insistence on one way to the truth and one which, while equally sincere, is welcoming of all faiths.

Wolfe offers one of his subjects, Mr. McLaughlin, as an example of the first kind of faith:

> For Mr. McLaughlin, if something is right and true for one person, it ought to be right and true for all; as he put it in our interview with him if you don't believe in God, or even if you believe in a God other then the Christian one, "you're going to be reading out of the wrong book."

In contrast, Wolfe describes another of his interviewees who reflects the second kind of religious perspective, one rooted in respect for individual freedom and individual rights

Because she is religious, Mrs. Thompkins believes that

there are right and wrong ways to act. But... she also thinks that however strongly one applies principles of right and wrong to herself, one ought to hesitate before applying them to others... the idea follows from a commitment to individual freedom; if we proclaim our religious ideas too publicly, we run the risk of interfering with the rights of others to believe in God the way they want to."

Wolfe's conclusions were powerfully confirmed and reinforced by an extensive series of two-hour interviews with 300 evangelicals, fundamentalists and other churchgoing protestants conducted around the same time by a team of 12 sociologists led by Christian Smith and published in the book, *Christian America—What Evangelicals Really Want.*

As Smith concluded, even among evangelicals and other presumably conservative Christians, many expressed surprisingly tolerant attitudes.

> Evangelicals are often stereotyped as imperious, intolerant, fanatical meddlers. Certainly there are some evangelicals who exemplify this stereotype. But the vast majority, when listened to on their own terms, prove to hold a civil, tolerant and non-coercive view of the world around them. For some readers this may be unexpected, perhaps even unbelievable. We ourselves—presuming we would hear more echoes of Christian Right rhetoric in our interviews— were surprised by the pervasiveness of this outlook in evangelical talk. Yet pervasive it was...

> ...For every one evangelical opposed to pluralism, there were about five other evangelicals who voiced a strong commitment to freedom of choice and toleration of diversity ...these open-minded and approving voices were the dominant viewpoint on the matter.

Smith quotes a wide range of comments from his interview subjects, including the following:

> I would respect their beliefs, just because I want them to respect mine.... I'm not going to insist that they come over to my way as long as they have their religion. It's not right. We are made up of different personalities, different ways, different beliefs. But if we can know in society how to blend, not telling everybody to believe like I do, we can live like that. Respect each other. Live and let live.

This fundamental division within American religion between tolerant and intolerant interpretations of Christianity is deep and pervasive. It is quite clearly reflected in the different ways religious faith is expressed in "Christian" and "County" radio.

In many of the explicitly Christian radio stations religious faith is extremely public, demonstrative and confessional, with the entire programming focused on eliciting a firm commitment to a particular doctrine. In its attitudes toward those who do not accept the particular doctrines being promoted, the commentary on these stations is often powerfully self-righteous, sanctimonious and judgmental. The programming is very deeply imbued with assertions about the vast difference between the Godly and righteous "us" (once we commit) and the sinful and even diabolic "them".

Religion in country music, on the other hand, is extremely private, personal and rooted in forgiveness rather than condemnation. In country music, God is frequently imagined as a deeply loving father who is the source of wise advice *("remember what the good book says")* and who offers understanding, forgiveness and perhaps a second chance for the inevitable human failures and weaknesses of ordinary men and women. In countless country songs, it is the lonely long-haul trucker who offers quiet and private late-night thanks to God for the miracle of his new-born child or the enduring love of a devoted wife. In country music, God is linked to the listeners' most private, tender, human and empathetic feelings rather than to their most sanctimonious and judgmental ones.

The 2000 election brought religious conservatives into new positions of power but it did not significantly diminish this deeply rooted current of tolerance among American Christians. As a 2001 report by the Public Agenda Foundation, *For Goodness' Sake—Why so Many Want Religion to Play a Greater Role in American Life*, noted:[2]

> "Civil libertarians who have dedicated their careers and their lives to the domain of separation of church and state may not be reassured by how ordinary Americans discuss the issue. If one asks people to discuss separation of church and state in focus groups one had better expect a vague, ill-defined conversation that lacks passion and certainly clarity." What people do understand, however, is tolerance for different values...

> ...Americans strongly equate religion with personal ethics and behavior, considering it an antidote to the moral decline they perceive in our nation today... However, alongside this conviction is an equally strong respect for religious diversity that translates into a strong tolerance for other peoples beliefs...

> ...The view of almost the entire survey sample—96 percent— is that "one of the greatest things about this country is that people can practice whatever religion they choose"...

> ...This is no mere lip service on the public's part nor is it an abstract ideal that disintegrates the moment it is tested. Americans seem to have an ingrained expectation that that they will encounter people with different ideas about religion in their daily lives, and the idea of tolerance is so well accepted that it has been absorbed into daily standards for social conduct...

Americans have developed finely tuned and evolved sensibilities about how to handle religion in their daily social interactions...people instinctively take care not to offend and are sensitive about when and how and whether to talk about religion...interviews indicate people seem to collect experiences—good and bad—which they use to build and fine tune their approach to the issue and develop a list of do's and don'ts.

Since 2000 this support for tolerance has been repeatedly demonstrated in the response to a wide range of different survey questions. On various surveys robust majorities agreed, for example, that:

- "Different religions worship the same God",

- "A good person who does not share your religious beliefs can still go to heaven",

- "You can be a good American and not have religious faith",

- "You can teach values without teaching religion".

The most systematic and comprehensive attempt to measure religious tolerance was developed by Gallup. Their analysis led to the development of a tolerance index based on a series of 5 specific items:

- I always treat people of other religious faiths with respect.

- Most religious faiths make a positive contribution to society.

- I would not object to a person of a different religious faith moving next door.

- People of other religions always treat me with respect.

- In the past year I have learned something from someone of another religious faith.[3]

140

By this more practical set of criteria, Gallup found 87 percent of Americans were tolerant and only 13 percent substantially intolerant in 2004.

The issue of prayer in public schools dramatically illustrates how this religious tolerance is expressed in practice. When people are simply asked whether they support school prayer, majorities of 60-70 percent generally agree. Yet most Americans are extremely aware that religious activities in school can all too easily infringe on the individual rights of children and parents of different faiths. 52 percent of the Public Agenda survey agreed that spoken school prayer "Embarrasses and isolates students whose religion is different or who are not religious at all" and 57 percent agreed that "School prayer is unfair to parents who think they should be the ones to decide what to teach their children about religion, not the schools".

In fact, the major studies that conducted personal interviews or focus groups repeatedly found the following pattern. When asked simple questions about their desire for greater religiosity in American life—such as their support for school prayer or the public display of religious symbols—many respondents immediately agreed. But when the ways in which such steps might violate other individuals' rights to religious freedom were pointed out, they quickly modified their positions.

As the Public Agenda study noted:

> A strong majority wants to see a softening of the strict separation of church and state in the schools. Many also seem to resent efforts that appear to eradicate all trace of religious sensibilities in the schools. At the same time, however, most people are sensitive to the fact that children of all creeds attend the public schools and want a policy that is as inclusive as possible. This explains the popularity of a moment of silence over other, more explicitly religious options like spoken prayer."

In fact, when people are given a set of choices about school prayer that include both "tolerant" and "intolerant" options, the results are striking. In the Public Agenda study, for example:

53 percent favored a moment of silence.

20 percent favored prayer that mentions god but no specific religion.

6 percent favored a Christian prayer that mentions Jesus.

19 percent favored having no observance at all.

Questions regarding the display of religion in public places follow the same pattern.

58 percent – it is acceptable to display Christian symbols as long as others are displayed too.

10 percent – it is acceptable to display only Christian symbols.

29 percent – it is unacceptable to display any religious symbols.

What is most striking about this pattern of results (which, in the case of school prayer, have been repeatedly confirmed in other surveys such as the yearly polls in the National Election Service series) is the fact that imposing an explicitly Christian prayer or displaying exclusively Christian symbols is favored by a remarkably small minority.

The Pew Religious Landscape Report updates these results to 2008 and reveals the profound division between tolerance and intolerance that exists beneath the broad support for religious and cultural traditionalism:

On the one hand, the report clearly reveals the near-universal acceptance of core traditional religious views among American Protestants. According to the Pew study, 98 percent of Protestants express a clear belief in God with 78 percent expressing the belief with "absolute certainty." 84 percent of Protestants express a belief in Heaven and Hell and 79 percent believe in angels and demons. 75 percent send their children to some form of religious education and a similar number read scripture with their children or pray with them.

These views do directly influence political opinions. Another important recent opinion study, *American Grace—How Religion Divides and Unites Us*, found that two key issues—abortion and homosexuality created a "God gap" between Republicans and Democrats with more religious individuals strongly preferring the former rather than the latter.[4] In essentially every area, evangelicals tended to be more devout and conservative than mainline denominations. But when one looks more closely, one quickly begins to see the divisions between tolerant and intolerant views—even within the ranks of evangelicals. Quite surprisingly, in 2007 one quarter of evangelicals thought homosexuality should be accepted by society and one-third thought abortion should be legal under some circumstances.

REGARDING HOMOSEXUALITY		
	Homosexuality is a way of life that should be accepted by society	Homosexuality is a way of life that should be discouraged by society
Evangelical Churches	26%	64%
Mainline Churches	56%	34%

Source: http://religions.pewforum.org/reports#

REGARDING ABORTION				
Abortion should be:	Legal in all cases	Legal in most cases	Illegal in most cases	Illegal in all cases
Evangelical Churches	9%	24%	36%	25%
Mainline Churches	20%	42%	25%	7%

Source: http://religions.pewforum.org/reports#

The gap between tolerant and intolerant interpretations of Christianity is even more dramatic in regard to questions about faith itself. The results quite dramatically echoes the conclusions of the *Christian America* survey a decade earlier.

On the one hand, a majority of evangelicals do support biblical literalism—and in this regard they are quite distinct from the mainline denominations.

	Bible is word of God, should be taken literally word for word	Bible is word of God but not everything should be taken literally	Bible is a book written by men
Evangelical Churches	59%	25%	7%
Mainline Churches	22%	35%	28%

Source: http://religions.pewforum.org/reports#

But when asked about their belief that their view represents the "one true way," the situation changes dramatically. A majority of evangelicals express a tolerant view rather than an intolerant one. This tolerant perspective is reflected across two quite different question wordings.

	My religion is the one, true faith leading to eternal life	Many religions can lead to eternal life
Evangelical Churches	36%	57%
Mainline Churches	12%	83%

Source: http://religions.pewforum.org/reports#

	There is only one true way to interpret the teachings of my religion	There is more than one true way to interpret the teachings of my religion
Evangelical Churches	41%	53%
Mainline Churches	14%	82%

Source: http://religions.pewforum.org/reports#

This is really quite striking and shows the quite significant divide between tolerant and intolerant views even within the evangelical community.

Even more striking, however, are the views of evangelicals regarding the obligation to help the poor and needy. A clear majority take a "progressive" view and their opinions are entirely indistinguishable from those of mainline denominations.

	The government should do more to help needy Americans, even if it means going deeper into debt	The government today can't afford to do much more to help the needy
Evangelical Churches	57%	34%
Mainline Churches	58%	33%

Source: http://religions.pewforum.org/reports#

Even when the role of government is posed directly as choice between a "big" or "small government, the division between more conservative and more progressive views is closer to 50-50 and is quite similar to the division within mainline churches.

	Would you prefer a smaller government with fewer services	Would you prefer a bigger government with more services
Evangelical Churches	48%	41%
Mainline Churches	51%	37%

Source: http://religions.pewforum.org/reports#

Finally, although many important figures in the religious right including Michelle Bachmann, Rick Perry and the leaders of major conservative religious organizations have expressed quasi-theocratic views and been associated with quasi-theocratic movements, genuine support for theocratic goals and policies are not widespread.

To be sure, when the question is posed as simply whether churches should have the right to "express their views" on political matters, two thirds of evangelicals and half of mainline Christians agree.

	Churches should keep out of political matters	Churches should express views
Evangelical Churches	32%	64%
Mainline Churches	50%	46%

Source: http://religions.pewforum.org/reports#

But when questions are more specifically focused on using the government to promote religious views, a significant division becomes clear even within the ranks of evangelicals.

	The government should do more to protect morality in society	I worry the government is getting too involved in the issue of morality
Evangelical Churches	50%	41%
Mainline Churches	33%	58%

Source: http://religions.pewforum.org/reports#

This lack of enthusiasm for theocratic policies is supported by other major opinion studies. The *American Grace* survey estimated that only 10 percent of religious Americans can accurately be defined as genuine "true believers," locked in an echo chamber where they only listen to others like themselves.

Equally, a 2007 Gallup survey found the following:

> "Only a small percentage of highly religious Americans—15 percent—believe the best way to spread their religion is to change society to conform to their religious beliefs.... Most highly religious Americans appear content to live the best possible personal life on the basis of their religious beliefs or to engage in traditional attempts at one-on-one conversion."[5]

Seen in the context of society as a whole, Gallup's survey divides the population as follows:

37 percent—about a third—of Americans consider themselves to be extremely or very religious. This group is divided between 18 percent who do not feel it is necessary to spread their beliefs, 10 percent who seek to spread their faith by personally converting others and only 6 percent who believe that Christians must change society to make it follow their religious views.

The conclusion is clear. There is indeed overwhelming support for basic religious traditions and beliefs within working class America. But inside this cultural consensus there is a profound division between tolerant and intolerant views. There is a substantial group of genuinely religious Americans who support religious diversity and tolerance on theological matters, "progressive" rather than conservative views on several key social and economic issues and who do not support to demands for Christian theocracy.

In short, like other Americans, white working people are overwhelmingly cultural traditionalists in regard to religion but they are not all religious conservatives. They are deeply divided between some who are essentially tolerant and even "progressive" in their Christian faith and others who are not.

Racial Attitudes About Immigrants

White working class racial attitudes regarding the mostly Mexican and Latino recent immigrants in America follow the same pattern as is evident with religion. There is near-universal acceptance of certain basic traditional cultural norms, but within that broad consensus there is a deep divide between tolerant and intolerant individuals.

The basic and almost universally shared "traditional" view of immigration is that immigration should be a gradual "one at a time" process that is strictly controlled by law and legal authority. Even in the 1980's only the oldest generations of Americans could remember the earlier "invasions" of European immigrants in the first decades of the 20th century and the profound racial and ethnic animosities that were provoked by the immigrants' arrival. On the contrary, for most Americans "immigration" was visualized as a matter of particular individuals filling out many forms, studying for and passing difficult citizenship tests and participating in formal ceremonies of naturalization.

The arrival of Mexican and other Latin immigrants in the 1980's and 1990's fit none of these models. It was a sudden and unregulated immigration of large groups that seemed to rapidly transform entire neighborhoods and communities into ethnic enclaves. The first wave in the 1980's was concentrated in small towns and areas where industries like meat packing, poultry processing and textile and carpet manufacturing rapidly shifted their workforce to immigrant workers. The second wave filled neighborhoods in larger towns and cities and job openings in food service, dishwashing, janitorial work, gardening and landscaping, and small scale construction.

It was an immigration of large masses, not individuals, and it represented a breakdown of law and order that authorities seemed unable and unwilling to try and reverse. As immigrant's children became more visible in local schools and parks and frictions developed between immigrants and non-immigrants, suspicions about the likelihood of future burdens on municipal services and social services became inevitable. More affluent Americans could view these problems as relatively remote. Working class Americans perceived them from a far closer vantage point.

One University of Minnesota study reviewed a variety of studies that investigated how working class Americans reacted to the trends:[6]

> Fennelly and Leitner (2002) conducted focus groups with white working-class individuals in a rural town with a large meat packing plant. The quote in the next paragraph is from a White worker who was employed at the plant until the mid-1990s, when it shut down, the union was disbanded, and the company reopened with a workforce that was almost exclusively made up of immigrants on the processing lines.
>
> > *Daniel: They shouldn't be treated better than we are. We're the ones that are payin' for what they're gittin. If they're gonna run around act like they're better than we are, we ain't gonna, we ain't gonna appreciate that at all.*
>
> ...In Fennelly and Leitner's study, the most strident anti-immigrant sentiments are voiced as a reaction to the perception that immigrants get special tax and social welfare breaks. In the present study, 58 percent of respondents overall agree with the statement that "immigrants do not pay their fair share of taxes," and 46 percent agree that "immigrants are a burden on our country because they take our jobs, housing and health care".
>
> Surveys and focus groups conducted by Greenberg and Greenberg (2004) with suburban residents in Minnesota provide further illustration of this tendency. For example, a middle aged white woman in a suburban community expresses outrage over what she perceives as unfair

advantages for immigrants:

> *The groups are getting very large and it seems when they come over here they are getting all the tax breaks. They get all this help. They get this, they get that,... and those of us who have fought for this country, who have paid our taxes, who raise our children and who live in this country and in this state are the ones that are paying for all those people to get all those breaks and our children and our lifestyles are not increasing, they are staying stagnant. Some are still staying at poverty level because these people who are coming into Minnesota from other countries are getting what us as Minnesotans or American citizens ought to be having.*

Another participant in a group of white middle-aged men from the same county voices similar concerns:

> *They got health care. I mean my father-in-law, he's worked here his whole life, and he's gotta pay for... He broke his back, he had to pay for his own medical. And there's these people that just move over here and (inaudible). They come in and they say they're depressed, well then they get five more years of Welfare.*

... A middle-aged, married woman shows the ways in which strong anti-immigrant statements and support of complete and unidirectional 'assimilation' may be prefaced by protestations of egalitarianism:

> *I agree with diversity too, but I think no matter where you are coming from, you should speak the language here, you should make adjustments to what is here. I think it is great, you know, keep the things from your own nationality, I think that is great, but if you live here,*

you should learn how to speak English and not have everything adjusted to fit you. You need to adjust.[16]

These comments reflect a broad consensus among working class Americans that illegal immigration represents a violation of traditional cultural norms about how immigration is supposed to occur. But within this consensus there are two quite distinct groups—individuals who are racially prejudiced against Latino and other non-white people and individuals who do not have such attitudes.

One way that overt racism is frequently expressed in this area is in the wide variety of derogatory terms that are used to refer to immigrants from Mexico:

Bean bandits, beaners, border bunnies, border niggers, burritos, cockroaches, chili-shitters, crimigrants, field rats, four-footers, gravel-bellies, greasers, jumping beans, latrinos, mexcrement, mexicoons, nachos, river niggers, roaches, spicaninnies, tacos, taco-monkeys.

These terms exhibit the classic dehumanization and identification with animals that is characteristic of racist ideologies. One particularly repulsive example of this is the very frequent application of words usually applied to dogs and other animals—words like "whelps", "spawn" and "mongrels"—to describe the infant children of illegal immigrants. It is particularly important in the rhetoric of racist immigration opponents because it invalidates any image of immigrant children as vulnerable and helpless victims who should be treated with pity and compassion.

Racially prejudiced individuals are generally careful to avoid displaying overt racism in public settings but the kinds of bitter, overt and explicit bigotry that is usually expressed only in private often spills out in call-in's to right-wing talk radio shows and in comments written on conservative political web sites. In California, for example, two right-wing radio hosts incited their listeners to call the voicemail of a leader of the Dream Act movement in California (which would make college available for the children of illegal immigrants) to *"let him have it."*

These were some of the responses:

> "You goddamn traitor to our nation. What the f*** are you doing? Go back to Mexico and fix your s*** over there...."

> "How dare you come to this country? I hope somebody shoots your ass."

> "How dare you, how dare you take American taxpayer's money for illegal aliens. Why don't you go back to wherever you came from and take those people with you?"

> "The Illegals are never gonna be welcomed in this country. You guys are breaking the law and you're stealing the taxpayer's money."

> "You guys are the worst scum of the earth I have ever seen. I can't stand you guys."

> "I want to thank you for stealing my hard-earned tax money to support all your Third-World illegal immigrants from Mexico... You guys better pack your bags. You don't belong here."

> "Speak in the f*** English, a**hole."

> "Jorge, you need to stop encouraging people to steal our money for illegal aliens. Shame on you. Go back to Mexico, you make us sick."

> "Get your people out of the United States. You are not American, you are a disgrace."[7]

There is a visceral distaste and revulsion against Mexicans as human beings that is clearly being reflected in these remarks and not simply expressions of anger about an unjust social policy. Several million Mexican-Americans have lived in California for generations, a fact that white Californians know perfectly well. For them to insist that Mexicans should all "go back home where they belong" represents an absolutely extraordinary expression of racial stereotyping.

On the other hand, however, there are also a substantial number of basically tolerant working class Americans who have no physical aversion or distaste for Mexican or other Latinos.

In Texas and other relatively rural and traditional areas of the Southwest there is a very unique and particular kind of relationship that has developed over generations between many Mexican-Americans and white Americans. In small towns, farms and ranches many families have known each other for generations and not infrequently intermarried. Until the 1980's, when large numbers of new immigrants began to cross the border, ethnic relationships between the two groups were stable and there were traditionally a wide variety of very relaxed and unselfconscious friendships and relationships that developed between the non-prejudiced whites of these communities and Mexican-Americans. Two relatively recent Hollywood films—*The Three Burials of Melquiades Estrada* and *Lone Star*—very accurately portray inter-ethnic friendships of this kind.

In more urban areas where many Mexican and other immigrants have settled, blue collar workers actually have had much more contact with them than most other Americans. As Mexicans have increasingly come to dominate the lower paid occupations in construction, large numbers of worker-contractors have come to know them as employees and co-workers. In a very large number of cases, people in the construction industry have come to have quite positive attitudes toward these immigrants as individuals. Mexicans and other Latinos are widely viewed as "hard-working" men who respect and embody traditional working class values like *"doing a full day's work"*, seeking to do a good job and aiming for high quality. These are values and characteristics that are respected and honored in working class life. On a personal level Mexicans and other Latinos are seen as polite, unassuming and deeply family oriented. For many years, in fact, it has been widely recognized among people in the construction industry that most immigrant workers more deeply embody traditional "family" values than many white workers—they labor long hours for low wages, do not complain and send a substantial amount of their relatively meager earnings to their parents and other family back home.

An in-depth 2005 study, *Prejudice Toward Immigrants in the Midwest*, conducted extensive focus groups with carefully selected groups of high-status, middle class and working class individuals in order to study the different ways that immigration affected the three distinct social groups. In discussing the working class participants in their study the authors noted: that "many may have friendly relations with some individual immigrants, while simultaneously harboring resentment and supporting broad negative stereotypes of groups."[8]

The study presented Daniel as an example:

> On the one hand Daniel expresses anger and resentment toward immigrants who 'shouldn't be treated better than we are'; on the other hand, he mentions going out for drinks with Vietnamese and Mexican co-workers and acknowledges that not all immigrants are the same, and that *"just like white people, there's good, there's bad, ugly."*...
>
> These sentiments are echoed by other Working Class group members at the end of their conversation... Although the Working Class group members made openly negative comments about immigrants, they also made many empathetic statements. *In fact this ambiguity is a principal finding of our study;* it is inaccurate to simply classify individuals' attitudes toward immigrants on a linear scale that ranges from low to high prejudice, because all of the group members tended to make positive statements in some contexts, and negative ones in others.[19]

The study quantified the comments the working class participants made about immigrants:

EVALUATIVE COMMENTS MADE ABOUT IMMIGRANTS				
Positive Statements	Positive In- terjections	Empathetic Statements	Negative Statements	Negative Interjections
75%	5%	12%	113%	15%

Source: 2005 study above, p. 78

As the study noted, there were a striking mixture of both positive and negative statements, often by the same individuals. The most common pattern was a balance between entirely positive evaluations of individuals along with hostility to the "invasion" of large numbers of immigrants.

It is this distinction between the widely shared outrage at the viola- tion of the traditional process of immigration and how it is differently processed by racially prejudiced and non-prejudiced individuals that underlies the pattern of results that are observed in opinion polls.

On the one hand, when the question directly invokes questions of law, authority and punishment, working class Americans respond in an extremely "conservative" way.

One sample was asked the question: "Which of the following two statements do you agree with?"

1. *Democratic leaders propose comprehensive reforms including tougher enforcement at the border and workplace but also providing a path to citizenship for law-abiding undocumented immigrants who pay fines and back taxes and get to the back of the line.*

2. *Republican leaders propose much tougher enforcement at the border, to arrest and deport many more illegal immigrants and to prohibit those here illegally from benefiting from any taxpayer funded social services. This is not the time for immigration reform.*

The results were as follows:

First Statement Strongly	First Statement Somewhat	Second Statement Somewhat	Second Statement Strongly
24%	35%	7%	50%

Source: Less than college respondents, sample size – 342 unpublished d-corps data

Even with the first statement "toughened up" with a series of semi-punitive conditions, half the sample of working class respondents strongly supported the second alternative which rejects any path to citizenship or legalization of the status of currently illegal immigrants. Given a forced either-or choice between punitive action and a path to citizenship, the weight of opinion was clearly weighted toward the former.

Yet, at the same time, when a similar sample of working class voters was asked the more general question *"which would you prefer: better border security, creating a path to citizenship or both,"* the results were as follows:

	Better Border Security	Creating a Path to Citizenship	Both
College Grad	29%	26%	43%
Some College	38%	19%	41%
High School or Less	37%	18%	42%

http://people-press.org/2011/02/24/public-favors-tougher-border-controls-and-path-to-citizenship/

Given this set of choices, 20 percent of working class individuals in this sample favored creating a path to citizenship and 40 percent favored a combination of both increased security and legalization of the status of currently illegal immigrants. Thus, the majority appears "tolerant" and "progressive" rather than conservative. When the issue is framed in such a way that both the restoration of traditional rules and legalization of status are offered at the same time, they gain majority support.

As a result, the conclusion is clear. As with religion, there is a broad consensus in favor of a return to a culturally traditional approach in working class America. But the consensus conceals within it a split between tolerant and intolerant individuals—in this case between those who are racially prejudiced and those who are not.

Attitudes Toward the Military

The final area of "values" is in regard to the military. In this case the split between tolerance and intolerance is in relation to the world rather than America—the willingness to accept the existence of different global cultures versus believing the United States has the right to impose American values and institutions on other nations.

As with the previous two cases, there is essentially universal support and respect for the basic social institution of the military itself. It is not only the general cultural traditionalism of working class Americans that supports this view but a key sociological reality as well: working class Americans perceive America's military as a distinctly—and profoundly—working class institution.

As a 2002 *New York Times* article headlined, *"Military Mirrors Working Class America"* noted:

> The soldiers, sailors, pilots and others who are risking and now giving their lives in Iraq represent a slice of a broad swath of American society—but by no means all of it. Of the 28 servicemen killed who have been identified so far, twenty were white, five black, three Hispanic—proportions that neatly mirror those of the military as a whole. But just one was from a well-to-do family, and with the exception of a Naval Academy alumnus, just one had graduated from an elite college or university.[9]

Indeed, while virtually all the enlisted men and women in the armed forces have high school diplomas, in 2002 fewer than 3.5 percent were college graduates and only 10 percent had ever attended college. In demographic terms, this makes the armed forces one of the most homogeneously working class institutions in America.

These young people, whites as well as minorities, come disproportionately from blue-collar homes and neighborhoods in large cities or from small towns, and tend to be from the South, Midwest and Mountain West. Not only parents and relatives, but neighbors and schoolmates in these areas and communities recognize the men and women in uniform as people much like them.

Beyond this, working people also feel an additional psychic bond with the men and women in the armed forces because the soldiers uphold very deeply held and distinctly working class values: ruggedness and bravery, teamwork and group solidarity, loyalty, heroism and self-sacrifice. In the rest of American culture these virtues are given a much lower value than intellectual ability, ambition, competitiveness and the achievement of material success. For high school educated young men and women who are often not "successful" in these latter terms, the armed forces provides them with the opportunity to be seen as role models and heroes to their families, friends and communities. When American working people refer to "our boys in uniform," they are expressing an intensely felt emotional truth as well as a metaphorical one—that the soldiers and other personnel are not only often quite literally their children but are also the representatives of the some of the best values of their culture.

This intense identification with the members of the armed forces leads working people to feel that there is only one legitimate point of view from which to think about issues of war and peace—that of the ordinary soldier. Working people may feel sympathy for other groups, such as Iraqi civilians, or recognize a need to understand other groups like devout Muslims. But the idea of actually trying to view international problems from perspectives other than that of the front line troops feels profoundly disloyal to the sacrifices the soldiers are making.

The identification with the troops also generates an emotional need for working people to believe that the Armed Forces are doing the right thing. They therefore tend to adopt the ethos of the Armed Forces themselves, an ethos that places a very high value on following orders and trusting superior officers.

This broad consensus, however, does not prevent a clear division between two ideologies—a militaristic view that believes in America's right to impose American values and institutions on other countries using force and a cautious view that wants to avoid foreign wars unless genuinely necessary for the security of the United States.

One can see this division at both abstract and specific levels.

For example, when given the choice between agreeing that *"America's security depends on building strong ties with other nations"* and *"Bottom line, America's Security depends on its own military strength"* working class Americans responded as follows:

First Statement Strongly	First Statement Somewhat	Second Statement Somewhat	Second Statement Strongly
30%	8%	10%	45%

Source: DemocrocyCorps unpublished data

Although tending to agree with the second statement more than the first, less than half agreed "strongly."

And when the specific issue of the war in Afghanistan was probed at the time of the 2010 elections, there was a clear split. When the choice was given between agreeing that *"We need to start reducing the troops in Afghanistan"* and *"We must stay the course to achieve stability and finish the job in Afghanistan"* the results were as follows:

First Statement Strongly	First Statement Somewhat	Second Statement Somewhat	Second Statement Strongly
40%	7%	15%	31%

Source: DemocrocyCorps unpublished data

Once again the pattern is clear: there is vast support for the military as an institution but a clear split between those who accept militarism as a philosophy and those who do not.

Thus, in all three areas—attitudes toward religion, immigrants and the military—the pattern is the same. Working class Americans are overwhelmingly cultural traditionalists but within this cultural consensus are deeply divided between tolerant and intolerant individuals and between conservatives and progressives.

CHAPTER
8

Working Class Hostility to Government – a New Kind of "Class Consciousness"

At first glance it might seem odd to consider white working class attitudes toward government before examining working people's views about the economic system as a whole. But the rather ironic reality is that anti-government sentiment now holds such a central place in white working class thinking that all of working people's attitudes toward economic issues are, in effect, filtered through the lens of their perception of government's role in the economy.

In a 2007 article in *The American Prospect*, pollster Stan Greenberg provided a particularly cogent description of the profound political problem that the decline in trust of government poses for the Democratic coalition:

> There is a new reality that Democrats must deal with if they are to be successful going forward. In their breathtaking incompetence and comprehensive failure in government, Republicans have undermined Americans' confidence in the ability of government to play a role in solving America's problems. Democrats will not make sustainable gains unless they are able to restore the public's confidence in its capacity to act through government.
>
> …the scale of damage done to people's belief in government is enormous… 62 percent in a Pew study said they believe

that whenever something is run by the government it is probably inefficient and wasteful. By 57 percent to 29 percent Americans believe that government makes it harder for people to get ahead in life rather than helping people. 85 percent say that if the government had more money it would waste it rather than spend it well.

Although people may favor government action on critical issues like health care, education and energy their lack of trust in governments capacity to spend money properly means that *their first priority is to cut wasteful spending and make government more accountable*. People are desperate to see accountability from Washington, not just in the spending of tax dollars with no discernible results but also in politicians' behavior... To have any chance of getting heard on their agenda, Democrats need to stand up and take on the government—not its size or scope, but its failure to be accountable—and deliver the results that people expect for the taxes they pay.[1]

A more recent strategy memo by Greenberg's Democracy Corps focuses on the overwhelming distrust and contempt with which Congress in particular is viewed:

Voters are disgusted with 'business as usual' in Washington. There is a deep and pervasive belief, particularly among independents, that special interests are running things and Members of Congress listen more to those that fund their campaigns than the voters that they are supposed to be representing. Three quarters believe that special interests hold too much influence over Washington today while fewer than a quarter believe that ordinary citizens can still influence what happens in politics. Similarly, nearly 80 percent say that Members of Congress are trolled by the groups that help fund their political campaigns while fewer than a fifth believe that Members listen more to the voters.[2]

In much of the Democratic discussion about the reasons for working class hostility to government the dominant tendency has been to view anti-government sentiment as the product of a well-established conservative media campaign energetically updated and promulgated by Fox News, the grass-roots conservative movement and the Republican Party.

This is undeniably true, but a more in-depth understanding of the problem must also take account of the underlying sociological trends that began to generate working class hostility to government in the early 1970's—Vietnam, inflation, school bussing, quotas and regulations—and also the decline of the Democratic political machine in the northern industrial cities.

The Fall of the Democratic Machine and the Rise of TV Politics

In fact, what had happened was the collapse of two unique community institutions that had emerged in a new form after the New Deal—the big city political machines and the trade unions. In the 1950's every major northern city had a network of local union halls and local Democratic Party offices which many blue-collar workers and other non-affluent democrats saw as an important and integral part of their community.

These institutions offered average citizens a real and distinct sense of inclusion and representation. Big city Democratic voters knew that local union representatives and neighborhood party workers—men who they knew personally—sat around the table with the local politicians who then played an important role in the selection of candidates for city and state offices and participated in the definition of the positions that were taken on issues. The complex local apparatus of political patronage and the provision of municipal jobs and minor services to constituents by the Democratic Party political machine was, to ordinary Democrats, evidence of their recognized role and position, however small, in the party as a whole.

But, beginning in the mid-1960's, this system gradually disintegrated. The giant manufacturing plants of the Northern and Midwestern cities gradually began to shrink, and the continual growth of the suburbs meant more and more Americans worked in jobs and moved to neighborhoods where there were no unions or union halls and no block captains or political clubhouses.

What replaced those institutions was TV. Political candidates and political campaigns became distant images on a screen with which an average voter never had any meaningful personal contact.

The system was inherently ripe for corruption. Increasingly large sums of money were needed to run for office and Democratic politicians no longer had a block and precinct organization that linked them directly with individual voters and neighborhoods and which could build support for them without massive TV advertising. Running for office became a multi-million dollar business investment and a politician's "job" became increasingly defined as successfully delivering benefits to his major financial contributors. The outgrowth was a burgeoning cynicism about congress and government among ordinary Americans.

A New Form of Class Consciousness

Thus, by 1995, when political scientists John Hibbing and Elizabeth Theis-Morse began an in-depth series of focus groups to study the details of public attitudes toward the political system, research published under the title, *"Congress as Public Enemy"*, they were not surprised to find that anger at the political system was focused on politicians as a group and what they called the "Washington system" of campaign finance and special interest groups. What they did not expect, however, was the powerful and very clearly articulated expression of what they said had to be described as a form of "class consciousness" among the people they studied.[3]

Hibbing and Theis-Morse noted two distinct ways this attitude was expressed by their subjects:

First, the huge sums of money needed for major campaigns had increasingly made politics a "rich man's sport" basically insuring that only the wealthy could participate. As one respondent in their focus group noted, "the wealthy put their own in office. And as long as it's like that we are not going to get represented... they might go back to their community, but it's the rich community they go visit". Another added, "Forget about the poor person. The poor person doesn't stand a chance. The congress is, they're all those people who were born with a silver spoon in their mouths, where they've got it made."

Second, the need for large sums of money provided an obvious and almost irresistible pressure toward influence peddling and corruption. As one focus group member stated, "Why would [a member of congress] want to come and talk to us this morning? Could we get a pot of money together? So why would he want to waste his time. But you let a bunch of executives or corporations sit around, he knows there is going to be millions of dollars thrown in his pot." Another added, "I think there is too much influence in the congress on the congressmen by, not the people, but by the special interest groups and the PAC's that put them in office". Another concluded simply, "Big money has bought them [congress] out".

After presenting their findings, Hibbing and Theis-Morse concluded that *"The American people have come to believe that the political system is run by a powerful professional political class (cut off from ordinary people) and that votes no longer make much difference because money rules...People believe the Washington system runs on greed and special privilege."*

In fact, the connection between this new anti-government sentiment and the previous pro-union, New Deal era "class consciousness" was underlined by the fact that for most ordinary working class Americans, the popular Roosevelt era caricature of the immoral top-hated millionaire, swilling champagne while orphans starved had by the 1980's been completely replaced by the vision of the venal and corrupt politician, making back room deals with cynical lobbyists in return for fat campaign contributions.

Why Attitudes About Government Are Uniquely Complex

Working class attitudes toward government, however, cannot be completely reduced to this one factor. Unlike many other, more specific topics, opinions about "government" involve a dauntingly complex variety of issues.

The attitudes people express about "government" may reflect views about different levels of government—federal, state or local. They may reflect views about distinct governmental functions— passing laws, issuing regulations or managing government agencies. They may refer to different branches of government—Congress, federal agencies or the courts. And they may reflect views about fiscal and economic issues like taxes, spending and deficits. Any and all of these subsidiary topics and issues may be what survey respondents are actually thinking about at the moment when they answer questions about their attitudes toward "government" in general.

This complexity makes the interpretation of polling questions fraught with difficulty. On other major issues such as illegal immigration, for example, it is usually the case that a dozen key questions and four or five alternate question wordings can be adequate to capture the main outlines of public attitudes on the subject. Additional questions and question wordings then add relatively little additional information. Regarding "government" in general, on the other hand, there are easily fifty or more distinct opinion poll questions that probe important dimensions of attitudes on the subject and literally hundreds of different questions that are directly relevant to attitudes about more specific aspects and activities.

The way to cut this methodological Gordian knot is to look at ethnographic field data—to examine how working class Americans conceptualize the general issue of "government" when they talk about it spontaneously in their homes and communities rather than when they are responding to specific questions on opinion surveys. Since John Zaller's 1992 analysis, *The Nature and Origins of Mass Opinion"* it has been accepted that people responding to survey questions on social and political issues will in many cases essentially "construct" or "compute" entirely original opinions based on the information contained in the question and the way it is framed rather than by retrieving any set "opinion" from a cubbyhole in memory. These "computed on the spot" opinions are, however, very often not what these same individuals actually use in spontaneous conversation, in their community activities or when they make serious political choices such as voting on Election Day.

In fact, the attitudes of working class Americans toward government that are reflected in much of the ethnographic field literature closely parallel the kinds of general and abstract anti-government sentiment reflected in common, "bumper sticker" expressions such as: *"government is the problem, not the solution"* or *"I love my country but I don't trust my government"* or *"big government is ruining this country."*

Three Interlocking Attitudes About Government That Foster Distrust

The ethnographic literature suggests that there are, in fact, three major attitude clusters that underlie white working class distrust of government:[4]

1. **"Government is bureaucratic and inefficient."** This is a perennial complaint continually refreshed by personal experiences. During the 1930's there were widespread criticisms of "men leaning on shovels" in the WPA and every subsequent generation has had negative views of government work and workers reinforced by grumpy or rude clerks at the

Department of Motor Vehicles, long lines at the post office, clusters of municipal sewer workers standing around an open manhole apparently doing nothing and so on. In the common view, these characteristics of government employees are consequences of the lack of competition and the civil service protection they enjoy. This perception is particularly deep-rooted because individual examples that disconfirm the stereotypes—for example, dedicated public health specialists heroically preventing epidemics or diligent inspectors preventing the sale of contaminated meat—are cognitively categorized as something other than government employees— as "doctors" or "health inspectors"—while every negative personal experience with government workers is mentally classified as an example of "typical government inefficiency."

2. **"Government is corrupt and dominated by special interests."** This perception, like the first, has always been present, but, as we have seen, a profound change occurred in the 1970's and 1980's when political campaigns became primarily waged through TV commercials rather than through face-to-face voter canvassing by block and precinct level party organizations. Hibbing and Theis-Morse's term "the Washington system" (rather than "government") captures the resulting perception of politics as having become a "rich man's sport" dominated by big money and special interests rather than average voters.

3. **"Government is dominated by liberal elites who channel government benefits to undeserving groups and attempt to impose alien values."** This third perception of government was not widespread until the "white backlash" against welfare, school bussing and quotas occurred in the late 1960's and early 1970's. It grew during the 1970's as the range of issues widened with the 1973 Supreme Court decision on abortion

and an increasing flow of environmental and occupational health regulations were issued by the EPA, OSHA and other agencies. In the late 1970's the focus widened once again with the emergence of various "tax revolts" and demands for general reductions in the size and scope of government that became common during the Reagan era. Because of the police power of the state, this "alien values" view also necessarily implies that government presents a major, constant threat to freedom.

One important reason for the unique depth and intractability of popular distrust of government is the fact that vast numbers of working class and other Americans hold all three of these conceptions simultaneously to some degree. Challenges to or disconfirming evidence against any one of the three does not significantly weaken the interlocking and reinforcing effect of the three in combination. For many Americans these three perspectives are not seen as alternatives but rather as a single overlapping and interlocking set of problems. Progressive proposals—which generally focus only on the second element—do not induce broader attitude change because they do not attempt to provide any solutions to the problems expressed in the first and third components of the view.

Conclusion

The quotation from Stanley Greenberg that began this chapter also summarizes the situation precisely:

> Although people may favor government action on critical issues like health care, education and energy their lack of trust in governments capacity to spend money properly means that *their first priority is to cut wasteful spending and make government more accountable*. People are desperate to see accountability from Washington, not just in the spending of tax dollars with no discernible results but

also in politicians' behavior... To have any chance of getting heard on their agenda, Democrats need to stand up and take on the government—not its size or scope, but its failure to be accountable—and deliver the results that people expect for the taxes they pay.

After the 2012 election, Greenberg's polling organization Democracy Corps conducted a survey of opinion regarding the political system and found massive support for change. As he said in his summary:

> A very clear and powerful theme emerged in this survey: voters are hungry for reforms that would increase citizens' access to and control over their political system and for reforms that would reduce the influence of big campaign contributors and lobbyists who control how policy decisions are made. This is apparent in their support for plans to expand access to voting, limit money in politics, and eliminate lobbyists' influence over politicians...
>
> ...The upshot is that small reforms no longer match the scale of the problem. Voters now want a fundamental overhaul, rather than modest changes, to the way elections are financed and run.[5]

Greenberg emphasized that this was an issue about which white working class voters cared deeply and noted that they would be extremely receptive to candidates who promised to champion political reform. As a result, in chapter 15 a specific proposal is offered for "a common sense populist" strategy to reverse working class distrust of government and win their support for a platform of progressive reform.

CHAPTER
9

What Working People Think About the Economy – Seeing the End of the "Middle Class"

For most working class Americans, opinions about business, government and economic issues are not learned in a classroom and mentally organized into the kinds of coherent ideological frameworks that are taught in economics or political science classes. On the contrary, for Americans who do not attend college many of their opinions about economic life are gradually built up out of daily experiences in the world of small- and medium-sized businesses and during real world interactions with bosses, customers, suppliers, co-workers, sub-contractors, city inspectors, bookkeepers and so on and through the informal exchange of opinions shared within the workplace.

As these individual experiences and conversations are gradually synthesized into more general attitudes, there are typically five distinct kinds of cognitive frameworks or schemas that develop: (1) a specific cluster of opinions about what appear to be "facts" or "common sense" about business and economic life, (2) a cluster of opinions about various positive principles and values that are inculcated by the business world, (3) a cluster of opinions expressing generally positive generalizations about markets and business, (4) a cluster of opinions about the limits of markets and the proper role of government and (5) a cluster of opinions about the role and values of the "rich and powerful".

For most ordinary voters, these five cognitive frameworks or schemas operate largely independently of each other. There is little conscious examination or effort to insure consistency. Invoking one opinion within a particular cluster generally activates a number of other opinions within the same cluster but generally does not bring to mind all the other cognitive frameworks related to economic life.

There are extraordinarily few opinion studies that have attempted to define and understand attitudes toward the economic system as a whole rather than toward specific economic issues. The classic study that did take a comprehensive approach is now almost 30 years old—Herbert McCloskey and John Zaller's, *"The American Ethos: Public Attitudes Toward Capitalism and Democracy"* which appeared in the mid 1980's. The study was an attempt to understand Americans' basic views about the economic system and to evaluate if the rise of Reaganism actually signaled a sea-change in American opinion. The American Ethos examined such an unusually wide range of economic opinions that it was possible to identify in it elements of all the major cognitive schemas noted above.[1]

1. Opinions based on "Common sense"

Some opinions reported in *The American Ethos*, for example, expressed what people basically saw as "facts" or "realities", about issues like competition, private property and the profit motive. 88 percent of the respondents in one study, for example, agreed that, "It is having to compete with others that keeps people on their toes" and 81 percent held that competition, "leads to better performance and a desire for excellence". Similarly, 54 percent of the people in one sample agreed that, "the profit system teaches people the value of hard work and success" and 85 percent agreed that, "giving everybody about the same income regardless of the kind of work that they do would destroy the desire to work hard and do a better job".

Average citizens do not consider opinions like these as

necessarily expressing their personal ethical values or philosophy. Rather, they see them as statements of "common sense" or "just the way things are." People do not necessarily think that these social facts are entirely desirable or always the appropriate things to encourage. But they perceive them as realities about social institutions and human conduct that it is simply foolish to ignore.

2. The positive values of business

At the same time, many people also strongly approve of some of the key values instilled by small business. Independence, hard work, ambition, self-discipline and individual initiative are considered positive character traits by most Americans and lead to support for a variety of small business values. 95 percent of the people in one sample agreed that, "there is nothing wrong with a man trying to make as much money as he honestly can." 78 percent agreed that, "under a fair economic system people with more ability would earn higher salaries" and 58 percent agreed that, "the way property is used should mainly be decided by the individuals who own it".

Although these views have significant social implications, the specific questions make it clear that they are more accurately seen as generalizations from small business experience and not the expression of a formal ideology. The questions focus on particular individuals and express beliefs about how such individuals should be treated, rather than views about society as a whole.

3. Positive views about free enterprise

McCloskey and Zaller did find a variety of more general social or ideological attitudes favoring free enterprise and the free market. 63 percent of the respondents to one survey agreed that "the free enterprise system is generally a fair and efficient system". 84 percent agreed that "private ownership of property is necessary for economic progress" and 82 percent supported the view that "our freedom depends on the free enterprise system".

These positive attitudes toward the market remain strong among Americans in general. As the 2009 CAP American Political Ideology study showed, 55 percent of the working class respondents agreed that limited government is always better than big government, 57 percent agreed that free market solutions are better than government at creating jobs and economic growth and 44 percent agreed that the primary responsibility of corporations is to produce profits and returns for their shareholders, not to improve society.[2]

Seen in isolation, these opinions might appear to be ideological statements based on a clearly held and fully consistent conservative economic philosophy. But when viewed in the context of the other opinions McCloskey and Zaller studied, it becomes clear that, for many Americans, they are more reasonably understood as informal extensions or generalizations of their specific, common sense views about small business. This kind of belief system differs radically from views based on a formal ideology because it is rooted in common sense observation rather than abstract theory.

4. The limitations of the market and the need for government

This difference became dramatically clear when McClosky and Zaller turned to consider the attitudes of most Americans toward the proper relationship between the market and government for society as a whole. It quickly became clear that the same "common sense" that makes many people accept many seemingly conservative propositions about the values of work, rewards and incentives also makes them completely unwilling to accept the notion that markets can actually be left to themselves or do not need extensive government oversight and wide-ranging regulation.

McClosky and Zaller noted that even in the 1950's only 25 percent of the American people believed that "Most things would run pretty well by themselves if the government just didn't interfere". In the late 1970's, 85 percent rejected the idea that, by itself, business would "strike a fair balance between profits and the interests of the public."

In that same year, a plurality agreed that "government regulation of business is necessary to keep industry from getting too powerful," and 62 percent held that "The way business is behaving, we need the government to keep an eye on them".

As with the positive attitudes about the market, the belief that the market requires oversight and regulation also remains strong today. The 2009 CAP study showed that 73 percent agreed that government regulations are necessary to keep businesses in check and protect workers and consumers, 79 percent agreed that government investment in education, infrastructure and science are necessary to insure America's long-term economic growth, 69 percent agreed that Government has a responsibility to provide financial support for the poor, the sick and the elderly and 59 percent agreed that government must step in to protect the national economy when the market fails. Even today, despite the dramatic growth of the Tea Party ideology within the Republican coalition since Obama's election, other recent surveys show broadly similar trends.

5. Attitudes toward "the Rich and Powerful"

At the same time that McClosky and Zaller found majority support for the right of individuals to become wealthy and do whatever they wished with their wealth, they also found that 67 percent also agreed that "corporations and people with money really run the country", 72 percent agreed that "when it comes to taxes, corporations and wealthy people don't pay their fair share and 55 percent supported the proposition that "in the American court system, a poor man usually gets treated worse than a rich man."

The CAP study again echoed these findings. 60 percent agreed that rich people like to believe they have made it on their own but in reality society has contributed greatly to their wealth, 65 percent agreed that government policies too often serve the interests of corporations and the wealthy and 62 percent agreed that gap between the rich and poor should be reduced, even if it means higher taxes for the wealthy.

The essential distinction in this area seems to be that Americans feel that individuals have the right to become wealthy, but not to use their wealth to gain unfair advantage. People have a very distinct reaction to the term "the rich and powerful" than they do to the terms "people who have become rich" or "wealthy people". It is the combination of both wealth and power that triggers this particular "populist" schema and distinguishes it from the cluster of attitudes about wealth alone.

After reviewing this and a wide variety of other data, McClosky and Zaller concluded the following:

> "Popular support for laissez-faire capitalism appears surprisingly weak even at a relatively abstract level"… [Only a] small group—perhaps 10-20 percent—wants a return to laissez-faire and a sharp reduction in government regulation of the economy. The balance—a substantial majority of Americans—seems reasonably satisfied with the present intermingling of business independence and government intervention".

When McClosky and Zaller presented this conclusion in the mid-1980's, it seemed startlingly at odds with the Reagan-era common wisdom that the American people had actually become much more conservative and supportive of a radical free-market point of view. But—again despite the rise of the Tea Party ideology—this basic conclusion has been repeatedly reconfirmed by other major studies since that time. Substantial numbers of Americans do have strongly positive opinions about small business and approve of a number of the social and personal values that are associated with it. But the same "common sense" perspective that leads them to this view makes them also strongly reject the idea that free markets are ideal or self-adjusting and can be left to operate without substantial regulation and oversight by society as a whole. The common sense perspective that leads to the belief that many small business values are beneficial

176

to society also leads to the view that, by its nature, business is entirely governed by "the bottom line" and will inevitably ignore or undermine goals or values that Americans think are "important", "good" or "right" if they conflict with profitability.

These five distinct attitude clusters outlined above provide a useful basic framework for examining attitudes about the economy, but to develop a concrete understanding of how working class voters view the economy today it is necessary to engage in systematic empirical research—research that uses not only opinion polls but other techniques as well to capture the overall structure of working people's views about the economy.

Democracy Corps Innovative Approach to Studying Attitudes About the Economy

The organization that has taken the most systematic and innovative steps in this direction is Stan Greenberg's *Democracy Corps*, a project run by the international polling firm Greenberg, Quinlan, Rosen. Democracy Corps periodic Strategy Memos are frequently quoted in the media and often play an important role in debates within the Democratic coalition but what is not equally well-recognized is the increasing methodological sophistication the group has employed in recent years to go beyond conventional polling in the investigation of political attitudes.

Democracy Corps has an unusual organizational philosophy—it is entirely partisan but firmly objective at the same time. Most "partisan" polling, in contrast, is quite consciously and intentionally manipulative—it is done with the objective of producing a dramatic headline ("e.g. Most Jews Dislike Obama") or inflating the actual level of support for a policy (e.g., "99.9999 percent of Americans Reject Immigration Reform"). Rasmussen and Fox News polls are particularly well-known for asking outrageously misleading and flamboyantly manipulative questions that are designed to produce these kinds of results.

Democracy Corps, on the other hand, seeks to measure public attitudes accurately and does not shy away from publishing data that reflects unfavorably on Democratic policies and campaigns. The purpose of their research is not to produce politically useful headlines but rather to use the data they collect to guide the comparison and testing of alternative political messages in order to find the ones that most effectively promote a Democratic perspective.

Democracy Corps was one of the earliest political polling firms to incorporate focus groups into their set of research techniques and in the more recent "Economy Project" they incorporated an even wider set of information-gathering tools in an attempt to more adequately measure not only working class attitudes toward the economy but also the specific ways in which the economy was affecting their lives.

The motivation for the Economy Project was the recognition that conventional economic statistics like the unemployment rate and economic growth rate were providing a profoundly misleading image of the conditions and hardships average Americans were experiencing. The "unemployment rate" suggests the image of a distinct social group called "the unemployed" that is separate from other working Americans while the media focus on the monthly economic growth rate suggests the view that Americans experience economic hardship as either improving or worsening on a month to month basis and shift their political loyalties as a result.

The Economy Project integrates data from five different sources—in-depth interviews, focus groups, dial meter response testing, traditional political opinion surveys and newly designed polling tools that probe respondents personal experiences with economic problems like job loss, reduced wages, lost health insurance or defaulted mortgages. By combining the data from these five sources, Democracy Corp's most recent studies produce a uniquely deep and detailed picture of the economic experiences and political attitudes of non-affluent, average Americans—with particular attention to the views of non-college "working class" whites.

The two major recent Democracy Corps studies reveal five major clusters of attitudes that do not show up clearly in conventional opinion polls.[3]

1. Ordinary Americans do not see the current crisis as a crisis of "high unemployment"—they see instead a massive decline in living standards that has destroyed any hope for a "middle class" life.

- In contrast to the standard image of the unemployed as a distinct minority group, the D-Corp research shows average Americans perceive instead a much larger social and economic crisis that includes people having to accept lower-paid, lower-status jobs, more temporary jobs, no jobs for youth, increased reliance on multiple jobs to make ends meet, reduced wages or hours on the job and the loss of health care and other fringe benefits even after years of service. Taken together these conditions have caused a massive decline in ordinary Americans' standard of living and has led them to conclude that the "middle class" life of their parents' generation has permanently disappeared. It is this larger picture that represents the "economic crisis" for most Americans and not simply official defined unemployment.

- The extent of this decline is stunning. The Democracy Corps studies show that during 2008, 2009 and 2010 between 37 and 40 percent of Americans reported experiencing reduced wages or benefits; between 35 and 41 percent reported losing at least one job; 22 to 27 percent reported losing their health insurance and 13 to 22 percent reported falling behind on their mortgage.

- The respondents in the Democracy Corps studies saw no relationship between the monthly fluctuations in the unemployment rate or growth in GNP and their personal economic conditions. They saw instead a massive and permanent economic decline, one that had been developing for decades but which became even worse with the deep recession of Fall 2008.

2. The initial reaction to the crisis was shock. Now it's fatalism. The cynical view has grown that "no-one is going to help me; I'm completely on my own".

- As the Democracy Corps studies expressed it "Last year, the impact of job loss was described using the vocabular of shock: *everything went downhill, everything went to shit, and it was crazy.* By contrast, this year respondents feel lucky to have jobs—any jobs—and express a kind of willful pride in their ability to make things work despite dramatically changed circumstances... Their attitude is best described as 'stoic resolution.'"

3. People are deeply angry at corporate America but think nothing can be done

- The Democracy Corps studies note: "A lot of blame and in many cases, anger, is aimed squarely at the rich, CEOs, big business, and the greed that many believe infects our economic system. This is further enhanced by blame for the state of the economy with nearly one-third of all respondents saying that banking was directly responsible for where we are and almost half saying banks and/or big business."

- Outsourcing and job export are particular sources of anger. In the interviews and focus groups many of the people interviewed spoke with disgust at the fact that Corporate CEO's received big bonuses and lavish stock options when they downsized plants, shipped jobs overseas and shuttered American factories.

- There is a profound cynicism about corporate America. Despite this, the respondents simultaneously expressed a deep pessimism about the possibility that any change might occur. Large corporations were seen as so powerful and so remote that ordinary people had no hope of changing their behavior. The executives and decision-makers who run Wall Street and corporate America were perceived as living in a completely separate and insulated upper-class world of their own where they were able to write their own rules and completely ignore the problems of average Americans.

4. People are even more profoundly angry at government than at business because government is supposed to represent "the people." The level of anger, cynicism and disgust is almost impossible to overstate.

- As the Democracy Corps studies explain, "Government has emerged as uniquely illegitimate—as the nexus of money and power that spends excessively and without good will. The tax system disadvantages the middle class and loopholes are rigged for lobbyists and most privileged. A nexus of money and power means there are secret rules that determine what government will do and which disenfranchise ordinary citizens."

- In this bitter vision, Congressmen are seen as no more than paid shills for campaign contributors and lobbyists. Congress is seen as a vile cesspool of corruption rather than a source of solutions. Spending—any kind of spending—becomes illegitimate in this vision because by definition it will not be used to help ordinary citizens or the country.

- The participants in the Democracy Corps studies do not trust either party to do the right thing. Neither has stepped up in a way that has restored trust in government. As the reports note, "This is a dangerous stew for both political parties. No politician, political party, or corporation seems to be making things better."

5. People want better times and better jobs but they are deeply opposed to increasing government debt, deficits or spending because they don't think such actions will produce these results.

- The respondents in the Democracy Corps studies simply do not believe that "spending" creates good, "real" jobs. Government spending programs can create temporary "leaf raking" jobs like the WPA in the depression or the various manpower programs of the 1960's and 1970's. Government spending can also direct money to particular projects and companies. But, in the respondents' view, "leaf-raking" public jobs accomplish nothing in the long run and big government projects just end up being pork-barrel "bridges to nowhere." There is virtually no confidence that a hopelessly corrupt government has the ability or the integrity to create useful, well-managed public sector jobs or to direct money to the projects and investments America actually needs.

- The national debt is not viewed as a vague abstraction that is free of cost or consequence. The participants in the Democracy Corps interviews, focus groups and surveys believe that the debt will be passed on to the next generation of children and grandchildren, creating a burden on their economic future and leaving the country at the mercy of the Chinese. The sense of lost control of America's economic destiny is a tremendously powerful current of opinion and is closely linked to the concern about the loss of American jobs through outsourcing and job export and the consequent disappearance of the decent wages of the past.

- Deficits are not visualized by average Americans as "stimulative" tools for injecting purchasing power into the economy, On the contrary, they are seen as symbols of government irresponsibly, the waste and misappropriation of taxpayer money and the failure of congressmen and congresswomen to responsibly budget for the future to meet the real needs of their constituents.

- Even when informed that the bailouts of the financial and auto industries had been paid back, many people in the D-Corps' studies remained skeptical about the corporate greed and excess that necessitated the bailouts in the first place and the decision to help the wealthy and large corporations instead of ordinary Americans. The principle of providing taxpayer dollars to big corporations (with mentions of golden parachutes/executive compensation) was viewed as morally unacceptable.

The picture that emerges from this research reveals a complex mix of attitudes that does not neatly fit into either the standard Democratic or Republican narratives. Yet, at the same time, it presents a perspective that is instantly recognizable as extremely typical and widespread among ordinary working Americans.

To see how this complex mix of attitudes influences the way white working class people make political choices, however, it is necessary to look at a specific issue. From 2008 to the present, the most intense debate regarding white working class attitudes is the degree to which they favor creating jobs versus reducing the deficit.

CHAPTER
10

Working Class Attitudes about Jobs and Deficits – Progressive "Full Employment" versus the Republican "Free Market"

Elite Frames About the Economy

The Democracy Corps Economy Project is the most in-depth recent investigation of basic white working class attitudes about the economy but the cluster of attitudes it identified do not exist in a vacuum. When workers turn to TV and the rest of the mass media, they are presented with two basic narratives or "media frames" that present coherent ideological views of the economy.

In order to understand how white working people think about economic issues it is ultimately necessary to understand the process by which they compare their basic attitudes (as reflected in studies like the Democracy Corps research) with these media narratives and to consider how working people use "common sense" to reach a conclusion.

In order to do this, the first step is to outline these two narratives.

The first narrative is the basic conservative perspective that asserts universal and complete support for the "free market." It is an approach that is unified by the idea that when left alone, the free market automatically and inevitably produces the best possible outcomes. This view is not only presented in a popular form by Fox News and talk radio hosts but also by the Republican Party and most business groups in their publications and communication that are aimed at average Americans.

At the core of this view are a cluster of ideas that can best be summed up as *"pre-Keynesian."* The view is frequently simplified to one basic proposition—that government should be run according to the same principles that ordinary Americans apply to running a small business or a household.

The main ideas are:

1. Government spending cannot create "real" jobs. This is rooted in the widespread but superficial "common sense" notion that if there actually were any real demand for some particular service or product, a private business would inevitably arise to provide it. As a result, aside from a limited set of necessarily public jobs (the armed forces police, fire, etc.) there is no need for the government to be involved in any economic activity.

2. Government simply should not go into debt; it should maintain a permanently balanced budget. This idea, which in previous generations was called fiscal responsibility or "sound finance," is based on making an analogy between an individual household and the government. If going into debt is bad for an individual, it must be equally bad for country. The "common sense" notion behind this view is that borrowing money to buy things one cannot afford ("going into hock") is never a good idea on moral grounds. It undermines important virtues like thrift and hard work.

3. Banks are visualized as essentially profit-seeking businesses like any other and not as an abstract "credit system" that provides "finance" or "liquidity" to the economy. In this view, the fact that banks' particular business happens to be taking deposits and lending money does not entitle them to any

185

special treatment. In consequence, common sense dictates that they do not deserve to be "bailed out" when they fail any more than any other business.

4. Government regulation is seen from the perspective of a small businessman. As such it appears as a maze of annoying paperwork, licenses, permits, inspections, and so on. Since the 1970's when the demands on small businesses—and particularly the paperwork required of them—did actually increased exponentially, the view grew that many of these regulations were really created by government bureaucrats to keep themselves employed rather than as a sincere attempt to solve genuinely pressing social problems.

5. Taxes are seen from a very limited point of view—as money that is simply taken away from individuals by the government—and not visualized as part of a larger circular flow that returns in exchange services and a healthier society in which to live. The "common sense" notion simply is that "Taxes are my money and the government is stealing that money from me to give it to other people".

Before the 1930's, these views were part of the dominant social philosophy in America—a broad consensus that extended from the "neo-classical" economics textbooks of the era to the leaders of industry and government. Since the 1930's, however, in each of these areas a broader, "system-wide" economic view has taken hold, one which can broadly be defined as Keynesian.

1. This view sees a substantial part of government spending as investing—not just in national defense but in modern science, education, infrastructure development and other fields that have broad long-term benefits for the society as whole and multiple "spin-off" benefits for the private economy.

2. This view sees the management of government debt and

spending as part of maintaining the circular flow of income—of managing the business cycle and preventing mass unemployment or run-away inflation.

3. This view sees the credit system primarily as a critical mechanism for providing finance for private investment and growth. An individual bank's success or failure is seen as a secondary side-effect of this national economic function.

4. This view sees regulation as driven by genuine and significant market failures and vital to the economic system of any advanced country. From a broad social view, an advanced country simply cannot have babies dying of lead poisoning, stockholders routinely defrauded or "snake-oil" medicines sold without control. Regulation is seen as vital for creating the basic level of trust and economic stability needed to allow a complex modern economy to function.

5. Taxes are seen as the price of necessary public services. They are the "overhead costs" of living in a stable advanced country rather than a destitute third world backwater. When pre-Keynesian conservatives describe a place without taxes as Utopia, proponents of the Keynesian view suggest Ethiopia as a more realistic example.

By the 1960's, this Keynesian "big picture" view of the economy had become dominant among economists, corporate leaders and government officials—a dominance codified in the successive editions of Paul Samuelson's textbook which defined the field of economics for several decades. Even during the later Reagan and Bush administrations and until Obama's election, "serious" people—corporate executives, national politicians, mainstream media commentators, economic advisors and so on generally agreed that the first view was simplistic and that this second perspective was the only appropriate basis for making economic policy.

Alongside the establishment "Keynesian" perspective, there was also a third, related point of view: a liberal/labor progressive perspective that reflected the economic programs and outlook of the labor and civil rights movements and of liberal organizations and "New Deal" politicians. This "progressive" perspective basically accepted the establishment Keynesian framework but added three specific progressive amendments:

1. That trade unions were positive forces in the economy. Rather than representing "distortions of the free market" as conservatives claimed they actually provided a healthy "countervailing power" to management.

2. That economic policy had an obligation to aim at maintaining "full employment" which was traditionally defined as an unemployment rate of around 4 percent.

3. That the government had an obligation to provide a robust social safety net for the most vulnerable in society—the old, the sick and the poor.

One still finds each of these three perspectives—pre-Keynesian, Keynesian and liberal/labor progressive today.

The pre-Keynesian narrative can be found in the conservative media, in Chamber of Commerce booklets for schoolchildren—booklets with titles like, "What You Need to Know about the Free Enterprise System"—as well as in the pages of the *National Review* and the *Wall Street Journal* editorial page. It also appears in the political platforms of many conservative candidates.

The Keynesian narrative can be found in economic textbooks, in *Business Week* and *The London Economist* and on the editorial pages of the *New York Times*.

The liberal-progressive narrative can be found in the publications and resolutions of the AFL-CIO, in articles in *The Nation* magazine, in commentary in the *Daily Kos*, in the liberal sectors of the academic world and in the platforms of many Democratic candidates.

But the fundamental question is: "How do white working class Americans integrate and reconcile these organized media narratives with their personal views as revealed by the Economy Project?" To see how this process occurs, it is necessary to look at a specific issue such as unemployment and deficit spending because working people are rarely if ever called upon to evaluate the three major economic perspectives as a whole. Generally, they do not have the need or the opportunity to consider and judge the economy as an integrated system.

The Two Opposing Narratives On Job Creation

As was shown in chapter five, the specific opinions that individuals express on opinion polls are not stored in hundreds of separate little mental cubbyholes from which they are retrieved when needed but are rather organized into larger "knowledge structures"—various kinds of cognitive schemas, narratives, media frames and mental models that create a larger mental "picture" or "story" that explains a complex reality like the how the economy creates jobs. When people are asked a question on an opinion survey, they refer back to the larger mental framework and either locate a particular opinion that is held somewhere within it or use the information in the framework as the basis for essentially "deducing" or "computing" an opinion.

On specific social and political issues, these larger cognitive frameworks are often contained in speeches or similar narratives. In the case of jobs and unemployment, for example, at any time during the 1950's or 1960's there was a standard Democratic stump speech that generally went as follows:

1. America has a basic moral obligation and moral commitment to maintain high employment—an obligation first codified in The Employment Act of 1946. It is this commitment that has

undergirded America's prosperity since the Second World War.

2. The Great Depression demonstrated that reliance on the free market is not sufficient—government must play a central role in insuring jobs, growth and prosperity.

3. Full employment benefits everyone—business and workers— while tolerating prolonged mass unemployment not only harms individual workers but impoverishes society as a whole. Government spending during recessions increases consumer purchasing power and produces new sales opportunities for business, which leads to new hiring, greater revenues and increased profits.

4. There is therefore no excuse for inaction. All that is required is to set aside outmoded conservative myths that modern economics exploded many years ago.

To a remarkable degree these are still exactly the same arguments that many Democratic candidates give in speeches today. And there remains a large, solidly democratic audience that will hoot, holler and applaud this speech in union halls and other traditional democratic venues.

Outside the Democratic community, however, this view is widely seen as totally antiquated. In "red-state" America there is an alternative narrative that goes as follows:

1. Only the private sector can create real jobs—government spending simply shifts resources from the private to the public sector.

2. Business is always ready and willing to create new jobs. The only thing that prevents business from hiring more workers is the multitude of impediments imposed by government. Serious policies to create jobs are therefore measures that lower business taxes, remove regulations and eliminate all

other government imposed constraints on the private sector.

3. "Creating" jobs through government action, on the other hand, only creates a new kind of artificial welfare program. The belief that government can "stimulate" the economy is an illusion that is easily refuted by daily observation and good, old fashioned "common sense."

4. The only way to create jobs is to step back and let the free market work. There is no other alternative.

Like the Democratic narrative above, this narrative is widely circulated in the conservative world—in political speeches and advertisements, Fox News commentaries and talk radio.

How Voters Deal With Narratives That Conflict

As previous chapters have shown, there are two very distinct ways that voters react to opposing narratives.

First, a substantial group of voters will fully and categorically accept one narrative or the other. They form the committed "base" voters of both political parties and the ideologically committed partisans of the conservative and progressive movements. The defining characteristic of their perspective is an "all or nothing" view of the opposing narrative. The opposing perspective is totally wrong and all those who accept it are simply deluded. The other perspective's supporters have *"drunk the kool-aid," "been completely brainwashed," "are trapped in a propaganda bubble," "live on some other planet"* and so on. There is absolutely no sentiment among firm partisans of either narrative that there might be *"some truth on both sides."*

The second major group is the "ambivalent" or "open-minded" voters who are not fully convinced by either of the two narratives. They have *"not completely made up their minds,"* or *"see some truth on both sides,"* This group represents a smaller segment of the electorate than the two base groups but they are of critical political importance because they are the most persuadable "swing" voters who can be won by either side.

How Ambivalent Voters Decide

On the issue of jobs and unemployment, for example, a typical statement from a person of this kind would be something like the following.

> *Well, you know, I can't see any evidence that the stimulus really worked and I don't think just making phony leaf-raking jobs is a real solution. But I also think there must be some way the government can get people back to work and I don't think just laying off state employees or giving rich people lower taxes is the answer either.*

When a person using this *"on the one hand, on the other hand"* mode of thought is confronted by simple yes/no survey question, he or she cycles through these different kinds of considerations and weighs them in order to decide on a response. The person's choice will be deeply affected by the particular way the question is worded as well as whichever considerations happen to be uppermost in their minds at the particular moment they are surveyed. In any case, however, their "real" opinion will remain their inherently ambivalent mixture of positive and negative assessments and not the simple yes/no answer they provide.

How White Working Class Americans View the Issue of Deficits Versus Jobs

Ever since the package of emergency measures undertaken in the first weeks of the Obama administration in 2008—measures which included both the "Bailouts" and the stimulus package— were passed, the continuing debate over U.S. economic policy has become centered on the choice between stimulating the economy to reduce unemployment and cutting government spending to reduce budget deficits and debt. From 2009 to the present, the national political debate in the mass media between Democrats and Republicans has consistently framed this choice as representing an inescapable trade-off between conflicting objectives.

But there is a fundamental question that is not often asked: do average Americans actually see reduction of the deficit and debt on the one hand and reducing unemployment on the other as irreconcilable goals or do they see them as complementary objectives that should be simultaneously pursued?

Many policymakers and commentators automatically assume that most Americans view deficit and debt reduction and job creation during a recession as directly opposed because in a Keynesian conceptual framework they most certainly are. Every reputable econometric forecasting model clearly predicts that reducing government spending during a deep recession will inevitably increase unemployment.

But ordinary Americans do not visualize the two issues in these terms. As the Democracy Corps studies revealed, the issues of government spending and deficits are primarily conceptualized in relation to the larger conceptual framework about government corruption and inefficiency while unemployment is visualized in relation to the larger conceptual framework about the deindustrialization of the American economy and the decline of the middle class.

This more complex view does not fit comfortably into either of the two standard economic narratives, a fact that is easily obscured by poll questions that automatically assume that jobs and deficit reduction are in direct opposition. For example, forced choice questions inevitably produce results that appear to show that voters in general believe job creation and deficit reduction are antithetical.

Here is one example from the spring of 2011:

> *"Do you think large cuts in federal spending would do more to create jobs or do more to cut jobs in this country?"*
> *More to create jobs – 41 percent*

More to cut jobs – 45 percent
Neither (vol.) – 7 percent
Unsure – 7 percent

Taken at face value, one can easily misinterpret this data as proving that people "really" believe that jobs and spending reductions are incompatible rather than recognizing that it is the specific wording of the question that actually produces this result.

Just look at what happens when respondents are given a third choice.[1]

"If the government makes major cuts in federal spending this year in an effort to reduce the budget deficit, do you think these cuts will: help the job situation/hurt the job situation, or not have much of an effect either way?"

Help – 18 percent
Hurt – 34 percent
Not have much of an effect either way – 41 percent[2]

In this case the explicitly ideological pre-Keynesian view that deficit reduction will help to create jobs drops very dramatically to 18 percent. In contrast, a larger group of about a third of the sample takes a "Keynesian" view that spending cuts would hurt job creation. The largest group, however, feels that spending cuts would *"not have much of an effect either way"*.

A professor teaching a traditional Economics 101 course would say that those people who believe that cutting spending during a deep recession will not have any effect at all are not only factually wrong but are also technically expressing an "anti-Keynesian" view. But many of the people choosing the "not much effect" option are not really making a serious macroeconomic forecast (i.e., "I predict that the net effect of major spending reductions on the unemployment rate will be zero") but rather suggesting that they do not see the two things as directly related.

The best way to understand what average voters think is to use a research device called an "opinion thermometer" to separately and independently gauge voters' basic attitudes toward deficit reduction and job creation. In this kind of question respondents are asked to simply give an entirely subjective "warm" versus "cold" opinion about a given topic or idea on a scale of 0 (freezing) to 100 (boiling).

In January 2011, a Democracy Corps poll asked a thermometer question of this kind:

> When respondents were asked to rate *"a plan to invest in new industries and rebuild the country over the next five years"*, 57 *percent* of the respondents offered "warm" ratings in contrast to 16 percent who responded "coldly."

> When respondents were asked to rate *"a plan to dramatically reduce the deficit over the next five years"* 52 percent of the respondents expressed "warm" ratings of the idea in contrast to 20 percent who responded "coldly".

In short, both job creation and deficit reduction were given strongly positive evaluations with majorities favoring both goals.

The results are clear. Most average voters view both deficit/spending reduction and job creation positively—and the largest group is actually quite "hot" about both. More important, the majority who are "warm" or "hot" toward one are not simultaneously "cool" or "cold" toward the other which would indicate that they perceive them as antithetical.

This is confirmed when surveys ask white working class Americans if they want both objectives pursued at the same time or if they prefer choosing to focus on deficit and spending reduction alone. For example:

> *We need to prioritize both cutting the deficit and making growth–producing investments in American industry and small business to make us stronger and more competitive.*

Or

Since we cannot both cut the deficit and continue high levels of spending, we need to make cutting the deficit the higher priority to make the US economy stronger and more competitive.

The results were as follows:

First Statement Strongly	First Statement Somewhat	Second Statement Somewhat	Second Statement Strongly
57%	8%	7%	22%

White respondents with less than a four-year college degree, unpublished data from Democracy Corps)

In short, when asked in a way that allows them to express their view directly, white working class people do not see jobs and deficit reduction as necessarily opposed. This is, of course, what would be expected based on the Democracy Corps Economy Project research.

One can visualize a typical participant in that research summarizing his or her view in the following way:

"Today's crisis is nothing new. Factories have been closing and huge numbers of jobs have been exported to other countries constantly since the 1980's. The 2009 crash made things worse, but the good jobs and decent salaries that created the middle class life of the past have been going down the damn toilet for decades and nobody in Washington has ever done one damn thing about it".

"Government can't really solve problems. It always screws up anything it does. It can throw money around, but that's about it."

"The politicians in Washington don't give the slightest damn about people like me. They take care of their fat-cat contributors and big business lobbyists and sell the average person down

the river every chance they get."

"We gotta stop just getting deeper in debt. We're borrowing money from the Chinese and everyone else like a drunk on a binge and sooner or later the party has to stop."

Although it is more difficult, it is possible to use more sophisticated survey questions to explore in more depth how white working class people choose between the "pre-Keynesian" and "Keynesian" conceptual frameworks when they are forced to choose. In November 2012, immediately after Obama's re-election, Democracy Corps asked the following question to an unusually large sample of white working class voters:

Q.137: I want you to imagine you are listening to a debate on the topic of the economy.

In one concluding statement, Speaker A says: *Our country's highest priority should be growth that creates full employment and raises incomes at every level and that reduces the deficit in the long-term. Growth requires public investment in things like transportation, science, and education. Markets don't always produce the best outcomes, so we need to rein in corporate excess that harms consumers or the economy. We should tax the highest earners to address the country's key priorities.*

In the other concluding statement, Speaker B says: *Our economy works best when government is smaller and entrepreneurs and small businesses play a bigger role. So our biggest priority should be cutting government spending, including out-of-control entitlement spending, and removing government regulation that does more harm than good. We should be simplifying the tax code so government doesn't pick winners and losers and cutting taxes permanently for all taxpayers and corporations to spur growth.*

Source: Democracy Corps combined Post Election Survey, Nov 9, 2012

The results were as follows:

Speaker A strongly	Speaker A somewhat	Both/ neither	Speaker B somewhat	Speaker B Strongly
20%	17%	4%	22%	29%

Source: Democracy Corps combined Post Election Survey, Nov 9, 2012

Combining the categories produces the following summary results:

Total Agree Speaker A	Total Agree Speaker B
36%	51%

Source: Democracy Corps combined Post Election Survey, Nov 9, 2012

These results are clear in indicating that when faced with a forced choice between the broad pre-Keynesian and Keynesian narratives, by a substantial margin the white working class respondents agreed more with the pre-Keynesian "free market" view.

This is underscored by follow-up questions that D-Corps asked the people who responded to this question. The 51 percent of the respondents who agreed with the second, conservative pre-Keynesian statement very specifically indicated that they were most in agreement with the parts of the overall statement that expressed advocacy of "small government" and "giving small business a larger role". In contrast, the 36 percent of the Respondents who favored the first statement indicated that they were not most positively influenced by the call for "full employment" and "growth", but rather by the call for higher taxes on the wealthy and in favor of greater public investment.

The results make clear that, in general, the Keynesian, "full employment" goal, which was overwhelmingly popular among white workers in the 50's and 60's when the memories of the great depression were still strong, has now been substantially forgotten and replaced for many with a broad ideological approval of small business and hostility to big government.

It is important to note, however, that the intensity of this view is rather low. Only 29 percent of white workers agree with the pre-Keynesian view "strongly." A majority of 51 percent on the other hand were ambivalent, once again illustrating the significance of "on the one hand, on the other hand" mode of thought.

Further insight into the way white working people think about jobs on the one hand and deficits, debt and spending on the other can be gained by looking at the ways that white working class respondents react to a variety of different statements related to the subject. Each of the questions below is actually one half of two paired statements, the second half of each statement being calls to reduce deficits and spending.

Opinions on Jobs and Deficits	% Agreeing
It is important to cut seriously wasteful spending and abolish special interest tax breaks and subsidies so that we can invest in infrastructure and technology and make sure we can support education, Medicare and Social Security, which are key to the middle class.	71
The federal deficit is a big national problem but we should not make major changes or cuts in Social Security and Medicare.	67
The biggest priority after the election is for leaders to work to grow the economy	54
The wealthiest have used tax breaks and loopholes to pay lower tax rates than middle class families. Any new plan to address the deficit should start by closing corporate loopholes and raising taxes for those at the top. A deficit plan should not include cuts in Medicare or Social Security.	51
Given where our economy is, we should invest now in infrastructure, education and technology, and re-hiring teachers and firefighters to get people back to work to make our country stronger in the long-term	46
We should avoid immediate drastic cuts in spending, and instead, we need serious investments that create jobs and make us more prosperous in the long term, and that will reduce our debt, too	44
Given where our economy is, we should do everything we can to help the middle class, and that means protecting Medicare and Social Security	41

Slashing spending now is short-sighted. It will cost millions of jobs, force cuts in schools, child nutrition and Medicare and Social Security benefits. Our children will find jobs harder to find, and will lose skills vital to compete in global economy. And more people out of work will make it harder to reduce the deficit.	37
Our first priority should be putting people back to work. In a weak economy, laying off teachers, closing schools and firehouses, cutting health care for parents and grandparents makes it harder to reduce the deficit. Severe cuts will drive us back into a recession as Britain and Spain have learned.	36

There are several important conclusions that can be drawn from this chart.

First, it is clear that there are large differences which are caused simply by the specific wording of the questions. A strong majority of 67 percent, for example, agree that Social Security and Medicare should not be cut when the question is posed as a direct trade off with deficits. This support drops to only 41 percent, on the other hand, when the question is posed more vaguely in terms of helping the middle class. The contrast illustrates the degree to which specific question wording can influence the results.

Second, looked at more carefully, however, one basic trend is apparent. Statements that express very typical Keynesian arguments for "creating jobs" and "putting people back to work" receive relatively low levels of support while statements that express support for public investment and tax reform are substantially more popular In fact, the most popular option in the group of statements above combines a package of abolishing special interest tax breaks, investing in infrastructure, supporting Medicare and Social Security along with cutting wasteful spending.

This kind of result is very frustrating to liberal economists who would prefer to see white working class Americans express clear and unambiguous support for the traditional Keynesian "demand management" policies and perspective that were dominant in the 1960's. But the actual results make perfect sense as expressions of the views identified in the Democracy Corps Economy Project polling.

This dramatically illustrates the key conclusion that emerges. White working class Americans do indeed know the socially dominant mass media frames and narratives about the economy in general and the choice between jobs and deficits/spending on the other. But many white working class Americans—and particularly the open-minded—do not accept them completely or uncritically. They use "common sense" to weigh conflicting ideas and to pick and choose the ones that correspond and resonate with the reality of their daily lives. When asked simple yes/no questions on an opinion poll, they can seem to be expressing complete agreement with either the pre-Keynesian or the Keynesian media frames about jobs and deficits. But more careful investigation of their views inevitably reveals a more complex pattern that can only be understood by more detailed kinds of empirical research. No single survey question or set of simple yes/no responses can provide an adequate understanding of the opinions of white working class Americans.

Summary of Part II – How They Think

1. White working class Americans are overwhelmingly cultural traditionalists. In broad perspective, they respect and uphold the values of the four major social institutions in working class life— the church, the army, small business and the "American system of government" (which essentially includes the Constitution, Bill of Rights and democratic elections).

2. For many white working class Americans life experiences completely confirm and reinforce the values promulgated by the major social institutions—religious piety, patriotism, support for "free enterprise" and the "American way". For others, personal life experiences significantly modify or challenge these values systems.

3. The result is the continual formation of two characteristic groups—true believers who are firm and passionate supporters of traditional values and more open-minded individuals who analyze political issues using and "on the one hand, on the other hand" form of thought and who rely on "common sense" to reach conclusions.

4. When applied to social and political issues, this social and psychological series of processes produces three distinct groups: white working class progressives, white working class conservatives and white working class moderates. For Democratic strategy, the moderates are the key group of persuadable white working class voters.

5. In the area of "values" issues, the basic division between the "true believers" and the "open minded" overlaps a related split between tolerant and intolerant individuals. This split shows up in many areas including religion, immigration and attitudes toward militarism and war.

6. Hostility to government is an immensely powerful sentiment in white working class America. In part it reflects conservative critiques that portray the government as imposing alien, elite

programs and values, but for many other white working class Americans it actually represents a new kind of "class consciousness"—a sense that the rich and powerful control the government while ordinary people are left without any real influence at all. The intensity of anti-government sentiment is impossible to overstate. It is central to the world-view of many white working class individuals.

7. White working class views of economy are largely derived from practical experience in the world of small business. The resulting complex of attitudes combines a world-weary cynicism about "the way things are" in business life, an appreciation of many positive values inculcated by business, and a mixture of approval of private property and the market system alongside clear reservations about the limits of markets and the resultant need for a social safety net and regulation to protect workers and consumers.

8. In depth research by Democracy corps reveals that the events since 2008 deeply reinforced and deepened a sense of hopelessness about the possibility of the economy ever again providing the stable middle class life of the past and a profound cynicism about political system and the ability of government to effect positive change.

9. In contrast to the dominant "pre-Keynesian" and "Keynesian" narrative frameworks, white working class Americans do not see jobs and deficits as antithetical. They perceive them as substantially separate issues and wish to see both objectives pursued simultaneously.

10. The fundamental conclusion that emerges from the study of white working class attitudes is that within this social group there is a persuadable sector that is not now voting Democratic but whose support can be obtained. To gain these workers' support, however, will require substantial changes in the Democrats current approach.

Part Three

How Progressives Can Regain the Trust and Support of Working Class Americans

11

Eliminate Condescension: Two Attitudes That Undermine All Progressive Attempts to Win Working Class Support.

There are two profoundly condescending and destructive assumptions about ordinary working Americans that are widespread in the progressive world:

1. That progressives naturally understand the "real" issues that face ordinary Americans without having the need to do any serious "field" research to find out how ordinary people themselves define, understand and think about the issues.

2. That ordinary working Americans are basically gullible and can be easily manipulated by the messages they get from the media.

Stated this bluntly, most progressives would quite indignantly deny that they actually hold such views. But these views are rarely expressed this directly. Instead, they operate as unstated underlying assumptions behind other kinds of assertions that are far more widespread.

An Example

A June 11th, 2011 article in the *Huffington Post* presented an entirely typical example of how these views are expressed in progressive commentary.

Here is how the article expressed the first assumption—that progressives already know what ordinary Americans consider the "real issues" without needing any data:

> [Democrats] have become convinced by the new conventional wisdom in Washington, that Americans aren't really concerned as much about jobs as they are about the deficit.

> If you stop and think about it for a moment, that notion is absurd on the face of it. Is it really possible that Americans who have lost their jobs or fear losing them are more worried about an abstraction—the budget deficit in Washington— than about the realities of their lives—that they face a budget deficit around their own kitchen table at the end of every month when they're trying to pay their rent or make their mortgage payment on their rapidly depreciating home?[1]

Set aside for a moment the verbal sleight of hand by which *"Americans"* in one sentence becomes *"Americans who have lost their jobs or fear losing them"* in the next. The article's implicit argument is that "common sense" alone is sufficient to prove that the American people could never genuinely view deficits to be of equal importance to unemployment. The alternative can be dismissed as "absurd".

Polls or other empirical data, on the other hand, can simply be "rigged" to provide any answer the pollster wants. As the article says:

> Can a pollster who believes or wants to show that Americans are as or more concerned about the national debt than jobs or the economic insecurity they face every day write questions in such a way as to get what he or she is looking for? Sure. Does this reflect what working and middle class Americans feel as they watch their economic security disappear? Not in a million years.

Many progressives will tend to agree with this point of view on an emotional level. But when one steps back to view it more dispassionately it becomes clear that the basic assumption underlying this line of argument is that progressives can know what ordinary Americans consider the "real issues" they face by a process of simple introspection and logic. Data is unnecessary because the alternative hypothesis can be summarily dismissed as "absurd on the face of it" and could not be true "in a million years."

This view has its roots in the post-World War II conviction of both progressives and Democrats that, as the New Deal advocates and representatives of the "ordinary guys" and "average Joe's" of the 50's, they quite naturally understood the "real"—essentially "kitchen table" economic—interests of working people and could reliably distinguish between the "real" issues working people faced and the social and cultural issues that conservatives exploited to manipulate them. A recent and particularly lyrical version of this "real issues" versus "false consciousness" notion was expressed in Thomas Frank's 2004 book, *"What's the Matter with Kansas?"*

The problem with this perspective is that it too easily leads to the rather arrogant notion that progressives can "know" what working people actually need, want and care about by a process of deduction from their "real interests" rather than through open-minded field research and investigation of what they actually say.

Manipulated by the Media

Elsewhere the same article also expresses the second assumption—that the opinions of ordinary Americans can be manipulated with relative ease:

> ...when leaders on one side are voicing a strong opinion—in this case, the Republicans arguing that the sky is falling on the economy because of deficits, tax and spend liberalism, and over-regulation of business—and the other side is either silent or echoing GOP talking points—*the average voter hears what sounds like a consensus and starts to mouth it.*

Then pollsters start to pick up in their polls precisely the view they have been promulgating and *elites have been putting into the minds and mouths of ordinary citizens,* rendering elected officials all the more afraid of bucking what is now the conventional wisdom. And the result is a self-fulfilling prophecy.

The phrases, *"the average voter hears what sounds like a consensus and starts to mouth it"* and views that *"elites have been putting in the minds and mouths of ordinary citizens"* are quite clear in suggesting that the opinions of ordinary Americans can be relatively easily molded and manipulated. The alternative possibility—that ordinary Americans are expressing authentic, seriously held views—is simply not entertained.

In expressing these views the article is not in any way atypical or extreme. On the contrary, the near-universal progressive arguments about the national debate in 2011 that say *"The Dems allowed the Republicans to control the narrative and that's why the national debate switched from jobs to deficits"* or that *"if Obama had just used the bully pulpit in the spring of 2011, the American people would have supported him"* implicitly assume that media messages can quite easily shape what ordinary people think. The unstated assumption is that working people do not have stable, thoughtfully held views on issues like their priority between jobs and deficit reduction and can therefore be shifted relatively sharply toward either progressive or conservative stances depending on the media messages they hear coming out of Washington.

Both of these notions should disturb thoughtful progressives. This is essentially a completely "data-free" approach to political analysis and strategy and it is found in every corner of the progressive community. It assumes that progressive and Democratic understanding of what ordinary people think can be based on logical deductions and introspection rather than field research and empirical observation and that media messages determine what they think. These are both deeply and inherently dangerous assumptions.

And notice how the two assumptions above mutually reinforce each other to create an entirely circular argument. Since progressives feel confident that they know the real issues facing ordinary Americans without having to study peoples' opinions empirically, it follows logically that if such people express views or priorities that are inconsistent with what progressives know their real interests to be, they must necessarily have been manipulated by conservative messages and narratives—messages and narratives that energetic progressive counter-messaging should be able to reverse. From this vantage point, the statement that *"If Democrats had only presented the progressive perspective on [some issue] with sufficient energy and passion, the American people would have supported them"* becomes a completely vacuous assertion—one that can never be proved or disproved—rather than an empirical hypothesis that has to be confirmed by field research regarding the actual opinions of ordinary Americans on a particular topic. It is impossible for working class people to actually disagree with progressives in this perspective; if they do it is necessarily because they have been manipulated by conservative propaganda.

Yet, in fact, there is nothing inherently conservative rather than progressive in the views that the Democracy Corps studies unearthed. Those views reflect the reality of life for ordinary Americans today and express an anger, frustration, alienation and discouragement that is fundamentally justified. Casually dismissing these views as the mindless parroting of "conservative clichés" or gullible acceptance of "conservative propaganda" is not only objectively false but is also the most powerful driver of the widespread sentiment among many ordinary Americans that progressives are indeed "condescending elitists" who are completely out of touch with the realities of life for hard-working families. The conservative accusation resonates with them because there is a reality they can directly perceive that supports it.

The Democracy Corps research illustrates how progressives and Democrats can overcome this problem. The first step, however, is to firmly and categorically set aside these two profoundly destructive notions that are now a central roadblock preventing progressives and Democrats from being able to communicate with ordinary Americans.

CHAPTER

12

Beyond Populism – Appealing to "Common Sense" as well as Populist Anger

For most progressive Democrats it seems completely obvious that Dems have no choice except to adopt a firmly "populist" approach and strategy if they want to have any hope of regaining the support of white working class America. While some affluent "soccer moms" and white-collar "office park dads" might conceivably be attracted to a Democratic platform based on a mixture of "Republican-lite" economic conservatism and mild social liberalism, no faction within the Democratic coalition has ever seriously suggested that a political platform of this kind would have much appeal to ordinary working people.

And within the Democratic coalition as a whole there is now a consensus on the need to adopt a series of essentially "populist" approaches—on taxes, offshoring U.S. jobs and energetically defending the social safety net. There is, in fact, relatively little disagreement any longer among Democrats about the need for these particular aspects of a "populist" appeal.

But in the debate over Democratic political strategy many advocates of a populist strategy propose something substantially more than these measures. As they describe it, a populist strategy would embrace and champion the profound sense of anger and frustration and try to redirect it from hostility toward liberalism and government over

212

to anger at business, corporations, Wall Street and the wealthy. It is, in effect, a strategy to adopt the angry political style of the conservative "politics of resentment," but change the villains in the narrative from left-wing university professors, government bureaucrats and Democratic politicians to corporations, highly-paid executives, Wall Street and the banking system.

There are two specific recommendations for Democratic strategy that flow from this general approach. First, there should be absolutely no compromise with conservative ideas and concerns. A populist strategy must be clear and categorical in rejecting any search for a middle ground. Second, in regard to style, a populist approach should be militant, combative and indeed "rabble-rousing" in order to demonstrate authentic and genuine concern for working Americans.

The Argument For a Populist Approach

To many progressives under 30 the necessity for this kind of strategy seems self-evident. The Democratic political victories in 2006 and 2008 have been widely—and convincingly—credited to the more aggressive stance Dems took after their cautious, "Republican-lite" strategy in 2000 and 2002. In addition, both Al Gore and John Kerry's failure to win white working class support is generally attributed to their seemingly aloof and condescending manner, one which stood in marked contrast to George Bush's clumsy but ultimately successful impersonation of an "aw-shucks" Texan. Today, an identical frustration has emerged with Obama because he is seen by many as still too cerebral and detached to create an emotional connection with white working class Americans.

Beyond this recent history there are two additional reasons why it seems extremely plausible to assume that an aggressively "populist" approach ought to be effective in appealing to white working class voters. First there is the Depression-era tradition of the tough-talking, "rabble-rousing" union organizer—the gruff and pugnacious defender of the average working stiff exemplified by CIO president

John L. Lewis in the 1930's and Teamster leader Jimmy Hoffa in the 1950's. In popular memory, it was men like these who won the respect and support of industrial workers and built the American trade union movement. It therefore seems plausible to think that a similar approach might still work today. Second, there is the repeated success of right-wing populists in winning substantial working class support—a parade of right-wing populist politicians that includes George Wallace and Spiro Agnew in the 70's, Ross Perot and Pat Buchannan in the 90's and Sarah Palin today as well as the many radio and TV commentators like Rush Limbaugh, Bill O' Reilly, Glen Beck and their imitators.

Yet, simply citing these two cultural models suggests that important limitations exist on Democrats' ability to replicate them. For one thing, no major national labor leader or other progressive spokesman for working people in the rough-hewn Lewis-Hoffa mode has appeared in the last 40 years. Equally, although many progressive politicians have tried, none have been able to replicate the success of the long line of conservative populists who have achieved national prominence. Progressives will frequently cite radio commentator Jim Hightower and the late Senator Paul Wellstone of Minnesota as illustrations that progressive populists can and do exist. But unlike the conservative populists noted above, neither of these men achieved any major following or influence outside their home state or radio market. In fact, the best known progressive who expresses a solidly and consistently "ordinary guy" populist point of view today, filmmaker Michael Moore—although nationally known—is popular among liberals and progressives rather than among white working class Americans. As such, these figures indicate the limits of progressive populism at the same time that they demonstrate its existence.

In fact, there are five major conclusions that flow from the analysis that has been presented in this book that suggest the need for an approach that goes beyond a simple aggressive populism:

1. The recommendation of a traditional, aggressive "populism" is based on two popular "folk models" of how workers actually think about political issues—"cubbyhole" or "bin" models that suggest Democrats can appeal to a set of "real issues" that they themselves define and "media framing" models that suggest sheer volume and intensity can determine which message working people accept. These folk models tend to suggest a relatively narrow and inflexible approach to political strategy.

2. A more sociologically-grounded model—one that is based on the interaction of the basic social value systems workers internalize as they grow up and the individual experiences they have in their lives—leads to the conclusion that working class voters are in fact significantly split between two groups—a quite substantial group of rigid "true believers" and a smaller but politically pivotal "open minded" or "common sense" group.

3. Unlike the "true believers", the more "open-minded" group can be influenced on a wide range of issues and values by appeals based on "common sense" and "seeing both sides". They can be convinced by Democratic proposals and candidates if Democratic proposals are presented in a framework that argues *"there are reasonable arguments on both sides of this issue, but this particular idea is a good 'common sense' compromise."*

4. Working class Americans are also sharply divided between those who are tolerant versus those who are intolerant. The opinion data show that a significant minority of working class Americans fall in the former category and are therefore potentially open to Democratic appeals that reflect that perspective.

In cases where political issues involve questions of basic social values, these individuals' explicitly compare and balance the injunctions of their core value systems with their practical life experience. Democrats can successfully appeal to this group if their ideas and candidates are presented as sincerely rooted in and respectful of basic American values but as also facing up to real-world needs and challenges that ideologically rigid Republicans simply refuse to face.

5. Working Class Americans have a deep distrust of government coupled with complex economic ideas. They make political decisions by balancing a set of core ideas, and awareness of their current situation with the messages of elite media frames that are communicated through the mass media. These individuals can be reached with a "populist" style that is distinct from the traditional "angry populist"—a "reasonable, down to earth" style that stresses "common sense" rather than just a visceral and bitter "us vs. them" antagonism.

It must be emphasized as forcefully as possible that these conclusions do not imply a rejection of a traditional populist approach but rather an extension of it. There are a wide variety of issues and problems where the opinion data and the 2012 election clearly show that Democrats can and should proudly embrace traditional populist rhetoric and attitudes.

But, at the same time, there is also a legitimate role for a "populist" appeal that employs a "down-to-earth", "honest", "common sense" form of outreach to working Americans—one that respects the importance of basic American social values in working class political thinking and that recognizes that government corruption and serious government reform is a central issue for working Americans, one that Democrats must sincerely and authentically champion if they wish to win the support of working class Americans for any other progressive goals.

These two kinds of "populist" approach are not incompatible. On the contrary, they are complementary and can be combined to produce a more robust and inclusive populist appeal to working class Americans than can be achieved by either one alone.

CHAPTER

13

The Long-Term Solution – Giving Working People a Voice and Bottom-Up Representation in the Democratic Coalition

Regaining the support of white working class voters is now the most significant long term problem facing the Democrats. After the 2010 elections, Ronald Brownstein stated the basic reality bluntly:

"Democrats don't have to win a majority of the votes of white workers to compete. But they can't get annihilated on those battlefields either and that's exactly what happened [in 2010]."[1]

In the 2012 elections Obama won the support of 36 percent of white working class voters, just enough to insure his victory. But, because many people who vote in presidential elections do not do the same in off-year elections, it is predictable that the Democrats share of the white working class vote will decline to closer to the 33 percent they obtained in 2010. Without significantly improving Democratic performance among white working class voters to at least the level of the 40 percent Obama won in 2008, a Democratic victory in the next presidential election in 2016 will remain dangerously contested.

But what can Dems do to increase their white working class support? In the discussion of this question three main strategies consistently reappear:

217

1. **Offer different programs and policies** – Progressives generally argue for more radical and populist measures across a wide range of issues; other critics propose changes in priorities rather than new programs—in 2009, for example, choosing to prioritize additional job creation measures in preference to other liberal goals like health care reform or combating global warming.

2. **Improve communications** – Many observers fault Obama for failing to provide a clear and compelling narrative to counter the Republican attacks. More generally, Democratic candidates are frequently criticized for becoming too immersed in the details of programs and policies while failing to explain their goals in simple everyday terms.

3. **Choose more appealing candidates** – Not only Obama, but essentially all recent Democratic candidates including Al Gore, John Kerry and Howard Dean have been repeatedly criticized for being cold, aloof or condescending—individuals who create the impression of being out of touch, "wine track" elitists.

Regardless of whether the discussion focuses on Obama in particular or Democratic candidates in general, current proposals largely revolve around these three topics. The implicit assumption underlying these analyses is that some combination of improvements in these three areas can produce a major increase in white working class support for the Dems.

On the surface this seems a plausible view but there is also a radically different perspective to consider—that there is actually no possible combination of these three measures that, by itself, can overcome the current impasse that exists between the Democrats and white working class America.

To understand the argument for this second point of view it is necessary to step back from the immediate "what can we do right now" perspective and take a more long-range view. Although at first glance the three factors above seem to offer a reasonably comprehensive list of the Democrats' major problems with white working class Americans, they all actually reflect a particular underlying conceptual paradigm—the limited, essentially beltway-centric perspective of professional campaign management and advertising agencies. This is a view that sees politics as essentially an exercise in advertising in which the political candidate is the "product" and the election essentially a vast advertising campaign. Ever since Joe McGinnis' classic book about the 1968 election, *"The Selling of the President,"* whose cover featured a picture of Richard Nixon's face printed on a pack of cigarettes, politically aware Americans have been sharply aware of the profound influence the advertising perspective has on the day-to-day strategy and management of modern political campaigns.

And in fact—although it is not immediately obvious—the three factors listed above can actually be directly translated into three standard advertising agency recommendations and strategies for helping their clients sell more products – (1) *adding features and improving the product design* (better platform and policies), (2) *developing improved advertising slogans and ad campaigns* (better narratives) and (3) *selecting a more effective on-camera celebrity spokesman* (better candidates). From a professional campaign management perspective, these options are all part of the planning process that goes on around a conference table in an ad agency at the beginning of a political campaign.

Progressives, of course, emphatically reject the ad agency "candidate as product" advertising model because they do not seek to cynically manipulate white working class voters like the "hired gun" political campaign management companies that work for clients without regard to their ideology but rather to honestly win white working class support by offering progressive policies and programs that they sincerely believe to be in workers' best interests.

But as a practical matter when progressives discuss strategies for winning white working class support in specific elections they often tend to focus their recommendations on the same three factors—policies, narratives and candidates—that advertising agencies invariably target in political campaigns. A very common opinion among progressives, in fact, is that charismatic Democratic candidates with firm populist programs and clear progressive narratives could indeed win back the support of white working class America.

There is however, one reality that this approach does not take into account—that the fine-tuning of platforms, narratives and candidates was emphatically NOT the major method by which Dems won and then retained the support of white working class voters in the past. On the contrary, white working class support for the Democrats in the 1940's, 1950's and early 1960's was fundamentally based on two quite different factors – (1) that Dems from every sector of the party genuinely and sincerely viewed American workers as the heart and soul of their political coalition and (2) that workers had a set of important, bottom-up institutions that simultaneously represented their needs and interests on a day to day basis and simultaneously cemented their allegiance to the Democratic Party

Let us look at these two factors in turn.

In the 1950's Democrats genuinely respected workers as the heart of the New Deal coalition and sincerely wanted to represent them.

In the period after World War II, as the Democratic Party returned to peacetime political activity, most rank and file Dems as well as the political leaders and strategists within the party naturally and legitimately considered the Democrats to be the sincere champions and authentic representatives of the people they saw as "the common man", "the ordinary guy" or "the average Joe". Post-war Democrats sincerely identified with the hardships these men and women had endured during the depression and the enormous sacrifices they had made during World War II. The Dems also felt that they had demonstrated their concern for these voters, not only with the major New Deal programs, but also with the Wagner Act which made possible the growth of industrial trade unions and with post-war Democratic initiatives like the G.I. Bill. In major urban areas with local Democratic political clubs and ward-level political machines, Dems also sincerely felt that they were socially and culturally in close touch with average working Americans. The Republican Party, in contrast, was widely seen as a party of the well-to-do—of businessmen and executives, Chamber of Commerce luncheons, country clubs and midday golf games.

When Democrats tried to visualize exactly who these typical "average guys" or "ordinary Joe's" were, they thought about them in essentially occupational terms. Working class Americans—both men and women—were basically manual, physical workers, hard-working people who earned their living with their hands rather than their minds. They were blue collar rather than white collar, brawn rather than brains.

They included far more than just factory workers. The "average guys" and "ordinary Joe's" of America were not only automobile and steel workers but also carpenters and garbage collectors, truck drivers and policemen, night watchmen, bartenders, janitors and mailmen. Working class women were waitresses and cashiers, maids and cleaning women (they were also working class wives for whom—in an era when housework in non-affluent homes was still done with brooms, washboards, rolling pins and clotheslines—being a "homemaker" was a hard, full-time job).

This broad, "populist" way of conceptualizing the American "working class" was not confined to the Democratic Party but was widely shared in the culture as a whole. The two best-known working class characters portrayed on the television of the 1950's were Ralph Kramden and Ed Norton of "The Honeymooners," a bus driver and a sewer worker. Similarly, the three most sensitive portrayals of "ordinary Joe's" in the movies of the 50's were not of factory workers but of a butcher (Ernest Borgnine in "Marty"), a longshoreman (Marlon Brando in "On the Waterfront") and a pool shark (Paul Newman in "The Hustler").

Thus, the "working class" voters that Democrats sought to represent in the 50's were a very broad and heterogeneous group of "ordinary guys and gals" or "average Joe's" that Dems visualized as including a solid majority of Americans.

In this pre-civil rights era, neither African-Americans and other minorities nor voters with advanced educations were seen as separate interest groups with competing and conflicting agendas. Black support for the Democrats was not seen as a reward for specific legislation like the civil rights and voting rights acts (which would come later) but rather as a consequence of Black Americans' general position as an overwhelmingly working class group who would clearly benefit from the general progressive economic policies of the New Deal. In the 1950's the unique problems Blacks and other non-whites faced were widely viewed—quite naively, it must be admitted in retrospect—as simply the prejudiced attitudes of some individual whites. In popular plays and films of the period like *South Pacific*, *West Side Story* and the interracial chain gang melodrama *"The Defiant Ones"* the solution to prejudice was depicted as simply guiding racially-biased white people toward greater tolerance and understanding through patient and gradual persuasion.

Voters with advanced educations—a very much smaller proportion of the electorate in that era than today—were also not seen as a distinct "interest group" whose allegiance to the Democrats had to be won with specific policies and positions. Many educated voters were indeed attracted to the Democrats by "intellectual" politicians like Adali Stevenson and John Kennedy and by the party's generally more moderate stance on social issues. But the Democratic Party's educated supporters were basically viewed as "liberals" rather than "college professors" and their support for the Democratic party was fundamentally attributed to a sense of social concern and solidarity with average Americans rather than because they were a distinct interest group with a political agenda of their own. Most important, they were emphatically not perceived as a central pillar of the Democratic coalition that was equal to or even more important than ordinary Americans. While the Democratic Party received support from minorities and the educated in the 1950's, it still basically viewed itself as essentially the party of the ordinary working man.

Workers had a set of important, bottom-up institutions that represented their needs and interests and at the same time connected them with the Democratic Party.

The heart of the Democratic base in working class America were the industrial workers employed in the giant factories of the post-war era—automobile workers in Detroit, steelworkers in Youngstown, rubber and tire workers in Akron. Most of these workers lived in tightly knit urban ethnic neighborhoods near the plants. A number of these communities—Brooklyn in New York, "Southie" in Boston, Hamtramck in Detroit, the ethnic mosaic of Chicago's south side— became iconic parts of American culture because of their distinctive working class character.

These urban ethnic communities were knitted together by three major social and cultural institutions—the local church, the union and the local Democratic political club. The latter two played an important and active part in the daily life of industrial workers in the 50's and 60's that is now largely forgotten.

In the social world of the large factory, the union was not just a remote group of highly-paid union officials who negotiated contracts with management. On the contrary, the grievance procedure and the local shop steward system made industrial unions grass roots, representative institutions that defended individual workers in day-to-day disputes over arbitrary firing, dangerous working conditions and harassment by supervisors.

As now, Republicans in the 50's invariably characterized unions as nothing more than uniformly corrupt, crime-ridden institutions that simply took workers dues without providing anything in return, but the day to day reality was profoundly different. For industrial workers, "the union" was not so much the distant figure in a suit and tie emerging from contract negotiations as it was their co-worker who had been elected to serve as shop steward and who came to work every day with a grease-stained and well-thumbed copy of the union contract in his back pocket that he pulled out and quoted whenever an argument with the foreman arose.

The local Democratic clubs in the major northern industrial cities also had a grass-roots representative function. Although often disparaged as simply a cynical "machine" that delivered votes for Democratic candidates, at the neighborhood precinct level they were also a significant community service organization for urban working class Americans—a source of municipal jobs for relatives, for intercession with the city and state bureaucracy when problems arose on issues like veterans benefits or disability payments, for help with a wide range of urban issues and problems. They provided the equivalent of the "constituent services" many congressional offices offer today, but on a much more localized, street by street, "walk-in" basis. As a consequence, they created loyalty to the Democratic Party as an institution rather than to individual candidates.

The local Democratic clubs also gave urban workers a sense of political representation and participation because workers knew that the same precinct captain who listened to them and helped solve their personal problems in the local office also sat in the "smoke-filled rooms" with the higher level politicians when decisions about endorsements and candidates for city and statewide offices were made. Often, the most powerful endorsement a local political candidate could possibly get was simply the off-hand statement that *"Joe the precinct captain says he's OK."* Local union endorsements of political candidates frequently had a similarly informal *"Lou from the UAW says he's a solid guy"* quality.

These social institutions were central to the connection and loyalty that existed between working class voters and the Democrats. Workers would support a Democratic candidate not because his TV commercials were better or more frequent than the Republican's but because he was endorsed by two bottom-up representative institutions that workers trusted and felt a part of.

Beginning in the 60's and 70's all this changed.

First, with the rise of the automobile culture during the post war period, the predominantly working-class urban neighborhoods that had surrounded the industrial areas of major northern cities increasingly gave way to more occupationally and socially heterogeneous suburban communities. The second change was the profound decline of manufacturing in the northern industrial cities. Beginning in the 1960's factories began relocating—first to the South and then, in the 1970's to other countries.

By the mid-1980's the change was largely complete and the deeply rooted social and cultural institutions of working class life dismantled. The union locals and Democratic clubs that had been an integral part of daily social life in working class America became largely a memory.

Today Republicans Have Grass Roots Connections with White Working Class Voters – and Democrats Do Not

One perceptive analyst of the new and very different white working-class America that emerged from this transformation in the 1970's and 1980's is Joe Bagaent, author of the 2006 book, *Deer Hunting with Jesus*. He was born and raised in the working-class town of Winchester, Virginia. Bageant left the town and region as a young man and then returned in 2000, seeking to study and then sympathetically interpret his former home and neighbors to liberals and Democrats for whom it is largely an enigma.

One profoundly important fact that he found was that Republicans are familiar and active participants in local working-class community life while liberals and Democrats are not.

As he says:

> Republicans everyday lives seem naturally woven into the fabric of the community in a way that the everyday lives of the left have not been since the great depression... working class people encounter Republicans face-to-face at churches, all-you-can-eat spaghetti fund-raisers, fraternal organizations like the elks club and local small businesses... The GOP has a huge number of grassroots operatives. They turn up everywhere—at city council meetings and in the letters column of local newspapers...the nationwide grassroots network of zealous conservatives...recruits manpower for the entire GOP. At the humble level of the small towns, local candidates are raised and groomed for state and national office... and it is from these local grass-roots GOP business-based cartels that the army of campaign volunteers, political activists and spokesmen springs.

Bagaent offers a vivid portrait of one of these Republican grass-roots operatives:

> On a evening like this one you find people like Laurita Barr drinking a few beers with the proles at the [local] tavern... Laurita is one of the town's bigger—but by no means biggest—landlords, with two or three hundred residential units, many of them in the blighted North End. And she is of course a realtor...

> ...Laurita, age fifty, wears sharp business suites during the day and sports Max Studio and Nordy's casual afterwork wear...She runs the family real estate and rental business like a machine. "I do not fool around. The eviction process begins the minute they are late enough on the rent to start the paperwork" she says taking a sip of Sam Adams...

> ...She is a twenty-four hour-a-day Republican operative
> and enforcer. Along with her ceaseless activism in city hall
> against tenant's rights and property taxes... she also
> spends some bar-time bad-mouthing progressive politics
> and anything remotely related to the Democratic Party.
> Which is what she is doing this June evening.

Bagaent's observations form a critical foundation for any
discussion of Democratic strategies to contest Republican dominance
in white working-class America. So long as Democrats are
essentially invisible in the day to day life of the local community, the
battle is largely lost before it can even begin.

This is the fundamental underlying source of Democrats'
present difficulties. Without trusted grass-roots institutions as
intermediaries to defend policies, reinforce and interpret narratives
and produce "hometown" candidates, Democratic policies are easily
caricatured as wild-eyed radicalism, Democratic narratives are
easily ridiculed as the product of "limousine liberals" and Democratic
candidates easily scorned as elitists. Even the most exquisitely
polished candidate, platform and narrative cannot succeed if it is
not linked to grass-roots institutions and advocates in the everyday
community life of white working class America.

One observer who has clearly identified this reality is Michael
Kazin. As he notes in an article titled, *"To Mobilize the Indies, We Need
Stronger Unions"*:

> Of all the social groups essential to a winning democratic
> coalition, white working class people are the only ones
> who, for the most part, currently lack sturdy institutions
> that promote progressive ideas and policies... white
> working class men and women need new institutions
> that can speak to their discontents and offer compelling
> alternatives to the politics of anger and nostalgia. Nurturing
> them is vital not just to defeating conservatives in elections

to come. It is vital to the future of progressivism.[2]

Institutions of this kind cannot be built from a distance or with short bursts of door to door canvassing in the weeks before an election. Jane McAlevey, an innovative organizer for the SIEU, carefully distinguishes between sporadic "mobilizing" and ongoing "organizing":

> By "organizing," I mean an approach that has at its core a day-to-day, direct relationship with the base.... There are simply no shortcuts to this. We know this because we have spent the past twenty years looking for one and have not found it. Right now, the fashionable shortcut is using the Internet. Ten years ago it was direct mail, robo phones, phone banks, opinion research, and "sophisticated media." None of this is bad; of course it is a good thing to poll and message and phone and communicate in better ways. All of this is important, and all of it adds up to more wins and a stronger movement. But none of this can replace organizing. It must be in addition to it.[3]

The most important progressive initiative that is now attempting to do organizing along these lines is Working America, the community affiliate of the AFL-CIO. Although little known it is the largest, most dynamic and innovative progressive attempt to organize white working class Americans.

An article titled, *"Innovative Model Is Helping Save the Future of Unions and May Turn the Election"* provided a good introduction to this important initiative:

> Working America was founded in 2003 with the idea of reaching out beyond the ranks of organized labor. The idea, says Karen Nussbaum, the organization's co-founder and executive director, was one that people had been discussing for years but in 2003 they decided to give it one more try.

...What began as a pilot program in Cleveland, Ohio spread in the first year to Pennsylvania, Florida and Missouri, and recruited nearly a million members. Unlike labor unions, people become "members" of Working America simply by signing up so they can be part of a list, so that organizers can reach out to them again later, during an election or for an issue campaign.

...From those first few canvassing operations, the organization spread and has organized in around 25 states at one point or another. This year, they're in Ohio, Colorado, Massachusetts, Michigan, New Mexico, Oregon, Virginia, Wisconsin, North Carolina, Missouri, Pennsylvania and Minnesota.

In fact, Working America now has over three million members, most of them "moderate" white working class Americans.

...The people who sign up may have union backgrounds, Heck says, and be excited to be connected to the labor movement in some way. Others, he notes, don't have any experience with organized labor and don't really understand what it does.

Working America attempts to build its organizing strategy around the most important issues and problems the members themselves identify. But during elections they also engage in political action.

...In Ohio, they're working on the presidential race and Sherrod Brown's Senate race in particular, working to motivate voters who were active in the fight against Senate Bill 5 (Ohio's attack on collective bargaining, overturned by a ballot referendum in 2011). Working America was active in that fight, with four Ohio offices (there are now three) canvassing along every step of the way, gathering petition signatures and turning out voters. "We won by a margin of 22 points among the general population, among our members it was 44 points," Heck says. The organization actually ran a study during its SB5 operation and found that among people that spoke to a Working America canvasser, they gained almost 15 votes against the bill for every 100 conversations.

…"We've been organizing for nearly 10 years among working class moderates, the people who are most likely to be swing voters, those who have no other entry into the progressive movement…" Nussbaum notes. Those are the voters, it's worth pointing out, that pollsters constantly obsess over, particularly those swing, white, working-class men who have been courted so heavily the last two election cycles. When organized labor was strong, those voters tended to vote Democratic. If groups like Working America can build an awareness of economic issues among those voters, that could be game-changing.

…Theresa Bruskin, the field director in Columbus, who started out as a canvasser, notes that the success of the organization is tied to the way canvassers feel a part of the work—it's not a revolving door like so many canvassing jobs can be, where college kids work for a few months and then go back to school. The job includes listening as well as pitching, finding out which issues matter to people, and reporting those back.

…To get beyond that problem, Working America is now focused not only on meeting and signing up members door-to-door, but on getting current members to reach out to their own networks, to make sure they're engaging friends and neighbors on the issues. Signing up for an email list, as we all know these days, often isn't enough to get real engagement from people. Organizing, not just canvassing, matters....

"We feel like we've got a key to the future of the 21st-century labor movement and we all want to be a part of shaping that," Nussbaum says.[4]

As this description suggests, Working America does indeed provide a key model of the kind of grass-roots organizing and social movement perspective that will be necessary in order to build white working class support for Democratic candidates and policies. It is so important, in fact, that a far more detailed description of the organizations work and ethos is given in the next chapter.

Conclusion

There are three key characteristics that a social movement/ grass roots approach to building new community-based Democratic organizations must contain.

First, the approach must have the goal of providing "genuine representation"—a commitment to solving real people's problems in daily life. The classic model of this approach was the union shop steward in the industrial factories of the post-World War II era. The shop steward was the man on the shop floor who was the individual workers "rep"—the co-worker with the well-thumbed and grease-stained copy of the union contract in his back pocket who would pull it out to defend his co-workers interests and needs in the daily struggles with the foreman and the supervisors of the plant. This kind of representation was not representation in the abstract (i.e., *our tax plan is more progressive than their tax plan*) but rather representation in the immediate and concrete issues of daily life.

Working America is a pioneer and a major laboratory where the ways to bring this traditional kind of union representation into modern working class community life are being explored.

Second, the approach must incorporate the idea that the leadership

231

of the new grass-roots Democratic community organizations that are needed—whether political candidates or organizational figures—must emerge and be chosen and developed in an authentically democratic and bottom-up way. Democrats cannot copy the Republican model in which professional consultants take a well-funded candidate, give him a flannel shirt to wear, buy him a ranch and then attempt to market him as a cowboy. This fake authenticity can be made to work in some cases for Republicans (George W. Bush being a prime example) but the method is extremely unlikely to work for Democrats because they cannot rely on using familiar conservative rhetoric about traditional values to create an artificial "ordinary guy" identity and persona. For local Democratic candidates and local organizational leaders to be able to convince workers of their authenticity they must be able to honestly say, *"Damn it, I can represent you better than any Republican/conservative can because I really grew up in this neighborhood and worked in this factory and went to this school. I have lived and experienced the same problems as you in my own life and that's why you can trust me and not that other guy".*

The recruitment of these candidates and local leaders cannot be a top-down effort. The Democratic Party must recruit and foster local candidates who are drawn directly from the communities they will represent. This is a vast long-term challenge, but it is the only road to building white working class support for a Democratic future.

Third, the approach must recognize that white workers will need substantially more independence and autonomy within the Democratic Party and the progressive/democratic coalition than will other current elements of the Obama coalition.

The reason is that white working class people are sociologically and culturally quite distinct from the other segments of the Obama coalition. In a major mall or intown neighborhood in an American city it is possible to see all the sectors of Obama's base coalition walking by—African-Americans, Latinos, gays, students, young women, young urban professionals. Although demographically and ideologically very different, all these groups share the urban environment and feel able to coexist comfortably within it.

White working class people, on the other hand, live and work in a very different world—in the urban fringe or in small towns where factories have migrated. They live, shop and socialize separately from the current Obama coalition. They are geographically, socially and culturally part of Red State America not Blue State America.

The consequence is that working class Americans will need their own separate organization and identity within the progressive/democratic coalition. Within the Democratic Party the labels *"heartland Democrats"* or *"traditional values Democrats"* suggest the ways to define a separate space and identity for these voters—a way for them to assert that they have their own unique values and identity even as they participate in progressive social and political coalitions.

This distinctive "heartland" or "traditional values" identity would identify a distinct outlook that is culturally traditional, moderate on social issues and mildly progressive on economic issues. To build this independent identity these "heartland Democrats" will have to proudly and clearly assert their cultural traditionalism—not in an antagonistic way, but as a means of defining a separate cultural identity with which other white working class voters can identify.

It is important to note that the kinds of candidates that grass-roots Democratic organizations in white working class districts would produce would not be the same as many of the conservative "blue dogs" of 2006 and 2008. A significant number of those officeholders used the cultural traditionalism of their working class districts as an excuse to take positions that aid large corporations and Wall Street rather than the real economic needs of their working class constituents. Politicians who are genuinely recruited out of working class communities and remain responsive to their grass-roots supporters will be far less likely to attempt—or be able to get away with—defending the interests of Wall Street and large corporations rather than the interests of the people who elected them.

It is also important to underline that with the moderate sector of white working class America it will not be necessary to compromise central Democratic values or tolerate conservative ideas utterly alien to the Democratic ethos. The sector of the white working class that can feasibly co-exist within the Democratic party is the sector that is religiously and racially tolerant, non-interventionist in military affairs, pro-New Deal and suspicious of large corporations and the rich and powerful.

Despite these qualifications, there is no avoiding the reality that adopting this approach will require a radical change from the current, advertising-based and Washington-based paradigm of campaigning. It is, however, the indispensable step in order to overcome the Democrats long-term problems in white working class America.

The reality must be faced: rooms full of well-dressed professionals sitting around conference tables discussing the careful fine-tuning of candidates, narratives and policies will never solve the problem. Only the patient building of new community-based Democratic grass-roots organizations will do the job.

Of course Democrats do have another choice: they can go on hoping that new charismatic Democratic candidates will somehow begin to miraculously appear—candidates who will combine the physical magnetism of Russell Crowe, the soaring oratory of John Kennedy and the progressive platform of Paul Krugman. But it is now close to 50 years since Dems lost their working class support and Democratic saviors of this kind have still not come forth. It is better to finally accept that it is necessary to slowly, systematically and patiently rebuild the kind of community level institutions and organizations that provided the real foundation for winning white working class support for Democrats in the past.

CHAPTER
14

Getting Practical Part One –
An In-Depth Look at Working America

In a May 7th *New York Times* article Nicholas Confessore dramatically described the profound change in progressive and Democratic strategy that is now being debated among donors, campaign managers and political strategists—a change driven by the overwhelming financial advantage that Citizen's United has now given business and the wealthy in political advertising.

> "Instead of going head to head with the conservative super-PACs and outside groups that have flooded the presidential and Congressional campaigns with negative advertising, donors are focusing on grass-roots organizing, voter registration and Democratic turnout... Strategists involved in the effort said they did not believe they could match the advertising spending by leading conservative groups and instead wanted to exploit what they see as the Democrats advantage in grass-roots organizing."

The need for a reconsideration of progressive and Democratic strategy has become obvious. The Citizen's United decision has opened the floodgates to virtually unlimited spending by business and the wealthy and it is rapidly becoming clear that progressives and Democrats are at a profound disadvantage. In 2012, in several races totally unknown candidates with no prior political experience were catapulted into congressional seats by massive donations from single individuals or families, simply on the basis of saturation advertising. Democratic candidates for House and Senate seats are facing Republican opponents who have four-to-one and even five-to-one financial advantages in ad spending. Even at the presidential level, where ad spending is less decisive than it is in down-ballot races, massive negative ad bombardments allowed Mitt Romney to systematically overwhelm his primary rivals and essentially buy the Republican nomination.

But, as the *New York Times* story itself unintentionally demonstrates, there is a profound confusion within the progressive and Democratic coalition about what the term *"grass-roots organizing"* actually entails. In a wide range of recent discussions the three terms *"grass-roots organizing"*, *"GOTV/voter turnout"* efforts and *"door-to-door campaign canvassing"* are used interchangeably.

But these three terms are simply not interchangeable. GOTV and political campaign canvassing are short term efforts focused on promoting a single individual candidate that leave little or no long-term organization behind once a particular election is over.

The kind of grass-roots organizing that built the trade union movement in the 1930's, on the other hand, was designed to create enduring organizations and to support a vibrant, ongoing social movement. A trade union did not shut down and disappear the day after the first union contract was won. It remained as a permanent presence on the factory shop floor, providing day-to-day representation for the workers who built it and establishing deep roots as a local community service institution, headquartered in the local union hall, that provided individual workers with assistance with union pensions, health care provisions and job training and apprenticeship programs. Unions also provided their members with a union perspective on major political issues and endorsements of candidates.

It was the neighborhood and shop-floor representation provided by local unions and precinct level democratic machines that provided a firm social and political base for the Democratic Party in the northern and mid-western industrial states in the 1950's and early 1960's. Working people in those years did not vote Democratic because the Dems produced more or better TV ads; they voted for Democrats because the Dems were supported by two deeply rooted local community institutions.

As a result, the most important political initiative in America this year will not be any quickly thrown-together GOTV effort or additional political canvassing funded by liberal donors; it will be the organizing campaign that most faithfully and successfully builds on the traditional, grass-roots trade union model.

The organization that is most clearly following this approach is Working America—the community affiliate of the AFL-CIO. As a result, it is, in the long-run, the most potentially game-changing progressive project in America.

What is Working America

Every morning Working America's organizers—about 150 at the present time but substantially more during peak periods—gather in small meetings where assignments are distributed and goals set for the day's door-to-door canvassing and organization-building. The canvassers then fan out across neighborhoods in mostly white, blue collar areas of rust belt cities like Ohio, Wisconsin, Michigan and Pennsylvania as well as in similar areas in Colorado, Minnesota, Oregon, Virginia, Missouri and several other states.

The canvassers' job is to listen to the people they meet, explain Working America's progressive outlook and agenda and convince them to join the organization. Here's how David Moberg described the process in a 2008 article in *The Nation* Magazine:[1]

> [Working America] trains and continually briefs canvassers about both political issues and canvassing techniques (such as maintaining eye contact, keeping it short and simple, and using emotionally strong but friendly and optimistic language). At the door they quickly talk to people about a broadly defined issue. Now it's primarily affordable healthcare, but it can be good jobs, retirement security, overtime pay or local issues. Then canvassers ask potential recruits to take action, such as sending a letter supporting expanded funding of children's health insurance or signing a petition in favor of the Employee Free Choice Act to ease union organizing. And, of course, joining Working America.

Alec McGillis described the canvasser's "pitch" in more detail in a recent article in the *New Republic*:

> ...The overall pitch, drilled into the canvassers by rigorous trainings that I witnessed separately, was standardized: an introduction, a presentation of five issues listed on the canvassers' iPads—health care, education, and so on—to see which the resident cared most about, a bit of improvised chatter about that issue, and then the hook, which [the canvasser] gave like this:
>
>> "Our solution is just to put pressure on those politicians to make sure they're looking out for us and that they're doing their jobs. ...So we're asking people to join our citizens' lobby as members of the organization so that, when our lobbyists go to the capital, they can say we have strength in numbers."
>
> Signing up as a member was free, but canvassers added a forthright request for cash: "It takes money to fight money."

It is hard, grueling work. Canvassers encounter many people who turn them away. Even among those who are sympathetic to the issues and actions they present and to the idea of building a grass-roots "citizen's lobby" dedicated to giving ordinary people a voice in the political system, Working America's organizers confront massive misinformation and a deep and pervasive cynicism and a profound sense of powerlessness. At the end of the day the canvassers meet as a group once again to share their experiences, refine their message and renew their morale and commitment.

In the long run, the strategy works. Since its formation in 2003, Working America has grown to include over three million members, making it one of the largest (and simultaneously least-known) progressive organizations in America.

Every month Working America's canvassers have individual face-to-face conversations with anywhere from 10,000 to 20,000 and, at peak moments, even 30,000 Americans (a typical canvasser will knock on dozens of doors during a single day-long canvass and conduct from six to eight or sometimes even twelve or more face-to-face conversations). During 2011 close to 500,000 members of Working America took part in some direct activity like letter writing, phone calling, attending a meeting or participating in some action.

At first glance, these numbers seem so large that they appear implausible. But—as we will see—Working America is actually one of the most careful and meticulous progressive organizations in collecting and analyzing data about their members—the issues that concern them, the ways they participate in the organization and their opinions about a wide range of issues.

This focus on careful data analysis to understand what their members are thinking is actually vital for Working America because its major organizing efforts are aimed at winning the support of people who are not a typical part of the Democratic coalition—white working class people many of whom go to church every Sunday, own guns and—while they tend to be relatively moderate rather than deeply conservative—think of themselves as "ordinary folks" who are part of the "Real America" and not as "liberals" or "progressives."

Here is how Working America defines the kind of people it seeks to recruit and represent:

> Working America engages not the fixed 30-35 percent or so at each end of the political spectrum (including the firm conservatives who are not and will never be with us on the issues) but rather the 30-40 percent in the middle— working class moderates whose personal ambivalences make them swing voices in the public policy debates. Some of these individuals are present or former Democrats who have become disillusioned and some are persuadable blue collar or lower middle class Republicans.

The 2008 election gave some sense of the scale at which Working America can operate and the degree to which it can actually generate results. As an internal research summary concluded:

> In 2008, Working America knocked on more than 3 million doors and spoke to 1.8 million people. Our work produced results. Obama carried independents by 8 points and moderates by 21 points, but among Working America members who are independents, he won by 26 points, and among members who are moderates, he won by 49 points.

More Than Politics

But it is a mistake to think of Working America as essentially a political campaign organization. It is more correctly understood as an attempt to create a community-based organization that represents its members in the political system—a "citizens' lobby" that gives working class people who feel entirely helpless and disenfranchised a way to express their views and have an impact on the political system. It does not view them simply as voters that the organization wants to turn out on Election Day, it views them as members who it wants to represent on a permanent and ongoing basis.

More than anything else it is this that distinguishes an authentic grass-roots organization and social movement from the outreach efforts of a political campaign. The role of an authentic grass-roots organization is not merely to collect signatures on a particular petition or to increase voter turnout. To succeed it must give its members the tools to actively represent themselves on an ongoing basis and to provide inspiration and a sense of hope and confidence in the members own power of collective action.

Working America has gradually but systematically built this kind of momentum. As one organizer said:

> "The unanticipated outcome that's gotten us so excited is what organizing does not just for the people we sign up but for the people who sign them up. The people in [Working America] get so juiced up by their experiences that it gives us legitimate hope that there are many more people out there who are basically like us, and that the potential for solidarity is far greater than we thought."

To create and maintain this electric sense of possibility, the organization must constantly help the members generate new actions. As David Moberg noted:

> In some areas, Working America members join canvasses and phone banks to reach fellow members or, as a group of women did in Kentucky, gather to write personal letters encouraging Working America women to vote. Working America members also sign petitions or letters supporting unions (such as nurses organizing in St. Paul, Minnesota) or join labor rallies (such as backing Pittsburgh hotel workers in a contract dispute or Ohio union members

advocating labor law reform).

The full list of activities is long and varied. Members are encouraged to write letters (during the health care debate Working America delivered 75,000 handwritten letters to congressional leaders). They attend public events, rallies and demonstrations. They form local community action teams. They meet with lawmakers and write for blogs. During the Occupy protests Working America held a series of tele-town halls. After the 2010 elections they organized a *"buyer's remorse"* campaign in which voters returned imitation ballots to express their discontent with the newly elected politicians.

The sudden explosion of outrage against the "stealth" attack on unions by Gov. Scott Walker in Wisconsin and the anti-union SB-5 legislation in Ohio provided a rallying point for Working America's growing membership. As an internal memo reported shortly after the Wisconsin protests began:

> We're finding new energy at the doors, with working class moderates actively looking for ways to become involved and fight back. There's a heightened intensity of response from our members—people across the country asking us what they can do to help the Wisconsin workers, people increasingly mentioning specific policies or politicians they are upset about, and higher levels of anger and emotion being expressed.

- We recruited 25,000 new members in Wisconsin in just two months.

- We're collecting 3,500 handwritten letters, postcards and phone calls from members each week.

- Hundreds of members are going to rallies and lobby days and hosting meetings in their homes.

In Ohio, Working America played a clear and measurable role in defeating the anti-union SB-5 legislation. Voters who were reached by Working America were 14.7 percent more likely to oppose the measure, according to an independent study carried out by the Analyst Institute. This increase held for different age and gender groups and for both union and non-union workers.

Combining Research and Organizing on Social Issues

Working America's unusually strong emphasis on using serious empirical research as the basis for its campaigns is even more evident in regard to specific social and political Issues. Working America does extensive research in order to understand not only which issues are important to its members but the best language and approaches for its canvassers to use when they talk with them.

On the issue of jobs:

> An internal Working America memo notes: "In the three weeks from July 3rd through July 24th 2010, Working America's organizing canvass knocked on 141,924 doors and had 69,078 conversations focused in some way on jobs. Over the period we conducted several messaging tests about jobs and the economy with subsets of new and recently joined members."

> Some conclusions that emerged from this research included (1) that reducing outsourcing was the most frequently favored measure (2) that despite widespread hostility to "big government," in this area government was seen as a solution not a problem (a result which the researchers described as "an unexpectedly positive indicator") (3) that the issue of "fair taxation"—and specifically eliminating tax loopholes for companies that move jobs overseas—was a second highly popular remedy.

243

One specific application of this research was the creation of a "job tracker" application on Working America's website which showed the firms that were outsourcing jobs. This single feature of the website received 700,000 hits within a short time after it was introduced.

On Health Care

From April 25 to May 18, 2010—shortly after the health care bill was passed—Working America began a "Listening tour" in Ohio, Minnesota, New Mexico and Oregon. They conducted 1,200 informal conversations about health care with their members. At that point in time they found that 29 percent were supportive, 55 percent unsure/ undecided and 16 percent opposed. Based on the initial data they collected, they then tested a series of different messages, examining, for example, if members responded differently depending on whether the change was described as a "Reform" or a "Law."

Partially on this basis, Working America launched a campaign that resulted in 75,000 individualized letters supporting the health care reform legislation being delivered to congressional leaders.

On Immigration:

One particularly sophisticated project Working America conducted was a month-long outreach to working class voters in three Detroit counties: Wayne, Oakland and Macomb in December of 2009. Six experienced canvassers were given special briefings on the immigration issue and how to present a variety of messages favoring comprehensive immigration reform. The canvassers made extensive notes about what worked and what did not and developed a range of guidelines for future canvassers to use in discussing the issue.

The results were impressive. Of the 4,277 people contacted, 2,572 were willing to engage in an extended conversation with the canvassers about the issue (this represented 60 percent of those contacted). Of this latter group, an extraordinary 2,216 actually ended up by joining Working America (representing 86 percent of the completed conversations and 52 percent of all the people contacted). 2,004 of these voters completed postcards to be sent to Senator Debby Stabenow supporting comprehensive immigration reform.

As these examples suggest, Working America treats research as an absolutely critical part of their strategy for outreach and organizing. They view the knowledge it provides as vital for maintaining a close relationship with their lower middle class and working class members and they also have found that it provides a depth of understanding that simply cannot be obtained from conventional opinion polling. As one internal memo notes:

"What we hear at the doors often echoes the latest polling data but the responses we get from the field can also differ or add further insight because of the effect of the conversation itself. We often hear trends before they make it into polling questions—for example, we started hearing the heat around outsourcing months [before it showed up in the national polling]."

Digital Organizing Versus Face-to-Face Conversation

For many liberals and progressives, Working America's methods can seem highly admirable but at the same time rather antiquated and labor-intensive in the modern age of social media and the

"Netroots." After all, organizations like Move On have also developed memberships that number in the millions but have done so almost entirely by using digital communication.

For modern, "wired" and web-savvy liberals and progressives, this kind of purely electronic organizing can indeed be effective, but for working class Americans it is simply not a viable strategy. Intimate, face to face communication is absolutely indispensible for effectively presenting a progressive alternative to the Fox News/ Talk Radio perspective that is so widespread in the daily life and conversations of working class America.

Jane McAlevey, an innovative union organizer who worked for many years as an organizer for SIEU, carefully distinguishes between modern, electronic approaches and traditional "organizing":[2]

> By "organizing," I mean an approach that has at its core a day-to-day, direct relationship with the base.... There are simply no shortcuts to this. We know this because we have spent the past twenty years looking for one and have not found it. Right now, the fashionable shortcut is using the internet. Ten years ago it was direct mail, robo phones, phone banks, opinion research, and "sophisticated media."

> None of this is bad; of course it is a good thing to poll and message and phone and communicate in better ways. All of this is important, and all of it adds up to more wins and a stronger movement. But none of this can replace organizing. It must be in addition to it.

Indispensible as it may be, there is also no question that the traditional face-to-face, door-to-door organizing methods of Working America require tremendous commitment and dedication. Alec McGillis captured the hard, grinding character of this kind of organizing when he recently accompanied canvassers from Working America as they went door-to-door in working class neighborhoods in Ohio:

...I set out with Elisheva Aneke, an earnest Atlanta native with a very forceful knock, and Isaac Heard, an affable Ohioan whose front-step routine often included a request for a cigarette. I was struck by how resolute the pair remained despite setbacks:

- ...Heard coaxed Michele Zahel, who works in nuclear medicine, into scrounging up some money, and she reemerged with $6 in change. But, after Heard stepped away, Zahel told me that, despite being raised in a union family, she was now firmly opposed to organized labor and voted Republican....

- ...The next night out was in a much different area— Clintonville, a working-class neighborhood of tiny Cape Cod houses.... I was out with Theresa Bruskin, a brassy 24-year-old from New Jersey..."Our strategy is strength in numbers. It's how we won on Senate Bill Five in the fall, people like you and me fighting for working people," she told a home health aide still in her floral medical smock, who agreed to sign up but declined to give money.

- ...Bruskin's resolve was frequently tested, however. At one home, she spoke with Clarice Grinstead [who] signed up and said she might even be willing to chip in after her next payday. (Bruskin tried in vain to get a postdated check.) But, when I asked Grinstead about the election, she scowled. She had voted for Obama in 2008 but was leaning toward "Mitt Romney" this time.

- ...next door, we were greeted by David Schnepf, 49, sitting at the front door in his wheelchair as a dog and several cats lolled about. He, too, signed up, but he couldn't give any money—he had no ready cash and said he had gotten "in trouble with checks." Moreover, despite his good humor, he was not inclined to Bruskin's message. As much as he depended on the federal safety net, he said, he agreed with Republicans that entitlements needed to be reined in ….

- …At the next house, a slightly chaotic scene swirled around James Tichenor, a 50-year-old who works at a local McDonald's. A minivan missing a wheel sat jacked up on the driveway; an armchair lay on its side in front of the house; a 16-month-old boy, the son of Tichenor's deceased niece, cried inside the house. Bruskin forged ahead, taking it in stride when Tichenor said he had no e-mail address ("I don't know nothing about computers") and that he could not give any money ("Right now, I'm pretty well busted").

[Tichenor] told me he wasn't sure who he was voting for. I asked: Wouldn't Obama's health care law help him? He shook his head, saying he couldn't afford the $51 per week bare-bones health plan offered by McDonald's. I told him I was pretty sure that, if his employer didn't offer decent, affordable coverage, he would qualify for Medicaid, which Obamacare will greatly expand. He said he'd never heard anything about that: He worked nights and didn't watch the news.

McGillis concludes:

…Indeed, over my two evenings of canvassing—during which I met about a dozen different voters—what struck me most was the depths of the misinformation or resignation that needed to be bridged in order to turn opposition to [Ohio law] SB-5, as well as more general economic concerns, into solid Democratic votes."

This kind of traditional organizing is indeed hard, brutally hard and grinding work that requires vast reserves of dedication and commitment. But, for those in the trade union movement with long memories, it also recalls the history of how the last great wave of organizing in the 1930's finally achieved its success.

Echoes of the Past

If American history textbooks mention the trade union movement at all today, they note only a few climactic moments—the 1937 sit-down strikes at auto plants, the pitched battles in trucking and other industries. But the actual day to day reality of union organizing in the 1930's was in reality an endless succession of gradual one-to-one, face to face conversations—a process of slow persuasion and argument that was offered during lunch breaks on the factory floor or sitting in bars, churches, living rooms and union halls in the evening after work. Day after day, evening after evening, union organizers preached the progressive gospel of unionization, of the power of collective action to provide representation and dignity to working men and women and of the deep satisfaction produced by building and belonging to an institution that defended the interests of the "average Joe."

It is not surprising that precisely this same kind of organizing is needed once again today. In an extraordinary number of respects conservatives and big business have succeed in reversing the gains the trade union movement won in the 1930's and returning ordinary working people to the conditions of the pre-union era.

Today, few workers are any longer represented by unions on the job. Union pensions, union health insurance and union fringe benefits are for vast numbers of working class Americans only a memory. Job security, once common, is now almost impossible to find. Income is now in many respects as unequally distributed as it was in the turn of the century "gilded age."

And along with the reality of this return to the economic conditions of the pre-union era, the ideologies that dominated the era of the gilded age are also once again ascendant. Conservative economists today proudly promote pre-Keynesian turn of the century "neo-classical" economic theories that assert the ideal results of completely unregulated free markets. Ayn Rand's "objectivist" philosophy that extols the "virtue of selfishness" and the inherent inferiority of the ordinary working man is a direct 20th century echo of the "social Darwinism" of the gilded age and is proudly advocated today by members of the financial elite in downtown Manhattan and the Republican establishment in Washington and across the country.

In this grotesquely retrograde environment, the tools and strategies that progressives successfully employed in the past are once again the only viable strategy for reversing the conservative tide today.

The matter can be stated simply: there is absolutely no certainty that the traditional door-to-door trade-union style organizing Working America employs can succeed in organizing and mobilizing working people again on the scale that it did in the past. Social history offers no such money-back guarantees.

But one thing is certain. In the age of unlimited political contributions by corporations and the wealthy there is simply no alternative. If the appalling social recidivism of the policies and philosophies of this new gilded age are ever to be defeated, they will be defeated by the methods that Working America is pioneering today.

CHAPTER
15

Getting Practical Part Two – a "Common-Sense Populist" Progressive Strategy for Re-building Public Trust in Government.

Democrats need a coherent strategy for addressing the complex mixture of attitudes that lies behind working class hostility and distrust of government—a strategy that not only addresses the problem in a meaningful way but which can also be presented in a consistent and convincing communications campaign.

Beyond Advertising Campaigns

An effective Democratic strategy to overcome distrust of government must be substantially more than just a Madison Avenue advertising campaign—a fact which a 2011 *Harpers Magazine* forum with the creative directors of four major Madison Avenue advertising firms made dramatically clear. The day after the 2010 elections, the four ad men were brought together and challenged by *Harper's* editors to create TV ads for the Super Bowl that would build support for "Government" and diminish the lack of trust most Americans now feel.[1]

The *Harper's* forum presents the discussion among the four executives as they follow the standard procedure for developing an advertising campaign and then displays the actual storyboards and mock-ups that the four firms develop. One of the resulting ads uses the slogan, *"Our government is a lot like ice cream."* Another presents a montage of Americans talking about what the government makes possible *"Only in America."*

The ads are clever and amusing but they also make it entirely clear that, in isolation, ads and advertising slogans by themselves cannot begin to resolve the fundamental problem. In a roundtable discussion on rebuilding trust in government, John Halpin and Ruy Teixeira clearly express the limitations of this approach:[2]

> The recommended approach... is typically a combination of reminding people of all the good things that government already does and devising different language (or "framing") to talk about proposed new initiatives. There is, however, no evidence this approached has worked, or can work. People's views on government are not produced mostly by the way conservatives talk about government and they will not be substantially changed by the way progressives talk about government. Their views are far more solidly based, reflecting their experience with government and their assessment of government's output. In short, their views are rooted in the real world, not talk, and, even if unfair or mistaken in interpretation, cannot be dismissed as some form of false consciousness.

As a result, a meaningful Democratic strategy for addressing the profound lack of trust in government must in two important respects go beyond an advertising-based approach:

First, the strategy must be based on actual, workable reforms and solutions—solutions that people can plausibly believe will substantially improve government and its operation. A viable Democratic strategy must make it possible for people to say "Yeah, if you really do those particular things that really will change my attitude about government."

Second, the communications campaign that presents the proposed reforms must be more than a patchwork of slogans and advertisements. It must include both a single, coherent core narrative that tells the story of why the reforms are needed and how they will be put into effect and also a clear conceptual framework into which all of the individual elements of the strategy are organized. To be successful, the strategy should be one that a Democratic candidate can explain in coffee shop and living room conversations with ordinary voters at the same time that it can formally drafted and incorporated into the platform of the Democratic Party.

In the following pages an outline is presented of a strategy and communications campaign of this kind. It is designed to communicate three core messages: (1) that Democrats have a practical, common sense set of proposals for dealing with the problems of modern government, (2) that these proposals are based on a fundamental underlying principle—relying on the common sense of ordinary Americans—and (3) that this deeply Democratic approach proposes greatly increasing citizen participation, oversight and supervision of government.

Three Interlocking Attitudes About Government That Foster Distrust

As was shown in a previous chapter, the ethnographic literature suggests that there are three major attitude clusters that underlie white working class distrust of government:

(1) "Government is bureaucratic and inefficient."

(2) "Government is corrupt and dominated by special interests."

(3) "Government is dominated by liberal elites who channel government benefits to undeserving groups and attempt to impose alien values."

One important reason for the unique depth and intensity of popular distrust of government is the fact that vast numbers of working class and other Americans hold all three of these conceptions simultaneously to some degree. Challenges to or disconfirming evidence against any one of the three does not significantly weaken the interlocking and reinforcing effect of the three in combination. For many Americans these are not seen as three alternative perspectives, one of which can overshadow or dominate the others, but rather as a single overlapping and interlocking set of schemas. Progressive proposals—which generally focus only on the second element—generally do not induce broad attitude change because they do not attempt to provide any solutions to the problems expressed in the first and third components of the view.

What this correctly suggests is that what is needed is a basically new approach—one that addresses all three elements of today's anti-government perspective in a coherent and consistent way.

The Key to a Strategy for Reform: Genuinely Trusting the Common Sense of Ordinary Americans

Such an approach can be based on one very fundamental democratic and indeed "populist" notion—that reforms must be based on trusting the essential common sense of ordinary Americans.

This is a very deeply embedded part of the American ethos and one that has an overwhelmingly dramatic application in our national life—the essentially universal support that exists for the American jury system. Americans trust their most important personal rights and freedoms—the control over their life, death, liberty and imprisonment—to twelve entirely average and ordinary people like themselves rather than to some panel of experts or specialists. Why? Because Americans share a very deeply held core democratic value and belief that twelve ordinary people when given full information and the time to carefully reflect will usually make the right decisions—better decisions, in fact, than any experts or specialists. Experts and specialists may have their own distinct agendas and perspectives but most Americans believe that a randomly selected group of ordinary citizens will generally do what is reasonable and just.

This basic populist foundation leads to three guiding principles for reform.

- Let the people participate in writing the laws.

- Get big money out of politics.

- Let ordinary citizens supervise the bureaucrats.

Let us examine each one in turn:

1. Let the people participate in writing the laws.

The common sense core idea: Americans still deeply believe in the traditional ideals of citizen participation and direct democracy—the vision of the old-fashioned town meeting. In that vision ordinary citizens have the chance to hear debates, compare proposals and make their voices heard. That small town world may no longer be available in modern society but the ideal of public participation and town meeting democracy remains profoundly sound.

In modern society it is no longer possible for every American to participate in the equivalent of a town meeting. But, based on the same faith that Americans share in delegating twelve ordinary citizens to serve on a jury, it is still entirely possible to select a randomly chosen group of Americans to participate in a modern equivalent of a town meeting. There are many different ways such "deliberative democracy" town meetings can be structured but they all have in common the idea of allowing ordinary Americans to hear debates between advocates and opponents of new proposals, to question and demand facts and data, to examine and discuss the issues among themselves and with others and to reach conclusions that meaningfully influence the final decisions.

As one author noted in a contribution to a forum on restoring trust in government:

> "Eleanor Ostrom won the 2009 Nobel Prize in Economic Sciences for a career of work showing that laypeople can do an excellent job of managing public institutions. She has also found that decentralized, participatory bodies can produce better outcomes than either centralized, expert-led

bureaucracies or markets, even though participatory bodies often overlap, duplicate efforts, and reinvent one another's wheels."[3]

One recent example of deliberative democracy is the California system of redistricting, in which a lottery was deployed to choose 14 citizens (balanced by partisan self-identification) who drew the lines for the decennial remapping of state legislative and congressional districts.[4]

There are a very large number of other examples and well-developed models for conducting democratic deliberations on issues that have included immigration, renewable energy, social security reform and the redevelopment of lower Manhattan after 9/11. Many of these efforts have included several thousand participants. James Fishkin of Stanford University was one of the early advocates and developers of this approach but there are now dozens of specialists who work in this area. Three major organizations that work in the field and organize deliberative democracy exercises are The Center for Deliberative Democracy[5], the Deliberative Democracy Consortium[6] and America Speaks[7].

There are several indispensable criteria that are required to make deliberative democracy genuine and meaningful rather than just superficial "window dressing:" (1) the deliberations must involve genuinely random groups of ordinary citizens, as random as the groups of citizens who serve on juries; (2) the process must include a "bottom up" hierarchy of meetings, beginning with sessions held in local areas the size of towns or counties and then proceeding to state-level and national level meetings to consolidate and synthesize the decisions from the lower levels; (3) the process must involve a minimum of several thousand people in order to convince all observers that the results genuinely reflect the views of a representative sample of ordinary Americans (4) the process must allow for wide observation and discussion of the deliberations over the internet so that ordinary citizens can follow the proceedings in as much detail as they desire (5) the results of the deliberations must have a significant, clearly discernible influence on the shaping and final form of the law or other proposal that is under consideration.

2. Get big money out of politics

The common sense core idea: American politics has become the business of selling votes and influence in return for either campaign contributions, a high-paying job or "under the table" bribes. To stop this, the fundamental solution is a political process that is entirely funded by small donations from ordinary citizens rather than large contributions from corporations and other special interests. The basic rule of thumb is simple—a politician should not be allowed to accept any sum of money that is large enough to influence his vote. He or she should be financed by hundreds or thousands of small contributors, none of whom can or will expect any special favors in return for their support.

There is a tremendous range and variety of proposals for increasing the role of small donations and reducing the influence of large campaign contributions in American politics—so many that it is far beyond the scope of this analysis to list, much less compare them. One of the best known proposals for reform is the Fair Elections Now Act advocated by Lawrence Lessig and the organization, Change Congress but there are also many alternative schemes which include proposals with varying combinations of public finance and dollar limits on donations. Many organizations that work in this area have emerged relatively recently while others, such as Common Cause and Citizens for Responsibility and Ethics in Washington, have been in existence for many years.

Progressives frequently tend to view public financing itself as a desirable objective, but it is important to note that it is really just one particular method for increasing the role of small donor financing of political life—the donations in public financing being arranged by the government rather than obtained from voluntary contributions. In

257

either case the objective is a politics funded by small donations from ordinary voters rather than by large contributions.

3. Let ordinary citizens supervise the bureaucrats

The common sense core idea: With sufficient information ordinary citizens can apply effective "common sense" oversight to government programs and operations. Ordinary citizens are capable of clearly distinguishing between things that genuinely "just don't make sense" (e.g., a bridge to nowhere) and things that can be superficially ridiculed as frivolous (like "designing artificial hearts for pigs and monkeys") but which actually make perfect sense (this line of research led to the development of the device that is now keeping Dick Cheney alive).

There are literally hundreds of proposals for increasing citizen oversight of government agencies and operations. Many recent ideas for increasing citizen oversight involve the use of the internet to make widely available detailed "inside" information about government operations including data and even video. The Sunlight Foundation is one well-known organization that works in this area.

One of the simplest and most straightforward methods for increasing citizen involvement in supervising and reviewing bureaucracies can actually be found in state government agencies in many parts of the country, where officially constituted boards with required citizen membership exercise (in theory at least) genuine power over agency decisions. In Iowa, for example, citizens are encouraged to apply for board appointments that actually *control most agency activities, while enjoying complete access to agency records and data.*[8] A more open version of this type of structure, with randomly selected pools of citizen decision-makers, could be adopted for federal agencies as well. A combination of greater transparency, allowing all citizens to more closely examine the operations of government agencies, and greater direct citizen oversight and control could not only substantially improve public confidence in government but actually improve the operation of government as well.

This perspective is clearly evident in the Doing What Works project of the Center for American Progress. As the report summary states:[9]

> New information technologies provide government the opportunity to engage and interact with the public as never before. Thousands of extra eyes can be employed to spot problems, offer solutions, and bring fresh perspective. The public is ready for this role, but there must be tools to enlist them in evaluating performance and providing input to the decision-making process...such a government makeover would deliver more than policy results; it also promises to restore public confidence in government's basic competence.

These three ideas—*Let the people participate in writing the laws, Get big money out of politics* and *Let ordinary citizens supervise the bureaucrats*—can provide the basis for an effective set of programs and a Democratic communications strategy to reduce anti-government attitudes.

This Strategy Offers Democrats Several Key Advantages:

First, the three basic principles above—(1) let the people participate in writing the laws, (2) get big money out of politics and (3) let ordinary citizens supervise the bureaucrats—are easily presented as simple common sense. Unlike many Democratic proposals that are expressed as support for particular bills (e.g., "pass HR 1786") with which ordinary people are completely unfamiliar or for particular proposals ("support public financing for political campaigns") whose meaning and purpose are not immediately clear, this approach presents three principles that are essentially self-evident and self-explanatory. Even someone with absolutely no knowledge of the issues involved in government reform can examine these three principles and immediately feel that "Yeah, that makes sense" or "Yeah, I agree with that."

Second, this approach redefines the basic media "framing" of the issue. At present Republicans and conservatives are described in the media as being *"opponents of big government"* because they wish to shrink it while Democrats are described as government's *"defenders."* This framing automatically defines Democrats as supporters of everything that is wrong with the current system while Republicans appear as those who criticize the system's flaws. By shifting the axis of debate to, on the one hand, *"dramatically increasing citizen participation and control of politics"* versus *"keeping the current system (of unresponsive bureaucracy and special interest money) but making it smaller"* on the other, Democrats become the critics and advocates for change while Republicans and conservatives become the defenders of the deeply unpopular status quo. Obviously there are many individual Democratic officeholders who will be just as opposed to change as many Republicans. But for the parties as a whole, Republicans will in general be far more committed to defending the existing "Washington System" of back room deals and special interest money than will Democrats.

Third, this approach "scales" well at every level of political communication. Because the basic ideas are simple and self-evident, it can be applied at the door-to-door or "coffee shop" level of personal campaigning. It can also provide a consistent message for political advertisements, debates and interviews. It can be used both during specific campaigns and in ongoing, between-elections outreach. Once fully elaborated with specific goals and proposals it can be incorporated into state and national platforms and into general Democratic Party messaging by the DNC and other Democratic Party campaign committees.

Finally, this approach provides a way for Democrats to propose and defend new programs while at the same time promising that such new efforts will incorporate vastly more citizen involvement and participation than in the past and therefore avoid many of the problems that have plagued previous government programs.

It is important to note that the "common sense" based presentation of this approach also makes it possible to partially separate the discussion of basic principles of government reform from the details of exactly which methods of deliberative democracy, small donor campaign finance and citizen oversight will be employed. It thus makes it possible to clearly distinguish the basic philosophic approach of the Democrats—increasing citizen involvement and oversight—from the Republicans' program of cutting government services, programs and spending across the board. This will make it possible for Democrats to argue for the basic principles they are proposing without having to immediately defend every detail of complex proposals.

Before this communications strategy can be applied on a broad scale, however, the exact mechanisms for democratic deliberation, small donor campaign finance and citizen oversight will indeed need to be clearly specified even if they are not immediately to be put into effect. In this regard, however, it is important that this process of specification incorporate two rules of thumb:

First, Democrats must resist the tendency to formulate their specific promises as simply the titles of particular pieces of legislation or formal proposals. On the contrary, what Dems need to present voters is a list of specific goals or objectives, specified as concretely as possible (e.g., "all major new programs will be reviewed by citizen assemblies;" "stockholders will be given the right to approve all corporate advertising;" "all federal agencies will establish citizen oversight panels"). These objectives should wherever possible include specific numerical targets and deadlines for completion.

Second, Democrats must convincingly demonstrate the seriousness with which they take these reforms by directly tying their fate as candidates to the achievement of these objectives. The 1994 Republican "Contract with America" ended with the catchy phrase, *"If we break this contract, throw us out. We mean it."* If Democrats wish to convince the American people that the proposed reforms will genuinely produce better government, they must demonstrate a similar degree of personal commitment to making sure the new approaches are actually enacted and put into operation.

Republicans will, of course, point to the way in which the health care reform act was passed as proof that Democrats are entirely hypocritical in their endorsement of this new proposed approach and are still actually committed to the status quo. Dems must reply by making a clear and forceful promise—that in the future all major new programs and initiatives proposed by Democrats will include meaningful citizen involvement and oversight or they will not be proposed at all. This is the only way that Democrats can rebuild the level of trust that will be necessary to win popular support for new social legislation or political reform.

Part Four

Appendices – Academic Research and Progressive Political Strategy

APPENDIX

1

A New Research Strategy for Studying How Working People Make Political Decisions

There is a very substantial literature within political science that studies political ambivalence. One particularly comprehensive recent example of this research is R. Michael Alvarez and John Brehm's 2002, *Hard Choices, Easy Answers: Values, Information and American Public Opinion.*

When one attempts to apply this body of research to the challenge of increasing the level of white working class support for Democrats and the Democratic Party, however a substantial methodological limitation becomes apparent. The limitation arises because public opinion research within political science is entirely based on the mathematical analysis of polling data and does not also employ the kinds of structured interview techniques that are utilized in cognitive anthropology and other disciplines that conduct ethnographic field studies. As a consequence political science research generally does not try to directly study and understand the *"on the one hand, on the other hand"* method of cognitive processing that is characteristically employed when people deal with ambivalence.

A clear illustration of where this methodological limitation comes into play can be seen in a recent study by political scientist William Jacoby. As part of a 2005 analysis, "Public Opinion toward Government

Spending", (published in the collection, *Ambivalence and the Structure of Political Opinion* by Steven Craig and Michael D. Martinez), Jacoby constructed a summary measure of attitudes toward the size and power of government. He did this by combining individual answers to the following three separate survey items on the 1992 American Nation Election Study (ANES):

Choose which of the two statements comes closer to your own opinion:

- One, the less government the better; or two, there are more things that government should be doing.

- One, we need a strong government to handle today's complex economic problems; or two, the free market can handle these problems without the government being involved.

- One, the main reason government has become bigger over the years is because it has gotten involved in things that people should do for themselves; or two, government has become bigger because the problems we face have become bigger.

On the one hand, it is immediately evident that, in a normal conversation, a person who is ambivalent about these choices would naturally tend to employ an *"on the one hand, on the other hand"* style of reasoning in order to resolve his ambivalence. In order to make the data mathematically tractable for statistical analysis, however, Jacoby reduces the responses to these conflicting views into one summary index number for use in his subsequent analysis. This is a standard approach in political science research of this kind.

Jacoby is entirely clear and straightforward in acknowledging the trade-off that necessarily results from this approach. As he says:

"... [In the current study] the presence or absence of ambivalence has not been observed directly but rather inferred from patterns that appear in the empirical data. [As a result] is impossible to know for sure what mental processes actually generated the contradictory responses noted in the 1992 ANES.

The mental processes that are involved in the *"on the one hand, on the other hand"* reasoning of ordinary voters can however actually be directly studied by using the kinds of structured interview techniques that are employed in other social science disciplines. For example, a 30-45 minute interview protocol to examine this question can be structured as follows:

- The first segment can probe the overall *"personal philosophy"* or *"way of thinking"* of the interview subject on four major subjects— patriotism and the military, business and government, religion and moral values and the American system of government. These four topic areas correspond to the major value systems inculcated by the basic social institutions in working class life (the military, business, the church and the school system). A series of questions on these topics can directly extract and map an individual's strongest and most immediately accessible mental constructs in each of these four major areas.

- The second segment can ask the subject to explain how he or she applies his or her *"personal philosophy"* to a specific social or political issue such as health care reform. The responses to questions of this kind can reveal any additional concepts that the person needs to invoke and bring into play in order to cognitively process this specific topic and also indicate which core values, schemas and ideas play the largest role in the person's reasoning about the subject.

- The final segment can ask the subject to directly describe how her or she balances and decides between specific values and ideas that he or she finds to be in conflict in the particular area in question (e.g., a concern about big government on the one hand and support for affordable health care on the other). This can provide direct empirical information on how these individuals cognitively process and resolve such conflicting considerations.

It is likely that a relatively modest number of interviews of this kind (perhaps as few as 20 or 25) could be sufficient to begin revealing trends and patterns that could usefully inform Democratic communication and persuasion strategy.

The major difficulty in conducting structured interviews of this kind is the need for skilled interviewers. This is not insurmountable, however. The actual interview techniques are not substantially different from the structured discussion points that are commonly employed by focus group leaders in managing focus groups and there is an active research community within cognitive anthropology that works on developing methodologies for this kind of structured interview research (see, for example, cognitive anthropologist Naomi Quinn's, *Finding Culture in Talk: A collection of methods*).

APPENDIX

2

How Ethnographic Field Studies Can Contribute to the Development of Progressive Political Strategy

For many years, the more methodologically sophisticated polling organizations that study social and political opinion—notably Pew and Democracy Corps—have supplemented standard polling with tightly integrated focus group research.

The benefits are quite visible. The focus groups provide an independent confirmation that the yes-no answers to survey questions correctly reflect what the respondents actually mean to convey and provide a sense of the passion and intensity with which opinions are held. Focus groups also give some initial clues to the way in which specific opinions are cognitively structured and linked.

Ethnographic field studies can make a similar "add-on" contribution. They provide information about attitudes observed over an extended time period and in a real-world setting. This can provide a level of depth and context that cannot be extracted from polls or focus group sessions alone. Such studies can also offer an integrated vision of workers' attitudes about both the work environment and the community

The additional level of insight ethnographic field studies provide is dramatically illustrated by David Halle's 1984 study of workers in a New Jersey chemical plan—published under the title, "America's Working Man" which was described in chapter 3.

268

"America's Working Man" was the most impressively detailed ethnographic study of American workers up until the time of its publication. But ironically, rather than sparking an increase in such research, it marked the beginning of a massive decline. The chart on the next page shows the dramatic fall-off that occurred in ethnographic studies of the American working-class after 1985.

ETHNOGRAPHIC FIELD STUDIES OF WORKING-CLASS AMERICA			
	1970- 1985	1986-2000	2000- Present
Worksite	America's Working Man David Halle (fieldwork - 1974-1981)	Cutting into the Meatpacking Line Deborah Fink (1998)	Working Construction Kris Paap
	Manufacturing Consent Michael Burawaoy (1974-1975)	Talking About Machines (Xerox repairmen) Julian Orr (1996)	
	Cultures of Solidarity Rick Fantasia (1975-1976)	The Union Makes Us Strong (Longshoremen) David Wellman (1995)	
	Longshoremen: Community and Resistance on the Brooklyn waterfront William Difazio (1985)	Working the Waterfront Gilbert Mers (1998)	
	Work on the Waterfront William Finlay (1984-1986)	Kitchens: the culture of restaurant work Gary Fine (1996)	
	Chaos on the Shop Floor Tom Juravich (1985)	Kitchens: the culture of restaurant work Gary Fine (1996)	
	Royal Blue On High Steel A year in the Life of a Factory Maynard Seider (1773)	Dishing It Out:Waitresses in NJ Greta Paules (1987)	
	Blue Collar Charles Spenser (1977)		
	The Cocktail Waitress Mann and Spradley (1975)		
	One Sunset a Week –Coal Miner George Vecesy (1974)		

Community	Blue Collar Community William Cornblum (1970) Blue Collar Aristocrats E.E. LeMasters (1967-1972) Hard Living on Clay Street Joseph Howell (1970-1971) Norman Street Ida Susser (1975-1976) Ways With Words Shirley Bryce Heath (1969-1978) Getting Even Sally Engle Merry (1980-1984)	Working-class Heros Maria Kafalas (1993-1998)	
High School– Working- class Youth	Starting Out Steinitz and Solomon (1980-1982) Learning Capitalist Culture Douglas Foley (1973-1987) Jocks and Burnouts Penelope Eckert (1980-1984) Working Class without Work Lois Weis (1985-1986)	New Jersey Dreaming Sherry Ortner (1992-1994) Class Reunion Lois Weis (2000-2001)	
Plant Closings and Unem- ployment	The Magic City Gregory Pappas (1981-1984) Rusted Dreams Bensman and Lynch (1978-1982)	Farewell to The Factory Ruth Milkman (1986-1991) The End of The Line Kathryn Marie Dudley (1989-1990)	
Racial Attitudes	Canarsie Jonathan Rieder (1975-1977) The Inheritance Samuel Feldman	Racial Situations John Hartigan Jr. (1992-1994) Working-class White Monica McDermott (1996-1998)	The Color of Class Kirby Moss (2003)

Note: where possible, studies are grouped by when the research was conducted, not by the publication date. Further details (i.e., authors) are provided in the appendix.

It is worth noting that in the specific category of workplace studies the decline in studies of blue-collar workers is even greater than the chart initially suggests. In the 1970-1985 period there was only one study of "pink" or "grey" collar, rather than traditional blue-collar, work environments. From 1985 to the present, on the other hand, fully half the studies have been of "new" working-class job environments. While studies of the "new" working-class job environments are important, they should logically supplement rather than supplant new studies of traditional working-class work environments that are still major employers.

What accounts for this startling change?

Lois Weis, author of *"Working-class without Work"* and *"Class Reunion"*—two substantial ethnographic studies of working-class youth—notes the following:

> Discussion of the working-class and of social class in general has been tempered if not altogether ignored since the 1980's as scholarship targeted more specifically to issues of race and/or gender as well as to broader issues of representation has taken hold. Such scholarship, while critically important, has often delved into issues of race, gender or representation irrespective of a distinct social class referent, much as earlier scholarship on social class ignored gender and race...

> ...paralleling the eclipse of the working-class in prime time television (in the 1980's) academics simultaneously participated in the production of our collective ignorance around issues of social class.

In fact, the change was not simply a decline in attention. The studies of the 1970 and early 1980s were substantially motivated by a desire to delve below the clichés of "Archie Bunker" and "hard-hat conservative workers" and to sympathetically try to understand the forces that were motivating "the white backlash" and resistance to woman's rights. But the change in the reigning intellectual paradigm in academia—from "social class" to a tripartite framework of "class, race and gender" as overlapping modes of social stratification (a change apparent in most college course and textbook titles since the 1980's) made it substantially more difficult to analyze white working-class Americans sympathetically.

The reason is that using a tripartite framework of "class, race and gender" unavoidably tends to produce a vision of white working-class men as simultaneously victims and victimizers—victims of class injustice and perpetrators of racial and gender injustice. In the "society as prison" metaphor popular in critical social thought since the 1980's white working-class men seem to naturally fit into the role of quislings or "stoolies"—collaborators given special privileges by the guards in return for helping to maintain the status quo.

Once within the tripartite framework, it is hard to escape from the consequences of this kind of cognitive schema, a fact which the following more pointed example makes clear—In the same way that as it is much harder to make a sympathetic case for pornographic literature (based, for example, on the first amendment or the literary merits of D.H. Lawrence) if the topic of a debate is defined as *"pornographic literature, aggression and violence toward women"* rather than simply *"pornographic literature,"* it is similarly much more difficult to develop a sympathetic approach to the analysis of white working-class men if the defining framework is *"class, race and gender"* rather than simply *"social class."* The basic categorization framework exerts a profound "context effect" that shapes and constrains the subsequent discussion.

The underlying problem is that social scientists educated since the 1980's have no personal experience with any of the prior forms of working-class consciousness. None have personal memories of the dedicated and passionate union organizers of the 1930's and only a few can remember the solid working-class "union men" and "New Deal democrats" of the 1950's. With a personal historical memory that does not extend back beyond the "white backlash" years, it is understandable why, to them, the attitudes of white working-class men should appear to be fixed and unalterable results of their social position rather than more fluid and potentially malleable opinions shaped and conditioned by the contingencies of recent U.S. history.

As a result, it is vital that progressives and Democrats try to encourage the development of new ethnographic research in working class America. Democrats urgently need to figure out how to more effectively communicate with white working-class voters. But as long as this group is only defined in terms of abstract demographic categories like "non-college graduates" or "low socio-economic status voters," they remain impossible to visualize as three-dimensional human beings.

This presents a tremendous problem for all Democrats and particularly for Democratic speechwriters, advertising designers and other communications professionals. When major commercial companies are designing a new product, they will frequently create elaborate fictional profiles of their "target customers"—profiles complete with fictionalized biographies, photos, drawings, images, sketches of home furnishings and lists of other kinds of consumer products the imaginary consumers own and what they do on their weekends—all designed to assist the ad writers and others to better visualize the people who they are trying to convince to buy the new product. These profiles are often hung on the walls in ad agencies and design studios so that product and ad designers can continually refer to them as they work.

This is an area where ethnographic field studies of working-class Americans can add substantial additional insight and information to the opinion surveys and focus groups that Democrats currently use to understand political opinion. The best sociological and anthropological field research can provide precisely the integrated, three-dimensional picture of an individual or a groups' home, work, community and attitudes that other research tools cannot.

In order to adequately visualize the working-class "target voters" they need to reach, Democrats need to have at least a half a dozen (and preferably more) distinct, fact-based profiles of both male and female workers in a range of different occupational groups and settings—in traditional blue-collar jobs like construction workers, warehouse and loading dock workers, automobile repair and service workers and "grey collar" equipment repair and maintenance workers as well as in service sector working class jobs like restaurant workers, hotel workers, janitorial workers, hospital and health care workers and lower-level sales and clerical workers. These profiles also need to depict a number of different residential and community environments where these workers live—the Rust Belt, the South, the West, Urban, Small Town, etc.

At this moment, however, there is simply not sufficient ethnographic data to construct a full series of profiles of this kind and a new wave of ethnographic research desperately needs to be undertaken.

The academic community, however, does not currently provide adequate support for young ethnographers who wish to do socially relevant research on working-class Americans. Since universities do not provide the necessary support for this kind of research, the Democratic Party and the trade unions should consider commissioning, subsidizing and publishing such studies themselves. Considering the hundreds of millions of dollars that were spent on advertising in 2008, an investment of just a fraction of one percent could subsidize the creation of a half a dozen or even a dozen serious ethnographic studies that would dramatically enhance our knowledge of working-class voters and working-class America. This knowledge will be of particular importance for better understanding the younger working class voters who are for Democrats—the most promising sector of working class America.

Bibliography

General

Alvarez, R. Michael and John Brehm. *Hard Choices, Easy Answers: Values, Information, and American Public Opinion.* Princeton: Princeton University Press, 2002.

Bartels, Larry M. *Unequal Democracy: The Political Economy of the New Gilded Age.* New York: Russell Sage Foundation, 2008.

Cantril, Albert H. and Susan Davis Cantril. *Reading Mixed Signals: Ambivalence in American Public Opinion about Government.* Washington D.C.: Woodrow Wilson Center Press, 1999.

Craig, Stephen C. and Michael D. Martinez, Editors. *Ambivalence and the Structure of Political Opinion.* New York: Palgrave Macmillan, 2005.

Eichar, Douglas M. *Occupation and Class Consciousness in America.* Westport: Greenwood Press, 1989.

Fiske, Susan and Hazel Rose Marcus. *Facing Social Class: How Societal Rank Influences Interaction.* New York: Russell Sage Foundation, 2012.

Gilbert, Dennis. *The American Class Structure: In an Age of Growing Inequality.* Belmont: Wadsworth Publishing Company, 1998.

Greenberg, Stanley B. *Middle Class Dreams: The Politics and Power of the New American Majority.* New York: Times Books, 1995.

Greenberg, Stanley B. *The Two Americas.* New York: Thomas Dunne Books, 2004.

Hibbing, John and Elizabeth Theiss-Morse. *Congress As Public Enemy.* London: Cambridge Universty Press, 1994.

Jackman, Mary R. and Robert W. Jackman. *Class Awareness in the United States*. Berkeley: University of California Press, 1985.

Jensen, Barbara. *Reading Classes: On Culture and Classism in America*. Ithica: ILR Press, 2012.

Judis, John B. and Ruy Teixeira. *The Emerging Democratic Majority*. New York: Scribner, 2002.

Massey, Douglas S. *Categorically Unequal: The American Stratification System*. New York: Russell Sage Foundation, 2008.

Mayer, William G., Ed. *The Swing Voter in American Politics*. Washington D.C.: Brookings Institution Press, 2008.

Noelle-Neuman, Elisabeth. *The Spiral of Silence: Public Opinion – Our Social Skin*. Chicago: The University of Chicago Press, 1984.

Page, Benjamin I. and Lawrence R. Jacobs. *Class War?: What Americans Really Think about Economic Inequality*. Chicago: The University of Chicago Press, 2009.

Smith, Christian. *Christian America, What Evangelicals Really Want*. Santa Barbara: University of California Press, 2002.

Stonecash, Jeffrey M. *Class and Party in American Politics*. Boulder: Westview Press, 2000.

Teixeira, Ruy and Joel Rogers. *Why the White Working Class Still Matters*. New York: Basic Books, 2000.

Teixeira, Ruy, Ed. *Red, Blue & Purple America: The Future of Election Demographics*. Washington, D.C.: Brookings Institution Press, 2008.

Walsh, Joan. *What's the Matter With White People?* Hoboken: Wiley, John Wiley & Sons, 2012.

Williams, Joan. *Reshaping the Work-Family Debate: Why Men and Class Matter*. Cambridge: Harvard University Press, 2010.

Zweig, Michael. *The Working Class Majority: America's Best Kept Secret*. New York: ILR Press, 2011.

Ethnographic Field Studies

Applebaum, Herbert A. *Royal Blue: The Culture of Construction Workers*. New York: Holt, Rinehart and Winston, 1981.

Bageant, Joe. *Deer Hunting with Jesus*. New York: Crown Publishers, 2007.

Burawoy, Michael. *Manufacturing Consent*. Chicago: The University of Chicago Press, 1979.

Dudley, Kathryn Marie. *The End of the Line*. Chicago: The University of Chicago Press, 1994.

Dunk, Thomas W. *It's a Working Man's Town: Male Working-Class Culture in Northwestern Ontario*. Montreal & Kingston: McGill-Queen's University Press, 1991.

Durr, Kenneth D. *Behind the Backlash: White Working-Class Politics in Baltimore, 1940-1980*. Chapel Hill: The University of North Carolina Press, 2003.

Eckert, Penelope. *Jocks & Burnouts: Social Categories and Identity in the High School*. New York: Teachers College Press, 1989.

Fantasia, Rick. *Cultures of Solidarity*. Berkeley: University of California Press, 1988.

Fine, Michelle and Lois Weis. *The Unknown City: lives of Poor and Working-Class Young Adults*. Boston: Beacon Press, 1998.

Foley, Douglas E. *Learning Capitalist Culture: Deep in the Heart of Tejas*. Philadelphia: University of Pennsylvania Press, 1994.

Formisano, Ronald P. *Boston Against Busing: Race, Class and Ethnicity in the 1960s and 1970s*. Chapel Hill: The University of North Carolina Press, 1991.

Fox, Aaron A. *Real Country: Music and Language in Working-Class Culture*. Durham: Duke University Press, 2004.

Greenhouse, Carol J. *Praying for Justice: Faith, Order, and Community in an American Town*. Ithaca: Cornell University Press, 1986.

Halle, David. *America's Working Man*. Chicago: The University of Chicago Press, 1984.

Hamper, Ben. *Rivethead: Tales From the Assembly Line*. New York: Warner Books, Inc., 1986.

Hartgan, John Jr. *Racial Situations: Class Predicaments of Whiteness in Detroit*. Priceton: Princeton University Press, 1999.

Hartigan, John Jr. *Odd Tribes*. Durham: Duke University Press, 2005.

Heath, Shirley Brice. *Ways with Words* New York: Cambridge University Press, 1983.

Hodson, Randy. *Dignity at Work*. New York: Cambridge University Press, 2001.

Howell, Joseph T. *Hard Living on Clay Street: Portraits of Blue Collar Families*. Garden City: Anchor Books, 1973.

Kefalas, Maria. *Working-Class Heroes: Protecting Home, Community, and Nation in a Chicago Neighborhood*. Chicago: The University of Chicago Press, 2003.

Kornblum, William. *Blue Collar Community*. Chicago: The University of Chicago Press, 1974.

LeMasters, E. E. *Blue Collar Aristocrats: Life-Styles at a Working-Class Tavern*. Madison: The University of Wisconsin Press, 1975.

McDermott, Monica. *Working-Class White: The Making and Unmaking of Race Relations*. Berkeley: University of California Press, 2006.

Merry, Sally Engle. *Getting Justice and Getting Even: Legal Consciousness Among Working-Class Americans*. Chicago: The University of Chicago Press, 1990.

Milkman, Ruth. *Farewell to the Factory: Auto Workers in the Late Twentieth Century*. Berkeley: University of California Press, 1997.

Moss, Kirby. *The Color of Class: Poor Whites and the Paradox of Priviledge*. Philadelphia: The University of Philadelphia Press, 2003.

Ortner, Sherry B. *New Jersey Dreaming*. Durham: Duke University Press, 2003.

Ouellet, Lawrence. *Pedal To the Metal: The Work Lives of Truckers*.

Philadelphia: Temple University Press, 1994.

Paap, Kris. *Working Construction*. Ithaca: Cornell University Press, 2006.

Pappas, Gregory. *The Magic City: Unemployment in a Working-Class Community*. Ithaca: Cornell University Press, 1989.

Pilcher, William. *The Portland Longshoremen: a Dispersed Urban Community*. New York: Holt, Rinehart and Winston, 1972.

Rieder, Jonathan. *Canarsie: the Jews and Italians of Brooklyn against liberalism*. Cambridge: Harvard University Press, 1985.

Sherman, Jennifer. *Those Who Work, Those Who Don't: Poverty, Morality and Family in Rural America*. Minneapolis: University of Minnesota Press, 2009.

Silver, Marc L. *Under Construction: Work and Alienation in the Building Trades*. Albany: State University of New York, 1986.

Steinitz, Victoria Anne, and Ellen Rachel Solomon. *Starting Out: Class and Community in the Lives of Working-Class Youth*. Philadelphia: Temple University Press, 1986.

Susser, Ida. *Norman Street: Poverty and Politics in an Urban Neighborhood*. New York: Oxford University Press, 1982.

Theriault, Reg. *The Unmaking of the American Working Class*. New York: The New Press, 2003.

Torlina, Jeff. *Working Class: Challenging Myths about Blue-Collar Labor*. Boulder: Lynne Rienner Publishers, 1994.

Weis, Lois. *Class Reunion: The Remaking of the American White Working Class*. New York: Routledge, 2004.

Weis, Lois. *Working Class Without Work: High School Students in a De-industrializing Economy*. New York: Routledge, 1990.

Willis, Paul. *Learning to Labor*. New York: Columbia University Press, 1977.

Extended Interviews

Botsch, Robert Emil. *We Shall Not Overcome*. Chapel Hill: The University of North Carolina Press, 1980.

Bruno, Robert. *Steelworker Alley: How Class Works in Youngstown.* Ithaca: Cornell University Press, 1999.

DeGenaro, William, Ed. *Who Says?; Working-Class Rhetoric, Class Consciousness, and Community.* Pittsburgh: University of Pittsburgh Press, 2007.

Eliasoph, Nina. *Avoiding politics: how Americans produce apathy in everyday life.* Cambridge: Cambridge University Press, 1998.

Freedman, Samuel G. *The Inheritance: How Three Families and the American Political Majority Moved from Left to Right.* New York: Touchstone, 1996.

Gamson, William A. *Talking Politics.* Cambridge: Cambridge University Press, 1992.

Lamont, Michele. *The Dignity of Working Men: Morality and the Boundries of Race, Class, and Immigration.* Cambridge: Harvard University Press, 2000.

Lane, Robert E. *Political Ideology: Why the American Common Man Believes What He Does.* New York: The Free Press of Glencoe, 1962.

Lindquist, Julie. *A Place to Stand: Politics and Persuasion in a Working-Class Bar.* New York: Oxford University Press, 2002.

Reinarman, Craig. *American States of Mind.* New Haven: Yale University Press, 1987.

Rubin, Lillian B. *Families on the Faultline.* New York: Harper Collins, 1994.

Rubin, Lillian B. *Worlds of Pain: Life in the Working-Class Family.* New York: BasicBooks, 1976.

Russo, John and Sherry Lee Linkton, Editors. *New Working-Class Studies.* Ithaca: Cornell University Press, 2005.

Sennett, Richard and Jonathan Cobb. *The Hidden Injuries of Class.* New York: Alfred A. Knopf, 1973.

Walsh, Katherine Cramer. *Talking About Politics: Informal Groups and Social Identity in American Life.* Chicago: The University of Chicago Press, 2004.

Wellman, David T. *Portraits of White Racism*. Cambridge: Cambridge University Press, 1977.

Willman, Chris. *Rednecks & Bluenecks: The Politics of Country Music*. New York: The New Press, 2005.

Footnotes

Introduction:

1. http://www.tnr.com/article/politics/97972/false-choices-2012-election
2. http://www.thedailybeast.com/articles/2011/11/10/michael-tomasky-ohio-vote-shows-obama-winning-back-the-rust-belt.html
3. http://www.salon.com/2012/04/20/white_guys_vs_obama/
4. http://www.nationaljournal.com/columns/political-connections/obama-s-big-gamble-20120628
5. http://www.tnr.com/blog/electionate/106370/obama-isnt-the-only-candidate-whos-got-problems-the-white-working-class
6. http://campaignstops.blogs.nytimes.com/2012/09/23/whats-wrong-with-pennsylvania/
7. http://www.nationaljournal.com/thenextamerica/politics/coalition-of-new-old-equates-to-obama-win-20121107
8. http://www.brookings.edu/~/media/research/files/papers/2013/1/04%20presidential%20election%20galston/04presidentialelection
9. http://www.americanprogress.org/wp-content/uploads/issues/2009/03/pdf/progressive_america.pdf

Chapter 1

1. http://campaignstops.blogs.nytimes.com/2012/06/25/white-working-chaos/
2. http://www.brookings.edu/~/media/research/files/papers/2008/4/demographics%20teixeira/04_demographics_teixeira.pdf

Chapter 2

1. Eckert, Penelope. *Jocks & Burnouts: Social Categories and Identity in the High School.* New York: Teachers College Press, 1989. p 5
2. http://campaignstops.blogs.nytimes.com/2012/03/12/the-reproduction-of-privilege/

Chapter 3

1. http://www.huffingtonpost.com/2011/12/20/new-blue-collar-temp-warehouses_n_1158490.html?view=print&comm_ref=false
2. http://ed.stanford.edu/in-the-media/americas-affluent-and-new-bunker-down
3. http://articles.washingtonpost.com/2012-09-22/national/35495016_1_jefferson-county-voters-high-school-diploma
4. Bageant, Joe. *Deer Hunting with Jesus.* New York: Crown Publishers, 2007. p.3
5. Fox, Aaron A. *Real Country: Music and Language in Working-Class Culture.* Durham: Duke University Press, 2004. p.80
6. Ibid, p.66
7. http://papers.ssrn.com/sol3/papers.cfm?abstract_id=1770062

Chapter 4

1. Jeff Torlina, *Working Class: Challenging Myths about Blue-Collar Labor,* Lynne Rienner Publishers, Boulder and London, 2011, p 63-64
2. Fox, p. 32
3. Torlina, p. 2
4. Torlina, p. 155
5. Torlina, p. 146
6. Paap, Kris. *Working Construction.* Ithaca: Cornell University Press, 2006. p. 118
7. Ibid, p. 6
8. Ibid, p. 34
9. Applebaum, Herbert A. *Royal Blue: The Culture of Construction*

Workers. New York: Holt, Rinehart and Winston, 1981. p. 27

10. Ibid p. 116
11. Bagaent p. 12
12. Torlina P. 36

Chapter 5

1. Jennifer Sherman, *Those Who Work, Those Who Don't: Poverty, Morality and Family in Rural America*, University of Minnesota Press, Minneapolis, 2009. p. 8
2. http://www.americanprogress.org/issues/2009/03/political_ideology.html

Chapter 6

1. http://www.people-press.org/2011/05/04/beyond-red-vs-blue-the-political-typology/
2. http://www.people-press.org/2011/05/04/beyond-red-vs-blue-the-political-typology/
3. http://www.thedemocraticstrategist.org/_memos/tds_SM_Levison_Working_Class_American.pdf
4. http://pewresearch.org/pubs/1042/winds-of-political-change-havent–shifted-publics-ideology-balance
   http://www.gallup.com/poll/152021/conservatives-remain-largest-ideological-group.aspx
5. http://www.greenbergresearch.com/articles/2398/5488_TheVerySeparateWorldofConservativeRepublicans101609.pdf
6. http://www.thedemocraticstrategist.org/strategist/2011/10/progressives_there_are_two_pro.php

Chapter 7

1. http://religions.pewforum.org/
2. Public Agenda Foundation, "For Goodness' Sake – Why so Many Want Religion to Play a Greater Role in American Life":
   http://www.publicagenda.org/files/pdf/for_goodness_sake.pdf

3. http://www.gallup.com/poll/10666/new-religious-tolerance-data-paint-hopeful-picture.aspx
4. http://www.amazon.com/American-Grace-Religion-Divides-Unites/dp/1416566716/ref=sr_1_1?ie=UTF8&qid=1316053363&sr=8-1
5. http://www.gallup.com/poll/26674/necessary-highly-religious-americans-change-society.aspx
6. http://www.hhh.umn.edu/people/kfennelly/pdf/ruralresidence_determinant.pdf
7. http://www.huffingtonpost.com/jorgemario-cabrera/john-and-kens-fury-on-imm_b_949237.html
8. http://www.hhh.umn.edu/img/assets/3755/immigrants_prejudice_in_midwest.pdf
9. http://www.nytimes.com/2003/03/30/us/a-nation-at-war-the-troops-military-mirrors-a-working-class-america.html?pagewanted=all&src=pm

Chapter 8

1. http://prospect.org/article/democrats-are-back
2. http://www.prospect.org/cs/articles?article=democrats_are_back_but
3. http://www.amazon.com/Congress-Public-Enemy-Institutions-Psychology/dp/0521483360
4. See Appendix 1
5. http://www.democracycorps.com/attachments/article/930/dcor.pcaf.postelect.memo.111312.final.pdf

Chapter 9

1. http://www.amazon.com/American-Ethos-Attitudes-Capitalism-Democracy/dp/0674023315/ref=sr_1_1?ie=UTF8&s=books&qid=1238932100&sr=1-1
2. http://www.americanprogress.org/wp-content/uploads/issues/2009/03/pdf/political_ideology.pdf

3. http://www.democracycorps.com/wp-content/files/TheSelfSurvi-vors.pdf
   http://www.democracycorps.com/wp-content/files/A-Path-to-Democratic-Ascendancy-on-the-Economy-.pdf

Chapter 10

1. http://people-press.org/files/2011/05/Political-Typology-Topline.pdf
2. Ibid.

Chapter 11

1. http://www.huffingtonpost.com/drew-westen/democrats-identity-_b_880135.html

Chapter 13

1. http://nationaljournal.com/columns/political-connections/a-heartland-headache-for-dems-20101104
2. http://www.tnr.com/blog/critics/79361/mobilizing-independent-voters-unions
3. http://janemcalevey.com/
4. http://www.alternet.org/print/labor/innovative-model-helping-save-future-unions-and-may-turn-election

Chapter 14

1. http://www.thenation.com/print/article/labors-new-push
2. http://www.tnr.com/print/article/politics/magazine/103409/ohio-battleground-state-election-2012-labor-union-sb5-sher-rod-brown-john-kasich

Chapter 15

1. http://harpers.org/archive/2011/02/0083294
2. http://www.thedemocraticstrategist.org/_memos/tds_fo-

rum_0211_Halpin_Teixeira.pdf

3. http://www.thedemocraticstrategist.org/_memos/tds_forum_0211_Halpin_Teixeira.pdf

4. http://www.laweekly.com/2010-11-11/news/the-weirdest-lottery-of-all/

5. Center Deliberative Democracy, http://cdd.stanford.edu/

6. Deliberative Democracy Consortium, http://www.deliberative-democracy.net/

7. America Speaks, http://americaspeaks.org/

8. https://openup.iowa.gov/

9. http://www.americanprogress.org/issues/2010/02/pdf/dww_framing_exec_sum.pdf

About the Author

Andrew Levison is the author of two books and numerous articles on the political attitudes and social conditions of working class Americans. His first book, *The Working Class Majority*, was nominated for a National Book Award and serialized in *The New Yorker*. His articles and commentaries have appeared in the *Nation*, the *American Prospect*, the *Washington Post*, *The Los Angeles Times* and numerous other publications.

Since 2003, Mr. Levison has been both the Director of Business and Operations and also a Contributing Editor to two significant online political publications: Ruy Teixeira's *The Emerging Democratic Majority* and *The Democratic Strategist* whose founding Co-editors are Stan Greenberg, William Galston and Ruy Teixeira. Mr. Levison is the author of over 200 articles for these publications, including many that deal with the issues discussed in this book.

About the Book

The body of this book is set in Caslon Old Style. Chapter headings and table text are in Arial Narrow and Arial. The cover design is created in Photoshop. Cover and book design by Margaret Johns of Sage Design. Other designs and illustrations can be found at:

www.sagedesign.biz

291